The Canadian
MILITARY ATLAS

THE CANADIAN
MILITARY ATLAS

The Nation's Battlefields from the French and Indian Wars to Kosovo

TEXT BY MARK ZUEHLKE
MAPS BY C. STUART DANIEL

Published in 2001 by
Stoddart Publishing Co. Limited
895 Don Mills Road, 400–2 Park Centre, Toronto, Canada M3C 1W3
PMB 128, 4500 Witmer Estates, Niagara Falls, New York 14305-1386
www.stoddartpub.com

To order Stoddart books please contact General Distribution Services
In Canada
Tel. (416) 213-1919   Fax (416) 213-1917
Email cservice@genpub.com
In the United States
Toll-free tel. 1-800-805-1083   Toll-free fax 1-800-481-6207
Email gdsinc@genpub.com

10   9   8   7   6   5   4   3   2   1

National Library of Canada Cataloguing in Publication Data
Zuehlke, Mark
The Canadian military atlas: the nation's battlefields from the French and Indian wars to Kosovo
Includes bibliographical references and index.
ISBN 0-7737-3289-6
1. Canada — History, Military. 2. Canada — History, Military — Maps.
3. Battles — Canada — History. 4. Battles — Canada — History — Maps.
5. Battlefields — Maps. I. Daniel, Stuart C. II. Title.
FC226.Z83 2001   971   C00-932836-X
F1028.Z83 2001

Publisher Cataloguing in Publication Data (U.S.)
Zuehlke, Mark.
The Canadian military atlas: the nation's battlefields from the French and Indian Wars to Kosovo /
text by Mark Zuehlke ; maps by Stuart C. Daniel. — 1st ed.
[232] p. ; col. ill. ; photos ; maps : cm.
Includes bibliographic references and index.
ISBN: 0-7737-3289-6
1. Canada — History — Battlefields. 2. Canada — History, Military — Maps.   I. Daniel, Stuart C. II. Title.
355.409' 089971   21   2001   CIP

Jacket and text design: PageWave Graphics Inc.

We acknowledge for their financial support of our publishing program the Canada Council, the Ontario Arts Council, and the Government of Canada through the Book Publishing Industry Development Program (BPIDP).

Printed and bound in Canada

Contents

List of Maps

Acknowledgments

C. STUART DANIEL

I would like to thank Mark for believing in the idea of an atlas of Canada's military history and for making it happen.

Thanks to all the staff at Stoddart, but especially Jim Gifford, for their patience and indulgence with a project that just seemed to grow. Thanks to Elizabeth McLean for the incredible depth of her knowledge, and her sharp eyes and open mind. I would like to express my gratitude to several people who have influenced my work over the years: Dr. Sidney Jackman, who taught me how to "see" history; Bill Sinclair and Ron Deakin, who taught me how to put it on paper; and the late J.F. Horrabin, whose cartographic illustrations were exceptional examples of the art of leaving out. A very special thanks to John Russell, who has always given freely of his time and whose critical eye and encouragement have been invaluable.

And finally many thanks to Corinne and Mickey without whose support and companionship this project could not have been completed.

MARK ZUEHLKE

I would like to thank Stuart for mentioning a long-standing desire to create a comprehensive atlas of Canada's military history and then graciously agreeing to undertake the ambitious project when I hammered out an outline that was enthusiastically responded to by my literary agent, Carolyn Swayze, and military-history publisher, Stoddart Publishing. Many thanks to Carolyn for her usual excellent representation. Thanks also to the editorial team at Stoddart of Don Bastian and Jim Gifford. Elizabeth McLean, as has been the case with so many of my books in the past, deserves praise for her editorial attention to detail and style, for doing such excellent work in the face of tight deadlines, and maintaining much grace under pressure. Finally, I must thank Frances Backhouse once again for being so supportive and for making no complaint when her peaceful home is overrun with military history books and magazines, official histories and regimental histories, topographical maps, and the other essential material that gathers around the military historian.

Introduction
Mapping Canada's Military History

Before Europeans arrived, North America's First Nations used stone, paint, and the remembered word to record battlefield experiences. Peoples fought for honour, glory, revenge, spoils such as slaves and, later, horses, and only occasionally for control of ground or resources.

Europeans brought to North America the primacy of conflict motivated by territorial and resource domination. Delineating precisely which power controlled what territory and resource required the development of maps drawn to a variety of scales and including diverse details. Although the largely illiterate soldiers of the 1600s and 1700s undoubtedly still relied on the oral tale to pass on and remember their combat experiences, more enduring and comprehensive records combined maps, illustrations, and written accounts into a systematic whole.

While useful as historical tools, maps, of course, played a more immediate and vital function in the making of war. The ability to read terrain advantages or disadvantages from a map could mean the difference between victory and defeat. A ridge's dominating height, the natural defensive barrier of a river, or a route into the rear or flank of an enemy provided by a narrow track could be used to advantage, if a soldier could see on the map clutched in his hands the importance and opportunity presented. In the heat of battle, a hastily sketched map or finger brushed across a topographical map might send troops marching against a perceived weak point in the enemy position or to bolster a buckling defensive line. Failure to read a map correctly often determined defeat as soldiers arrived in the wrong place or at the wrong time.

The military importance of maps only increased with time and the resultant technological advances in weapons and tactics. The machine gun and mortar bomb forced soldiers to scatter and use every individual bush and fold in the ground for cover. Artillery and, later, aerial bombers relied on accurate maps to bring their weaponry to bear precisely against assigned targets. The phenomenon of friendly fire is too often the result of a map-reading error or of a poorly drawn, inaccurate map. On the modern battlefield, maps enable officer and trooper alike to render order out of chaos.

When the battle is done, maps also help lift the fog from events. Knowing where divisions or companies or even individual sections were positioned on a field of battle and where they moved to effect victory or blunder into defeat proves vital to overall comprehension. This is why the military historian and general reader love a good map. A map that visually captures the story of topography and movement unique to every battle is precious. But the cartographer's job is demanding, particularly when trying to capture the ebb and flow of battle. Too much detail mires the broad story in minutiae; too little and essence is lost, the whole reduced to a confused fragment.

The importance of maps to our understanding of Canada's battlefield experience has long been recognized by cartographer C. Stuart Daniel. His maps have brought lucidity to many books examining specific battles and wars. He is not the first mapmaker to realize the vital role maps play after the battle, but he is the first to undertake a comprehensive atlas of Canada's military experience through the centuries. Maps, illustrations, and written accounts have been compiled here to provide a record of a nation's wars.

While the maps constitute the heart of the atlas, containing the details of each selected battle or campaign, the text provides an overview that sets the maps in historical context. To keep the volume manageable in length, not every battle or campaign affecting Canada or in which Canadians were involved has been included.

• • • • •

Canada's history is full of military conflict. The extensiveness of the nation's experience of war may surprise those raised to believe the mythology that we live in, as historian William Kilbourn so successfully promulgated, "the peaceable kingdom," or that Canadians are, as George F. G. Stanley said, "an unmilitary people." Contrasted against this myth is the reality of a Canada born out of war and engaged throughout much of its brief 400-year existence in one war after another. New France's periods of peace were brief and relatively few. Peace also remained elusive for the British colony that eventually became an independent nation.

Seldom have Canadians hesitated to march to the martial drum, even for obscure causes — the South African War, the Korean War, the Gulf War, and the Kosovo War are all examples of conflicts Canada could have elected to avoid without particular difficulty. Instead, we sent men and women into harm's way. We will do so again and justify the action as being necessitated by external events beyond our control. While we again make war or peace through force of arms, our military will depend on maps to successfully carry out operations. When the latest military venture is done, we will again consult maps to understand what our soldiers, sailors, and air personnel did to succeed or fail.

The Canadian
MILITARY ATLAS

CHAPTER ONE

New France's
150 Year War

1609–1755

STRUGGLE FOR A FOOTHOLD

On June 29, 1609, Samuel de Champlain dreamed of a lake in which he saw "our enemies, the Iroquois, drowning before our eyes. I wanted to succour them, but our Indian allies said to me that we should let them all perish; for they were bad men." Awaking, he related the dream to his Huron Confederacy allies. "This," he later wrote, "gave them such confidence that they no longer had any doubt as to the good fortune awaiting them."

That evening, the 60-strong force paddled across Lake Champlain to face 200 Mohawk warriors, members of one of the five nations that constituted the Iroquois League of Five Nations. Following both accepted aboriginal and European military custom, the two groups traded personal and generic insults through the night and fought at dawn.

Wearing a white-plume-topped steel helmet and a plate corselet, Champlain strode out of a gap in the Huron line and advanced to within 30 yards of the Mohawks. Slamming the butt of his preloaded *arquebus* against his shoulder, he fired four bullets in rapid succession at the three war-party leaders grouped in the Mohawk centre. Two were killed instantly and the other mortally wounded. While Champlain ponderously reloaded his heavy, unwieldy *arquebus,* Mohawks and Hurons showered each other with arrows.

Suddenly a French soldier hidden in the woods discharged his gun into the Mohawk ranks. Threatened from the flank by the devastating French weaponry, the Mohawks broke, with the Hurons in pursuit. In the ensuing melee, 50 Mohawks were killed, and 10 to 12 taken prisoner. The captives were subsequently tortured to death. Champlain's party suffered only a few minor wounds.

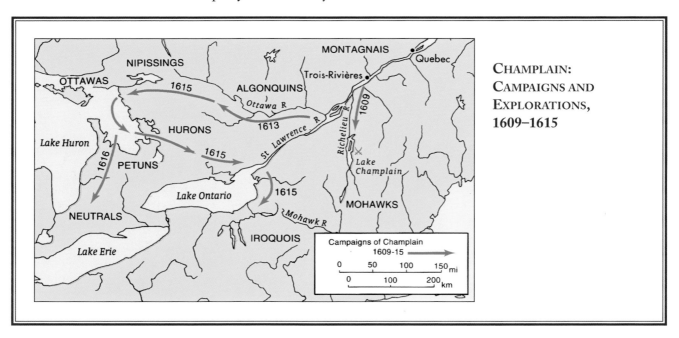

CHAMPLAIN: CAMPAIGNS AND EXPLORATIONS, 1609–1615

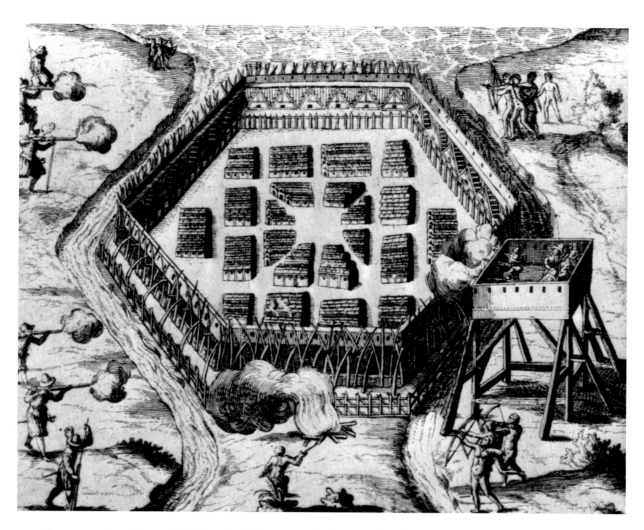

A year earlier, Champlain's colonizing party had arrived at the foot of Cape Diamond, east of the town of Quebec. They erected a structure to serve as a fort and trading post. Champlain's outpost stood amid a no man's land created by an ongoing war between the Iroquois League of Five Nations and the Huron Confederacy. After enduring a harsh winter, Champlain negotiated a formal trading and military alliance in July with the Huron Confederacy that was cemented by his participation in the Lake Champlain raid.

Champlain's purpose in North America was to trade for furs. His advantage over competitors was sustained by his willingness to campaign alongside the Huron tribes. In 1610, European pikemen and musketeers proved essential to defeat the Mohawks on a narrow neck of land between the St. Lawrence and Richelieu rivers. The victory forced a Mohawk withdrawal from the fiercely contested St. Lawrence Valley.

Over the next six years, Champlain struggled to ensure that New France prospered. During this time relative peace prevailed, although the Huron and Algonquin peoples clashed increasingly with the Iroquois Oneida and Onondaga nations in the Ottawa River Valley. In 1613, Champlain led his French soldiers in a campaign alongside the Hurons that probed deep into the Ottawa River Valley. This was

By deploying French infantry armed with arquebuses to fight alongside the Huron and Algonquin against the Iroquois, Champlain won their support for France's imperial ventures in North America. This highly stylized 1632 engraving shows French soldiers on the left and in the siege tower on the right, firing in support of Huron warriors attacking the Iroquois village of Onondaga Town in 1615.

followed by further forays in 1615 and 1616 that saw the Huron Confederacy, with support from Champlain, put as many as a thousand warriors into the field to secure the valley as a Huron preserve and to protect a vital trade route extending to Quebec.

If French dominance of the St. Lawrence was secure, the same was not true in Acadia, on the east coast. Although Port-Royal had been established in 1604, six years later it was sparsely settled and seen as a threat to England's Virginia colony. Virginian governor Sir Thomas Dale commissioned Captain Samuel Argall to raise a naval force of 60 soldiers and sailors to wipe out the French coastal settlements. In 1613, Argall struck and easily overwhelmed the ineffectual French defences. The English raid convinced the French to abandon plans for a permanent Acadian colony.

Both nations laid claim to Acadia and the St. Lawrence. Ignoring France's colonial claims, King Charles I granted Sir William Alexander charter to Acadia in 1621. Eight years later, Alexander's son sailed to the renamed Nova Scotia with two shiploads of colonists and soldiers and built Fort Charles on the site of Port-Royal.

While France lost Acadia, the St. Lawrence colony endured, even surviving English occupation from 1629 to 1632. The Treaty of St. Germain en Laye on March 29, 1632, restored France's North American holdings, but when Champlain died in Quebec on Christmas Day, 1635, the colony numbered only about 300 settlers and the population of its Huron allies had been devastated by smallpox and measles. Similarly reduced by disease, the Iroquois nations were also suffering economically because they had exhausted local fur supplies. Desperate, the Iroquois broke their truce with the Hurons. Although numerically equal to the Iroquois, the Hurons were seriously outgunned because French policy prevented trading weapons for furs. Dutch and British traders little hesitated to arm the Iroquois, and by 1644, the Mohawk alone could field 400 warriors armed with muskets.

Apart from a brief negotiated peace that lasted from 1645 to 1646, Iroquois raiding parties in the St. Lawrence Valley increased yearly, striking both Huron and French settlements. These raids differed strategically and tactically from earlier conflicts. No longer did the Iroquois line up outside Huron village walls to taunt the defenders into the open for a fight where only a few casualties would result. Instead, they launched surprise dawn attacks intended to destroy the villages. Long trains of Huron captives carried booty back to the Iroquois base in the Hudson River region. In 1643, hundreds of Huron were taken prisoner by the Iroquois or killed in raids. Between 1645 and 1655, the Iroquois undertook a massive military campaign, conducted summer after summer, that ultimately destroyed all rival peoples. More than 10,000 people of the Huron Confederacy were killed. By 1658, the last Huron remnants fled to Quebec for shelter.

With a population of barely 3,000 French, the colony existed in a state of siege. Outside the walls of Trois-Rivières, Montreal, and Quebec, the Iroquois controlled everything. More than 70 French were killed during summer raids in 1661.

THE ROYAL COLONY FIGHTS BACK

When King Louis XIV turned New France into a royal colony the following year, he decided France must send a regular infantry regiment to destroy the Iroquois. It took three years to organize, but on April 19, 1665, four companies of the Carignan-Salières Regiment sailed for Quebec under the overall command of 62-year-old Lieutenant-General Alexandre de Prouville, Marquis de Tracy. By early summer all 20 regimental companies, numbering 117 officers and 1,000 men, had arrived. Tracy's first step was to build a chain of forts from the Richelieu River mouth to Lake Champlain.

In January 1666, a force of about 500 men under French commander Daniel de Rémy de Courcelle, 200 of whom were regimental soldiers and the rest civilian volunteers, jumped off from these forts to attack Mohawk villages near Schenectady and Albany. Lacking snowshoes, poorly clothed, and badly supplied, soldiers and volunteers alike

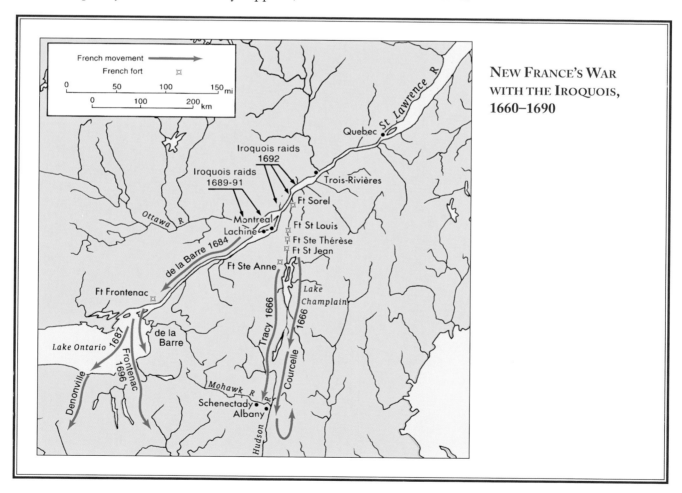

NEW FRANCE'S WAR
WITH THE IROQUOIS,
1660–1690

staggered through a frozen hell across 125 miles of dense wilderness. Chest-high snowdrifts made it difficult to cover 10 miles a day. Snow blindness, frostbite, hypothermia, pneumonia, and ever-worsening malnutrition due to increasingly sparse rations plagued the advance.

Finally on February 20, after a three-week march, the soldiers sacked a Mohawk village, but were attacked by 30 Mohawks armed with muskets. Advancing in fixed lines toward the enemy proved useless as the Mohawks moved quickly on snowshoes in small groups through the woods to snipe at the French. Despite the French numerical superiority, the battle's outcome hung in the balance until abruptly interrupted by Schenectady's British mayor, who stomped up and informed de Courcelle that his men were on English ground. Fearing an international incident, de Courcelle swapped prisoners for food and started a two-week retreat to Fort St. Louis on the Richelieu. On March 8, 100 men staggered into the fort. The remaining 400 lay dead in the forest, victims of starvation, sickness, or hypothermia.

Although the French adapted better to the conditions of land war in North America than did the British, both regulars and militia persisted in wearing, as shown in these sketches, European-style uniforms that greatly hindered them during campaigns and in combat.

De Courcelle returned to Quebec City to find France, allied with the Netherlands, at war with England. No longer having to fear British or Dutch reaction, Tracy decided on a full-scale campaign to crush the Iroquois. On September 28, 1666, a force of 1,000 regular troops, 400 *habitants,* and 100 Huron and Algonquin warriors under Tracy's command left Fort Sainte Anne, the most southerly Richelieu Valley fort, by boat and canoe.

After a tough 12-day march made worse by heavy rains and numerous crossings of streams, lakes, and a large swamp, the French approached the Mohawk villages under cover of darkness. Tracy's men made no attempt, however, to effect surprise. Instead they advanced boldly in column, drums pounding, and flags waving. Not surprisingly, dawn found the Mohawks had taken flight. Lacking an enemy to fight, the French claimed the villages and surrounding fields and crops for France by raising the flag and conducting a scorched-earth operation that left villages and fields destroyed. Seeing no way to force the Mohawks to battle, Tracy withdrew before winter set in.

Pressed from the south and west by the Mohican and Andastes peoples, who were trying to establish direct trading links with the Europeans rather than having to depend on the Iroquois to act as middlemen, the League of Five Nations signed a treaty in Quebec on July 10, 1667. New France now extended its influence south to the Mohawk Valley. The French position in America was further strengthened when the subsequent Treaty of Breda forced England to drop its claim to Acadia while the Dutch surrendered New York to England.

EXPANSION TO THE WEST

The success of 1667 sparked a rapid French expansion to the west that further excluded the Iroquois from participation in the French trading system and consequently led to their breaking the treaty and again taking up arms. Attempts by New France's Governor General Louis de Buade de Frontenac to broker a peace treaty collapsed and the Iroquois pillaged Fort Frontenac in 1681, resulting in Frontenac being fired in July 1682. As it took several months for a replacement to arrive, Frontenac used this time to bolster the colony's badly deteriorated defences, but he had only 1,000 militiamen in 1683 against 2,500 Iroquois warriors well armed with English muskets.

In May 1684, the Iroquois besieged Fort St. Louis, but its 46-man garrison staved off the attack with the help of Huron warriors. Knowing the French hold on the vast interior trading ground was tenuous, newly arrived Governor General LeFebvre de La Barre assembled 1,200 marines, militia, and aboriginal allies and marched from Montreal via Fort Frontenac toward the Ohio Valley, but soon retreated when Spanish influenza beset the column. Back at Fort Frontenac he asked the Iroquois for terms. They demanded free reign to destroy the Illinois First Nations people, who were actively trading with the French in the Ohio Valley region, in exchange for allowing La Barre's men to retreat to Montreal.

Incensed at being so humbled by savages, Louis XIV sacked La Barre for Jacques-Réné de Brisay, Marquis de Denonville. A well-regarded soldier, Denonville sailed for New France with about 550 marines and 150 male settlers in June 1685. Scurvy and fever killed more than 60 en route and another 300 were still dangerously ill upon arrival. When local nuns bled the stricken soldiers from their temples to treat the fever, many more perished.

Although his army was in tatters, Denonville was determined to re-establish France's North American interior. To the north, the English were occupying Hudson Bay and threatening the fur-trade grounds of the northwest while the English-backed Iroquois challenged French control of the western Great Lakes basin and everything south to the Mississippi. New France's western territories were caught in a giant English-controlled pincer.

Denonville sent a 105-man force overland to James Bay in 1686, where they captured three forts, effectively blocking further English activity in the north. In June of the following year, Denonville marched from Montreal at the head of a mixed 2,100-strong marine, militia, and aboriginal army against the most distant and powerful Iroquois nation — the Seneca.

By early July, the army closed on the Seneca villages adjacent to Lake Ontario and drove off the facing warriors after inflicting heavy casualties. Discovering the other villages abandoned, Denonville burned them and the surrounding cornfields, then withdrew to Niagara to build a fort where the Niagara River flows into Lake Ontario. Leaving behind a 100-man garrison, he marched back to Fort Frontenac.

Although Denonville's two-month campaign hurt the Senecas, it failed to reduce Iroquois military strength. Denonville estimated he needed a further 1,000 troops to destroy all the Iroquois nations. Failure to entirely eliminate the Iroquois, he believed, would lead to a murderous war of attrition that New France would lose. However, his hope of reinforcements was dashed when England, the United Provinces of the Netherlands, and the Austrian Hapsburgs allied to shatter France's European dominance in 1688. With war at home, Louis XIV could ill afford men for New France. Matters went from bad to worse when a smallpox epidemic killed more than 1,000 of the 11,000 soldiers and settlers.

NEW FRANCE UNDER ATTACK

With a violent hailstorm masking their approach, 1,500 Iroquois warriors paddled undetected past Fort St. Louis, then swept on foot across Montreal Island. Just before dawn on August 5, 1689, they dispersed in small bands through the Lachine settlements. With the first glimmer of light they struck, burning 56 homes, killing 24 *habitants*, and taking 90 captives. Denonville could only order the settlers to take refuge in nearby forts and to be armed while working the fields. Unable to adequately defend or supply Fort Frontenac, he ordered it abandoned. Finally, two months overdue, the annual French convoy arrived in mid-October. Aboard was Frontenac, sent back to replace Denonville.

Frontenac quickly took the offensive with three 200-strong mixed militia and aboriginal war parties that adopted aboriginal tactics to mount what he called *la petite guerre*, or "little war," against New York and New England frontier settlements and outlying farms. Men, women, and children were massacred or carried off as prisoners, while buildings and stores were burned. Schenectady and Salmon Falls were destroyed, as was Fort Loyal at Casco Bay. Frontenac's strategy was, however, badly flawed. First, it had no impact upon the Iroquois. Second, it united the normally divided northern English colonies against New France.

The English colonists responded with a two-pronged offensive plan. From Albany, a land force would capture Montreal while a naval flotilla from Boston captured Quebec. The Albany force was to number 855 militia and a large Iroquois force. Internal dissent so plagued the plans, however, that Captain John Schuyler eventually marched, in August 1690, with only 29 local militiamen and 120 Iroquois. They attacked a

OPPOSITE:
Huron warriors loyal to France fight off besieging Iroquois attempting to destroy Fort St. Louis in May 1684.

small settlement south of Montreal and destroyed it, killing 50 *habitants* and soldiers working the fields and then marched homeward.

Having detected the approaching English fleet well before it arrived at Quebec, the defenders had time to bring up reinforcements, dig trenches, and strengthen the palisades. When his 39 ships carrying 1,300 militiamen and manned by several hundred sailors hove within sight of Quebec, fleet commander Sir William Phips demanded the town's surrender. Frontenac rejoined that his reply would be "from the mouths of my cannon and muskets." An ebb tide forestalled Phips from mounting an immediate assault. That night almost 600 Montreal militiamen arrived, bringing Frontenac's strength to about 2,000 and giving the French numerical advantage over any English landing party.

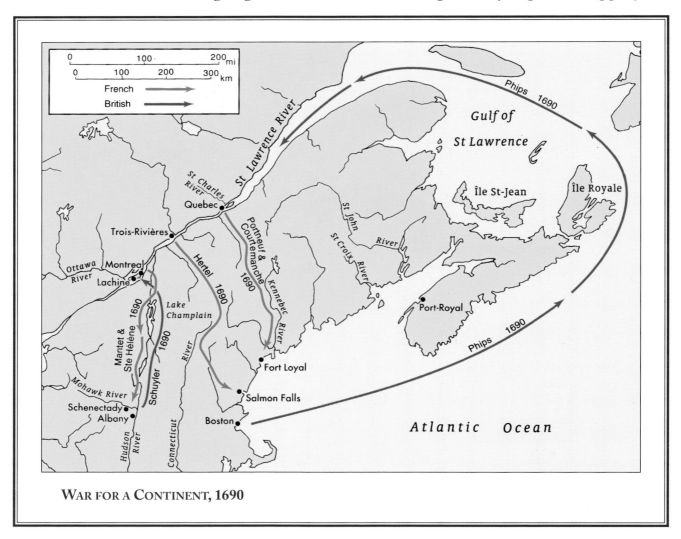

WAR FOR A CONTINENT, 1690

Two days later, the English landed the militiamen on the Beauport flats, across the St. Charles River from Quebec. After two days of sluggish fighting, the land force was evacuated. During Phips's retreat down the river, three ships were wrecked in storms and smallpox broke out on the rest. While only about 30 men were killed in combat, approximately 1,000 drowned or succumbed to smallpox.

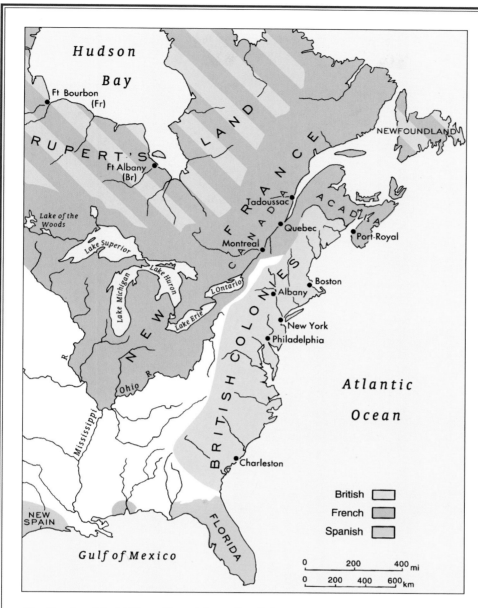

On October 30, 1697, at Ryswick, an English municipality in the western Netherlands Zuid-Holland Province, England, Spain, the Dutch republic, and the Holy Roman Emperor concluded a peace with France, bringing to an end the War of the Grand Alliance. While most of the treaty terms related directly to European causes of the war, the treaty also returned the colonial boundaries between France and Britain to the prewar status quo.

In the spring of 1691, about 1,000 Iroquois raided the St. Lawrence Valley region and destroyed many farms between Montreal and the mouth of the Richelieu River. The French, however, were learning to use *la petite guerre* tactics both offensively and defensively. By 1692, Iroquois raiders were as likely to walk into an ambush as to effect a surprise raid. French militia and aboriginal allies slipped through the woods as deftly as the Iroquois and struck out with their own war parties against Iroquois settlements. In 1693, a 625-man French force invaded Mohawk lands and destroyed their villages.

This offensive had a sobering effect and the Iroquois proposed a separate peace with New France's aboriginal allies. To French dismay, their allies were receptive. Faced with the possibility of a mass aboriginal defection that would cost France control of the interior, Frontenac ordered an all-out assault on the Iroquois. In July 1696, more than 2,000 regulars, militia, and loyal mission-based aboriginal warriors marched against the Onondaga and Oneida nations. The Iroquois faded away, either burning their villages or leaving them to be razed by the French.

The League of Five Nations' leadership was growing desperate. When the struggle for the western lands began, they had had a combined warrior strength of 2,800. Now they could barely field 1,300 against an ever stronger enemy. By 1695, despite heavy war-related casualties and many deaths to epidemics, New France's population had risen to 12,786. It was now within French power to crush the Iroquois entirely. Rendering the plight of the Iroquois even more desperate was British refusal to provide their former allies with support. In Europe, diplomats were finalizing a treaty that would bring peace between France and Britain by carving up the New World between France, Britain, and Spain. In September 1697, the Treaty of Ryswick was signed and through diplomacy Britain secured a return to the status quo in its colonial holdings. The Iroquois, cut off and friendless, finally sued for peace in 1700, leaving New France's hold on the western fur-trading regions largely unchallenged. The following year, however, brought a European war over the Spanish Succession and New France once again was at war.

WAR OF THE SPANISH SUCCESSION

In 1703, New France's recently appointed Governor General Philippe de Rigaud de Vaudreuil raided English settlements ranging from Wells to Falmouth, killing or capturing more than 160 settlers. Badly organized and inexperienced in *la petite guerre* tactics, the New England militia proved powerless to strike back. Meanwhile, the French demonstrated their competence at hit-and-run tactics on March 16, 1704, when 50 French and 250 Abenaki under Hertel de Rouville raided Deerfield, Massachusetts, after a 300-mile snowshoe trek. They killed 47 settlers, took 111 captive, and burned the hamlet and nearby farms.

Vaudreuil found the results of this terror campaign satisfactory, despite a retaliatory naval offensive led by Colonel Benjamin Church against the Bay of Fundy by warships bearing 550 Massachusetts militiamen that ravaged four defenceless seaside Acadian villages before being routed in front of Port-Royal by a small French fleet. Vaudreuil dismissed Church's raid as unimportant, continuing to harry British settlements with raids that culminated in a major effort in 1708. After that attack, Vaudreuil was able to boast that two-thirds of fields north

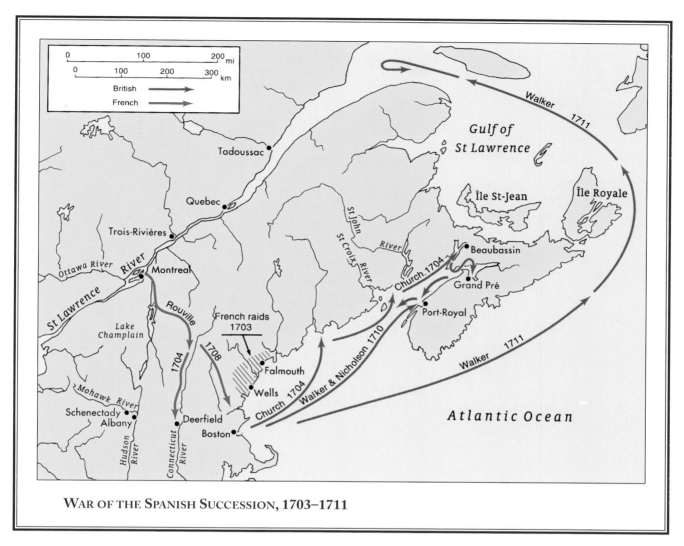

WAR OF THE SPANISH SUCCESSION, 1703–1711

of Boston were no longer tended because the settlers were too fearful of his raiding parties to venture out of their small forts.

But the terror campaign had belatedly stirred Britain to take events in North America seriously. On March 29, 1710, 500 marines and a small fleet commanded by Admiral Sir Hovendon Walker left Britain to capture Port-Royal. After linking up with a local New England fleet led by Colonel Francis Nicholson, it approached Port-Royal on October 5. The fleet consisted of 7 warships and 30 transports carrying almost 2,000 soldiers. Opposing it was a 258-man epidemic-weakened garrison.

The fortifications, however, were stout, prompting the English to rely on siege over direct assault. English cannon, firing from land and ship, hammered the fortress walls. The outgunned French responded with weak volleys. On October 13, 1710, the French surrendered, marching out of the fort with colours flying and drums beating. Ships transferred them to France. Acadian civilians within cannon shot of Port-Royal (soon renamed Annapolis Royal) were permitted to retain their land for two years without swearing allegiance to Britain.

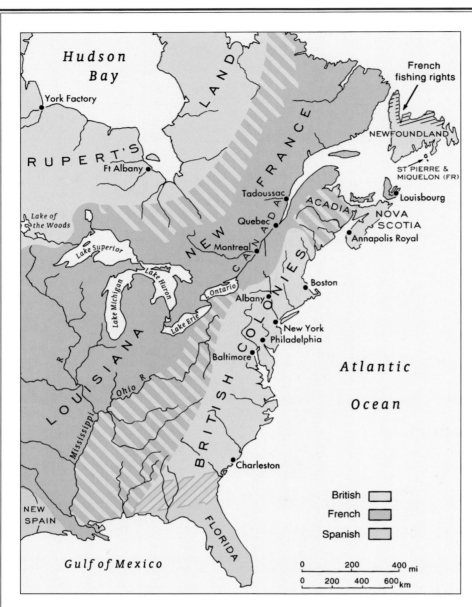

Between April 1713 and September 1714, a series of treaties signed in the Netherlands provincial capital of Utrecht brought a diplomatic settlement to the War of the Spanish Succession. In its treaty with Britain, France ceded Newfoundland, the Hudson Bay territory it had captured from Britain, and Acadia, which the British immediately renamed Nova Scotia. The treaty terms regarding colonial possessions in North America put France henceforth on the defensive, struggling to retain its remaining hold to territory on the continent.

With most of Acadia effectively in English hands, attention shifted to conquering Canada. On September 2, 1711, a fleet commanded by Admiral Sir Hovendon Walker became lost during a stormy, foggy night in the lower Gulf of St. Lawrence. Seven transports and a supply ship foundered on Egg Island with a loss of nearly a thousand lives. In the face of this debacle, Walker's nerve failed and he turned for home.

In 1712, the fighting in Europe ended badly for the French. For New France, which, with the exception of Acadia, had staved off English invasion despite being outnumbered and largely forgotten by Louis XIV's government, the terms of the 1713 Treaty of Utrecht were bitter. Newfoundland and the part of Acadia renamed Nova Scotia by the British were ceded to Britain, as was control of Hudson Bay and its river system. The latter concession opened a route for England to extend its fur-trading operations inland. Further damage to French intentions was dealt by a clause making all Iroquois British subjects, having the effect of providing England with direct access to the Great Lakes region. New France consequently faced being cut off from its trading operations in Illinois, Mississippi, and Louisiana. Strangely, the treaty was silent over control of the Ohio, Wabash, and Mississippi regions. The only bright spot for New France was its retention of Île du Cap-Breton (soon renamed Île Royale) and Île Saint-Jean (later Prince Edward Island).

The peace treaty did not end hostilities in North America. Rather, the fighting continued as successive governor generals sought to secure and strengthen control over the retained lands. The main thrust of campaigns during this period was to prevent interior native tribes from establishing trading links directly with the American colonies.

WAR OF THE AUSTRIAN SUCCESSION

In 1740, France saw an opportunity to restore its prominence by allying with Spain, Bavaria, Saxony, and Prussia against Austria. Fearing French hegemony in Europe, Britain sided with the Austrian Empire. On May 3, 1744, a declaration of war finally reached Jean-Baptiste-Louis Prévost du Quesnel, governor of Île Royale and commander of Louisbourg — a port that was unique, both as a community and a fortress, in the Americas. Built by French fortification experts, it was a thriving community that numbered about 2,000 civilians and soldiers, with another 2,500 settlers living on farms or in nearby hamlets. French and English alike regarded the fortress at Louisbourg as North America's strongest defensive position.

Du Quesnel was not content to rely on defence. While urging the Abenaki people to raid New England, he raised a 350-man fleet of privateers for coastal raiding. On May 24, 1744, the fleet fell upon the 120 British soldiers defending the fishing station of Canso, located in present-day Nova Scotia. The British surrendered and the prisoners were first taken to Louisbourg and then paroled to New England. Du Quesnel also unleashed the many French privateers who used Louisbourg as their primary North American port. Throughout the summer and autumn of 1744 they stalked British shipping lanes, netting 28 English prizes.

New England privateers striking against French shipping, however, captured one privateer named Dolabarats. When exchanged, Dolabarats reported to Du Quesnel that the Americans were planning an offensive against Acadia but planned to leave impregnable Louisbourg alone. Dolabarats was wrong. After repatriation, the British defenders of Canso reported that while from a distance the great fort's defences appeared significant, in reality they were badly decayed, poorly constructed, and ineffectually designed and sited. As well, its garrison was ill trained, poorly supplied, and demoralized.

THE SIEGE OF LOUISBOURG

Emboldened, Massachusetts Governor William Shirley dispatched an invasion force of 4,250 men under inexperienced militia colonel William Pepperrel. It sailed in April 1745 aboard a flotilla of 90 fishing boats. Three ships of the line commanded by Royal Navy Commodore Peter Warren supported the ragtag force that arrived off Louisbourg on May 11.

While Louisbourg's commander, the indecisive Louis Dupont du Chambon, dithered, the New Englanders immediately landed in nearby Gabarus Bay. Finally, with the landings almost completed by late afternoon, port commander Pierre de Morpain convinced Du Chambon to counterattack with 100 of his 1,300-strong garrison. This was too little, deployed too late.

After a sharp musket exchange that left Morpain among the wounded, the French retreated. Next, the Royal Battery commander drove spikes into the firing fuse holes of the cannon to render them inoperable and fled the key position that overlooked the harbour, the town, and the main citadel of the fortress. Soon the New Englanders stormed the battery with a small party of infantry and were astonished to find all military stores intact and the twenty-eight 42-pound guns ineffectively spiked. By morning, the guns were repaired and bringing down a fierce barrage on the French fort with support from an array of small cannon, mortars, and warship guns. Several days of bombardment destroyed much of the town, broke the right flank of the King's Bastion, ruined the Dauphin Battery, and breached Porte Dauphine and the neighbouring wall. Du Chambon could only hold on and pray for reinforcements from France.

His prayers went unrequited when the first French frigate turned back upon seeing British ships before the city. Shortly thereafter, the 64-gun *Vigilant*, having captured two English ships during its Atlantic crossing, hove near with the two prizes in its van. Its commander, seeing an opportunity to capture a small English ship that was straggling outside the bay, raced after it, and blundered directly into Warren's battle squadron. A sharp fight ensued, resulting in *Vigilant* striking its colours.

The New England militia's only reversal during the siege came when a surprise attack against Island Battery was detected while landing on the facing beach and cut to pieces by the battery's heavy cannon.

The successful defence of Island Battery proved only a minor setback. On June 8, the New Englanders started constructing a battery of their own on Lighthouse Point, effectively outflanking the French battery. These guns fired a 19-shell salvo against Island Battery on June 21 that destroyed several guns and ignited the ammunition magazine. Minutes later, the battery surrendered. With Island Battery's capture, a joint land and sea attack against the heavily damaged main citadel would be inevitable. Accordingly, Du Chambon sought terms on June 27.

New England invasion force landing in Gabarus Bay at the beginning of the siege of Fort Louisbourg

Two years later, European war weariness brought the conflict to an end. The treaty of Aix-la-Chapelle, signed in October 1748, led to the July 23, 1749, exchange of Louisbourg for Madras. Although the treaty returned North America to its prewar status quo, it was evident the American colonies were determined to expand their continental influence at French expense.

THE UNDECLARED INVASION

In 1753, France sent 2,000 marines and Canadian militia into the Ohio River Valley to build a series of forts, intended to control the region. Although the commander and all but 400 of the party starved or succumbed to illness, by year end three forts — Fort Presque Isle, Fort Le Boeuf, and Fort Machault — were completed. These forts effectively barred the Ohio to the Anglo-Americans.

When he learned of the French forts, the lieutenant governor of Virginia, Robert Dinwiddie, sent an eight-man party under command of Major George Washington to demand the French withdrawal from what he claimed to be British territory. That fall, Washington served his notice on Fort Machault commander Phillippe de Joncaire, who rebuffed the young major's demand. Washington returned to

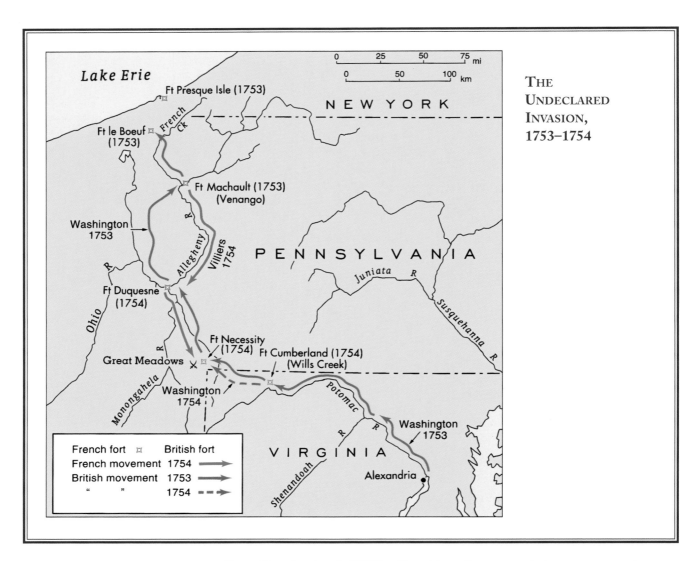

Fort Cumberland (Wills Creek) in January 1754 to report that
the French had claimed the entire Ohio Valley and could only be
removed by force.

That spring Dinwiddie responded by sending Washington at the
head of a motley party of militia and some native allies to construct
a fort at the junction of the Allegheny and Ohio rivers. Unknown to
the British, the French, who had reinforced their Ohio garrisons, had
already established Fort Duquesne at this strategically important position. Further, a strong French force, commanded by Nicholas Antoine
Coulon de Villiers, was advancing from the fort toward Washington's small column. After repulsing a French advance party at Great
Meadows, Washington realized he was outnumbered and attempted
to improve his odds by quickly erecting a makeshift fort appropriately
named Fort Necessity. The French lay siege and in early July, after
30 of Washington's men had been killed and another 70 wounded,
he surrendered and was allowed to withdraw his force intact when the
French uncharacteristically restrained their native allies from mas-
sacring the survivors.

BRADDOCK'S FOLLY

Refusing to cede the Ohio easily, the Americans appealed to Britain, which sent Major General Edward Braddock and two infantry regiments to their aid. Braddock was to launch a four-front attack against the Acadian frontier, Fort Niagara, Fort Duquesne in the Ohio, and Lake Champlain. The latter would enable the invasion of all Canada. By this move, Britain steered a new course in North America. Previously, war here had been an offshoot of European conflict. This time, Britain risked a European war over North America.

With so many objectives, Braddock had to divide his forces and allocate most command to local leaders. Militia Colonel William Johnson was to capture Lake Champlain; Massachusetts Governor William Shirley, Fort Niagara; and Lieutenant Colonel Charles Lawrence, Beauséjour in southern Acadia. Meanwhile, Braddock would march his British regulars against Fort Duquesne. Braddock organized a European-style campaign in the Ohio and left to the others their campaigns. In early June 1755, 2,200 men, resplendent in red coats with gold trim and even some tall bearskin hats, set out from the staging area of Wills Creek on a 110-mile march accompanied by supply wagons, a heavy artillery siege train, cattle, and women camp followers. Noticeably absent were native warriors, normally considered essential as guides and skirmishers.

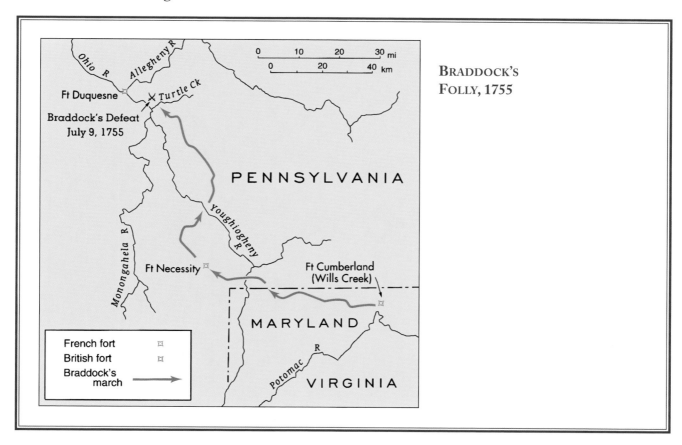

BRADDOCK'S FOLLY, 1755

Wagons and heavy guns soon broke down and had to be abandoned. Despite deteriorating morale, Braddock remained calm and assured, keeping his soldiers marching to drum and fife tunes that had accompanied British soldiers on countless European marches. By late June, he reached the ruins of Washington's Fort Necessity; a week later, the mouth of Turtle Creek. Fort Duquesne was about 10 miles away.

Against Braddock's column were only 108 regulars, 146 militia, and 600 aboriginal warriors. The fort itself was indefensible. On July 9, Captain Daniel-Hyacinthe de Liénard de Beaujeau arrayed his men with native warriors on either flank outside the fort's walls to face Braddock's vastly superior army. Advancing, Beaujeau's men suddenly confronted Braddock's advance scouts. Both were surprised, but the British reacted first with a volley. Struck in the head, Beaujeau fell dead.

The French line wavered and started to crumble. Just then Captain Jean-Daniel Dumas, joined by Charles Michel de Langlade, rushed forward to rally the French and seize a small wooded hill overlooking the main British column. From its cover, they poured heavy musket fire into the British forward elements, which reeled backward into the columns of the main formation trying to advance up the rough, narrow track. Braddock was unable to deploy his regiments effectively in the tangled woods that bore no resemblance to familiar European farmland battlefields. When Braddock was suddenly killed, the British panicked and fled, casting aside guns and equipment. The rout became a slaughter, until four hours later the scattered British survivors managed to break contact.

A greatly outnumbered force of French regulars, militia, and native allies routed Major General Edward Braddock's 2,200 British regulars on July 9, 1755.

The French suffered only 23 casualties in exchange for nearly 500 British killed and countless others wounded. Along with Braddock's military chest, all British cannon, supply wagons, cattle, and many horses were captured. The chest contained British plans for assaulting Fort Niagara and Fort St.-Frédéric. Knowing the British plans for Fort Niagara and Fort St.-Frédéric, the French quickly shifted reinforcements to bolster their defences. Johnson was turned back at Fort Carillon (called Ticonderoga by the British) and Shirley never marched on Fort Niagara at all. The American failures on three fronts left New France stronger than at the outset of 1755. Pivotal to this strength was the fort under construction at Fort Carillon, now Canada's first line of defence.

Only on the Atlantic coast did New France's enemies succeed, capturing Fort Beauséjour after a short 11-day siege, to gain control of all French Acadia. Nova Scotia Governor Charles Lawrence immediately enacted a mass deportation of 6,000 to 7,000 Acadians between September and December 1755. Only Île Royal remained an Acadian bastion. However, the small colony was anything but secure for Britain and France marched once again toward open hostilities — a war that came with the spring and lasted seven years.

CHAPTER TWO

The Seven Years War

1756–1763

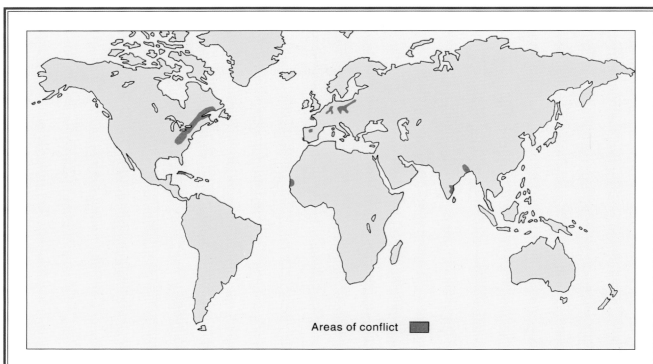

A FAR FLUNG WAR, 1757–1763

Sometimes referred to as the true "First World War," the Seven Years War was fought on many fronts around the world. In North America, the commitment of regular forces to battle reached a scale never previously seen. Both Britain and France recognized that in North America this war represented a final showdown, with the outcome determining which of the two nations would win uncontested control of an entire continent.

MONTCALM'S FIRST CANADIAN BATTLE

In May 1756, Britain declared war on France. French Governor General Pierre de Rigaud de Vaudreuil ordered military commander Marquis de Louis Joseph Montcalm to eliminate Fort Oswego.

Spring and early summer were spent in preparation. Not until August 10 did Montcalm's army of 3,000 men and 80 cannon beach their 200 boats within a mile and a half of Fort Oswego. The Americans soon opened fire with cannon positioned in a blockhouse known as Fort Ontario. It, and the blockhouses Fort George and Fort Oswego, constituted the American works. The harassing fire failed to deter the French from constructing in just 24 hours a corduroy road from the beach to a position overlooking Fort Ontario so the guns could be brought up. When the French guns opened fire, British garrison commander Lieutenant Colonel James Mercer realized the fort was as lost.

While some Fort Ontario gunners lay down covering fire on the French positions, the rest of the garrison retired to the remaining blockhouses. The gunners then spiked their cannon and fled. The French occupied Fort Ontario and brought Fort George under fire, while also deploying 1,200 Canadian militia across the river to sever the American communications with the Mohawk River Valley. By August 14, French cannon were battering Fort George and a chance shot beheaded Mercer. An hour later the defenders surrendered.

The French victory at Fort Oswego was significant. In addition to killing 80 of the enemy, taking 1,700 prisoners, and capturing 121 guns and all English shipping on Lake Ontario, the threat the American fort posed to Fort Frontenac was removed. All for the cost of only 30 dead and wounded.

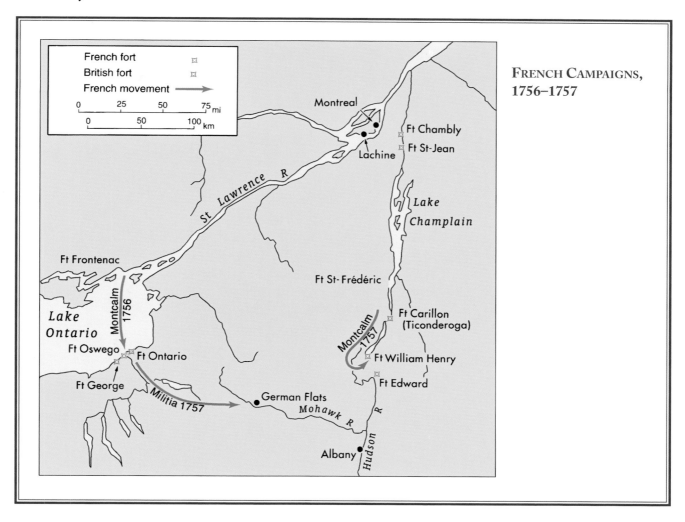

FRENCH CAMPAIGNS, 1756–1757

BRITISH REVERSES

Fort Oswego's loss in 1756 caused Massachusetts Governor William Shirley's dismissal as commander-in-chief of British-American forces. His replacement was the professional soldier Earl of Loudon, Major General John Campbell. The Earl immediately grasped that victory would only come by capturing Quebec. Loudon knew the advantage in numbers lay with the British and American colonials. Montcalm could summon no more than six regular battalions numbering about 6,000 men. Loudon had about 9,000 regulars with 8,000 more promised for the forthcoming spring. Each side could also call upon local militia, but neither Montcalm nor Loudon held these in regard.

Montcalm openly disdained the Canadian militia. Consequently, he forewent training them to fight alongside his regulars, mostly confining their duties to guarding his flanks or serving as support personnel moving supplies and guns. Neither the militia nor its leaders deemed either task sufficiently important, resulting in a schism between New France's militia and regulars. A similar schism soured Montcalm's relations with Vaudreuil.

New France's strength had been its ability to keep its enemies destabilized through a defensive-offensive war on the American colonial frontiers backed by occasional stabs deep into the American heartland. The British military buildup rendered deep raids impossible and Montcalm's disdain for the militiamen eroded their ability to wage *la petite guerre* against frontier communities and forts.

Initially, however, a string of military successes in 1757 disguised New France's increasing military weakness. Committed to his grand strategy to destroy first Louisbourg and then Quebec, Loudon drew his British regulars away from other theatres to a base camp in Halifax. Realizing the British were critically weak at Lake Champlain, Montcalm sortied out from Fort Carillon on July 30 with 8,000 regulars, marines, militia, and aboriginal allies backed by 188 cannon. After a six-day siege, the 2,400-strong Fort William Henry garrison capitulated. Vaudreuil ordered Montcalm to advance 15 miles more to take Fort Edward, but Montcalm, fearful of exhausting his supplies, vacillated. A frustrated Vaudreuil unleashed a militia-aboriginal raiding party down the Mohawk River to burn the frontier village of German Flats. Meanwhile, Montcalm returned to Quebec to survey the St. Lawrence's north shore and determine where gun batteries should be placed to close the river to any British naval assault.

That assault should have come with summer but unusually poor winds delayed the British fleet in England until May 8. Not until July were sufficient troops available at Halifax to entertain offensive action. Loudon realized it was no longer practicable to attack both Louisbourg and Quebec in one season. Further intelligence reports, indicating that Louisbourg was more heavily defended than expected, caused Loudon to hesitate while the campaign season passed by, leading to his being recalled.

1758: BRITAIN INVADES

While enjoying marginal success in 1757, New France's overall situation was deteriorating rapidly. Throughout the colony, food and other essential supplies were short. Even more critical was the manpower shortage. By spring 1758, Britain had more than 23,000 regular troops in North America. They faced only 6,000 French regulars. Montcalm, desperate for manpower, reconsidered his early stance against using Canadians and proposed drafting them into the regular forces. However, he intended to use them only as supply personnel. Vaudreuil refused

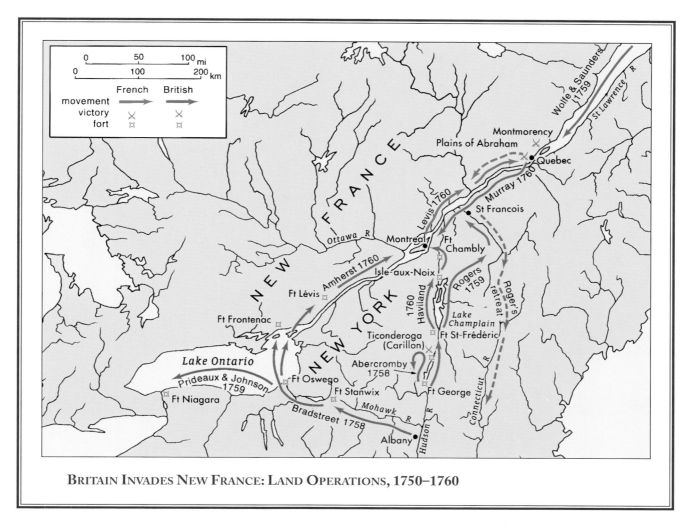

BRITAIN INVADES NEW FRANCE: LAND OPERATIONS, 1750–1760

this proposition, condemning it as an insult to the martial ability of the *habitants*.

Meanwhile, the British launched a three-pronged attack designed to overwhelm the thinly stretched Canadian strength. Loudon's replacement as commander-in-chief, Major General James Abercromby, envisioned a main effort against Louisbourg under the command of General Jeffrey Amherst in close cooperation with the Royal Navy. Simultaneously, Abercromby would follow the Lake Champlain and Richelieu River route to the St. Lawrence Valley. A subsidiary operation would be directed against the Ohio Valley's Fort Duquesne. This was the same strategy the British had tried so often with generally poor results. This time, however, the soldiers were mostly British regulars and far more numerous. "This is most certain," wrote Britain's Lord Chesterfield, "that we have force enough in America to eat up the French alive in Canada, Quebec and Louisbourg, if we have but skill and spirit enough to exert it properly."

Final Siege of Louisbourg

The Chevalier Augustin de Drucourt, commander at Louisbourg, was a veteran naval officer. Since assuming command in 1754, he had strengthened the aged fortress's defences. The garrison was also stronger: 3,000 regulars, 1,000 militia, and 500 native warriors. In the harbour floated 13 French ships manned by about 3,500 sailors. Against them the British fielded 12,000 regular troops and an equal number of marines and sailors aboard 23 ships of the line and 18 frigates and fireships. It required 100 transports to carry the invasion force. Amherst commanded the land forces and Admiral Edward Boscawen the fleet, with Admiral Charles Saunders commanding the elements of this fleet sent from Britain. The French were outnumbered four to one.

Drucourt's strategy was necessarily simple — hold out in the desperate hope the British would exhaust their supplies or be forced by late season storms to withdraw. The British strategy was equally simple — take Louisbourg quickly to allow the capture of Quebec in the same campaign season.

The British fleet hove into sight on June 1, 1758, but stormy seas precluded any landing attempt until the morning of June 8. Despite Gabarus Bay, due west of Louisbourg, being the most predictable landing site, Amherst decided to land his troops there.

Drucourt was well prepared. The most likely landing site in Gabarus Bay was 600-yard-long Cormorant Cove, bounded by two

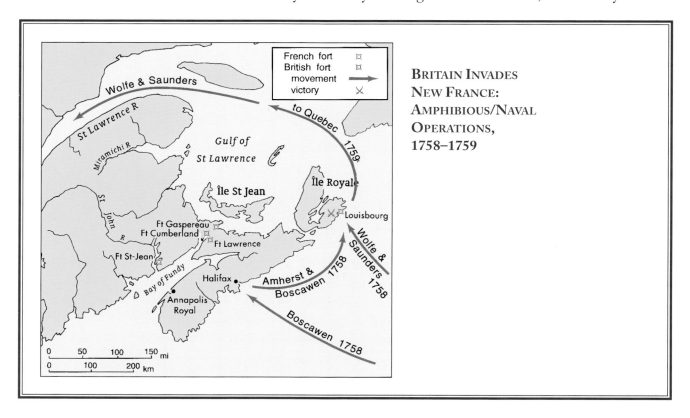

BRITAIN INVADES NEW FRANCE: AMPHIBIOUS/NAVAL OPERATIONS, 1758–1759

headlands. Here Lieutenant Colonel de Saint-Juhlien overlooked the beach with 1,000 entrenched men. To his east, Lieutenant Colonel Marin commanded 900 men and Lieutenant Colonel Henri Valentin Jacques d'Anthonay was positioned still further east with another 900 troops. The rocky gaps and headlands between sand beaches were, however, either poorly defended or undefended due to manpower shortages.

As the invasion force rowed its small craft through the rough surf toward shore, the French batteries laid down a withering fire. At Cormorant Cove, Saint-Juhlien ordered his men to hold fire until the charismatic thirty-year-old British army officer Brigadier James Wolfe's boats were well within range. The French fire slashed into the small British boats, shattering some. Dismayed, Wolfe ordered his boats to sheer off and retreat. But he soon noticed that three boats had escaped into a small rock-strewn cove. The soldiers aboard scrambled ashore seemingly undetected. Seeing an opportunity to outflank Saint-Juhlien's trench system, Wolfe ordered the remaining boats into the cove and Brigadier Charles Lawrence landed his men on Wolfe's left to support the attack. While some men were crushed between boats shattering on the rocks, the majority got safely ashore. Saint-Juhlien and his men were so blinded by their cannon and musket smoke they failed to detect the British flanking movement until a bayonet charge struck their flank and rear. Saint-Juhlien ordered his men to retreat into the woods. To avoid being outflanked, Marin also withdrew and soon the French beach defence collapsed.

With the British firmly ashore and the siege guns being landed, the outcome of the battle was sealed. Louisbourg could perhaps hold long enough to scuttle the British plan to also capture Quebec in 1758, but the fort would fall. Realizing the inevitable outcome, the French naval commodore Charry des Gouttes sought to flee for France. Drucourt refused permission. Gouttes responded by huddling his ships close to shore to afford them the protection of Louisbourg's mighty cannon. Only one small frigate, *Aréthuse,* took up position in the westerly portion of the harbour and brought its guns to bear on Wolfe's men, who had carried out an overland march to first capture Royal Battery and then sweep around Northeast Harbour to capture Lighthouse Point. Here, they were busily setting up a battery opposite Louisbourg when brought under fire to little effect by *Aréthuse.*

Eleven days after the successful landing, the British guns opened fire and the slow process of digging trenches and earthworks that crept ever closer to Louisbourg's walls began. The thunder of the guns was almost constant. Casualties mounted until, toward the end of July, one-quarter of the defenders were debilitated by wounds or battle fatigue.

On July 21, a bomb fell on the ship *Célèbre.* She and two nearby ships burned and an ensuing bombardment by British ships and

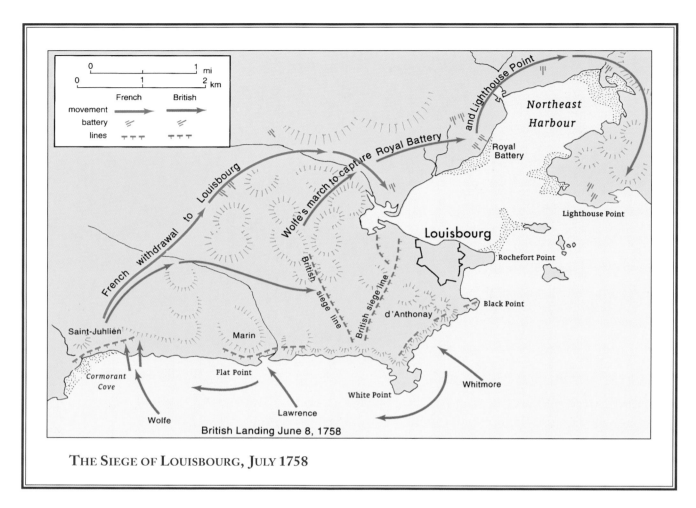

THE SIEGE OF LOUISBOURG, JULY 1758

batteries ashore destroyed all but two ships, *Prudent* and *Bienfasant*. *Aréthuse* successfully evaded the British dragnet and escaped to France, but on the night of July 25 a flotilla of rowboats manned by 600 sailors and marines crept into the harbour and seized the two remaining ships as prizes. When *Bienfasant*'s lines were cut she grounded and had to be burned. *Prudent* was successfully towed into the British lines.

That same evening, a demoralized Drucourt took stock of his defences. Few cannon remained operational, the walls were crumbling, and a serious breach at Dauphin Gate afforded an entry point for British infantry. The next day Drucourt sought a truce, but Amherst demanded unconditional surrender within an hour. Boscawen, no longer needing to fear the French fleet's guns, threatened to thrust six ships of the line into the harbour to join the bombardment. Louisbourg was surrendered.

The delay in the fort's fall bought Quebec reprieve, however. On August 8, Boscawen and Amherst reported that an attack on Quebec was "not practicable." They proposed instead to send three battalions of infantry and supporting ships to destroy French settlements at Miramichi, Gaspé, and other places as far up the St. Lawrence as the season would permit.

Command of the raiding party against Gaspé fell to Wolfe. Striking on September 4, he burned houses, 250 fishing vessels, and destroyed stored fish stocks. Colonel James Murray, meanwhile, destroyed Miramichi, while Lord Andrew Rollo completed the removal of Acadians from Île St. Jean, and Captain Moses Hazen razed Ste. Anne's at present-day Fredericton. Wolfe, disgusted with these attacks on civilians, wrote that the raids "added nothing to the reputation of British arms."

Carillon and Frontenac

While the siege of Louisbourg progressed toward its inevitable conclusion, British Brigadier Lord Howe accompanied by Abercromby moved on July 5, 1758, from Fort George against Fort Carillon with the largest force ever deployed on the North American continent — fully 16,000 men, of whom 6,000 were British regulars. Waiting for him at Fort Carillon, Montcalm had a mere 3,500 men, including marines, Canadian militia, and native warriors. Montcalm and his engineers had wisely abandoned the crumbling stone fort in favour of an entrenched camp with redoubts and abattis on high ground to the west. On July 6, the British landed and began marching overland toward Fort Carillon. En route, the advancing army encountered a small screening force of about 350 French and a short, sharp skirmish ensued, during which Howe was shot through the breast and killed instantly.

On July 8, Abercromby, having assumed command, and his chief engineer scanned the French works and decided a massed infantry frontal assault unsupported by artillery could easily overwhelm it. Just before noon, the British soldiers emerged from the woods in lines before the abattis. Three regiments led the way, including the 42nd Highlanders, who advanced behind the wail of pipers. In minutes, they were swept away by massed French musket and cannon fire.

Abercromby displayed his lack of generalship by failing to modify his tactics. Instead of calling up cannon and pounding the French works into ruin or bypassing Montcalm to capture weakly defended Fort St.-Frédéric and cut his communication lines, Abercromby ordered another unsupported frontal attack. Wave followed wave only to be repelled by the hard-pressed but determined French. After seven bloody hours, the British withdrew. They suffered about 500 dead and 1,450 wounded. The French had also suffered heavily — 106 killed and 256 wounded. Montcalm expected a renewed morning assault and doubted the French could prevail. But dawn patrols discovered the British had decamped in haste, abandoning supplies and boats. Having won a "miraculous" victory, Montcalm proceeded to dig in rather than pursue Abercromby's retreating army.

Meanwhile, Abercromby sent American Lieutenant Colonel John Bradstreet to re-occupy Fort Oswego. If practicable, he was to then

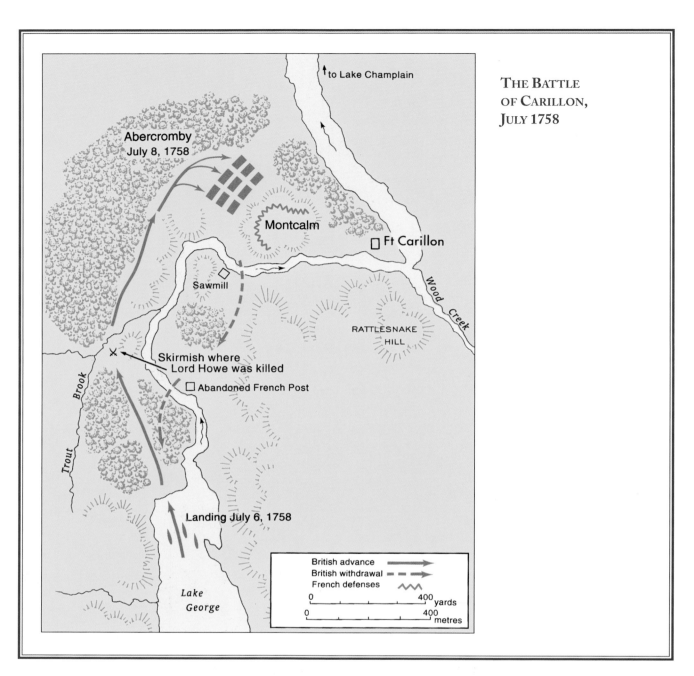

THE BATTLE
OF CARILLON,
JULY 1758

to Lake Champlain

Abercromby
July 8, 1758

Montcalm

Ft Carillon

Wood Creek

Sawmill

RATTLESNAKE
HILL

Skirmish where
Lord Howe was killed

Abandoned French Post

Trout Brook

Landing July 6, 1758

Lake
George

British advance
British withdrawal
French defenses

0 _____ 400 yards
0 _____ 400 metres

attack Fort Frontenac. In this way, Abercromby hoped to deter a
French counterattack from Fort Carillon against the Hudson River
forts. On August 11, Bradstreet marched with 3,000 men, arriving
at the Fort Oswego ruins on August 21. Barely pausing, he embarked
his men in 123 bateaux and 95 whaleboats and proceeded against Fort
Frontenac. The force landed on a small island opposite the fort on
August 25.

Detecting Bradstreet's approach, Pierre-Jacques Payen, Sieur de
Noyan, who commanded the fort's 110-man garrison, had begged for
reinforcements. A relief force was hurriedly organized and marched
for Fort Frontenac on August 27 from Montreal. Noyan, meanwhile,
hunkered inside the fort's walls and offered a desultory cannonade
whenever the enemy drew too close.

Possessing only 70 rounds per cannon, Bradstreet lacked sufficient artillery for a European-style siege. He decided victory would only come if his men could close on the palisades quickly. Under cover of darkness, he seized the high ground and his men started to dig a trench toward the fort. On August 28, the American cannon opened fire preparatory to an infantry attack. A chance round ignited ammunition near the magazine, causing several burn casualties and greatly demoralizing the defenders. Shortly thereafter, Noyan surrendered the fort, sparing Bradstreet an assault against the unbreached walls.

The British attempt to storm the French defensive works at Fort Carillon on July 8, 1758, ended in a bloody defeat.

Bradstreet destroyed the fort and then, fearful of the rumoured relief force, withdrew. Learning of the destruction of Fort Frontenac, Montcalm reported that French superiority on Lake Ontario was now lost, perhaps permanently. His pessimism was heightened when news reached him on November 23 that Fort Duquesne had been destroyed to avert its capture. At year's end, French dominance of the western frontier was imperilled and the way open for an attack on Quebec the following spring.

During the British attack on Fort Frontenac, a chance cannon round set off the French munitions magazine, greatly demoralizing the defenders.

THE DECISIVE YEAR

The Royal Navy prevented all but a few French ships reaching New France with vitally needed supplies in the spring of 1759. With them came only 400 regular soldiers to reinforce Montcalm's shrinking army. The general had five battalions totalling 2,900 regulars, 3,800 Montreal militia, 1,100 Trois-Rivières militia, 3,000 Quebec militia, a garrison of 600 in Quebec fort, and a dwindling number of aboriginal allies — fewer than 15,000 men to defend the colony against a four-front invasion.

Opposing the French was a combined British-American army numbering about 50,000. The British plan mirrored past campaigns. Major General James Wolfe would capture Quebec while Amherst campaigned against Fort Carillon, Fort St.-Frédéric, Montreal, and

DECISION ON THE PLAINS OF ABRAHAM: THE SIEGE AND CAPTURE OF QUEBEC, JUNE–SEPTEMBER 1759

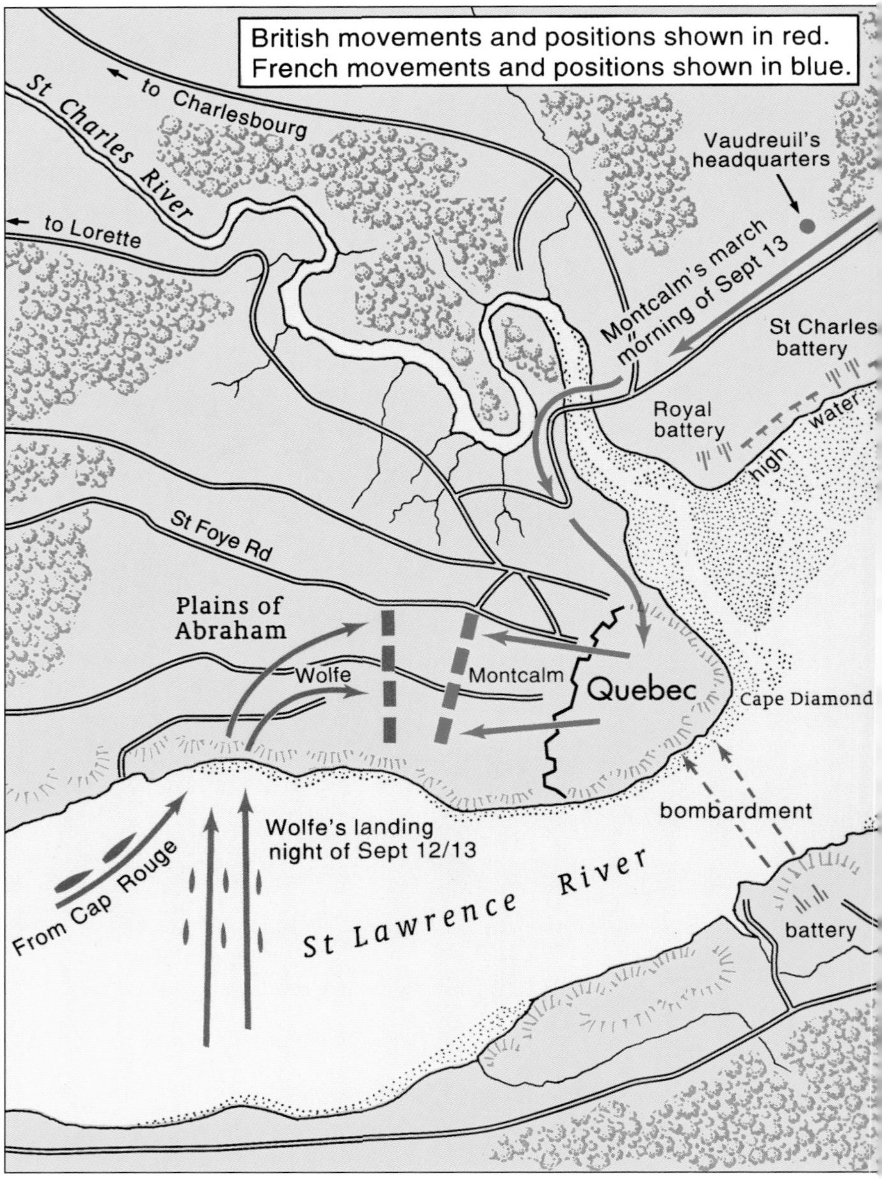

British movements and positions shown in red.
French movements and positions shown in blue.

to Charlesbourg
St Charles River
to Lorette
Vaudreuil's headquarters
Montcalm's march morning of Sept 13
St Charles battery
Royal battery
high water
St Foye Rd
Plains of Abraham
Wolfe
Montcalm
Quebec
Cape Diamond
bombardment
Wolfe's landing night of Sept 12/13
From Cap Rouge
St Lawrence River
battery

Fort Niagara. A new variation added to no real effect was the dispatch of about 600 frontiersmen, known as Roger's Rangers, under Major Robert Rogers from Lake Champlain overland to St. François on the St. Lawrence River. Although this force reached its objective, it was quickly repelled and forced to undertake a long, difficult retreat to the Connecticut River.

Meanwhile, the two major offensive forces finally got underway with 5,000 men led by Brigadier General John Prideaux marching in late June toward Fort Oswego to establish a jumping-off point for attacking Fort Niagara and opening up a route for invading the St. Lawrence Valley. Required to leave men behind to secure communication lines and rebuild Fort Oswego, Prideaux arrived on July 6 before Fort Niagara with about 2,500 men. The dilapidated fort's

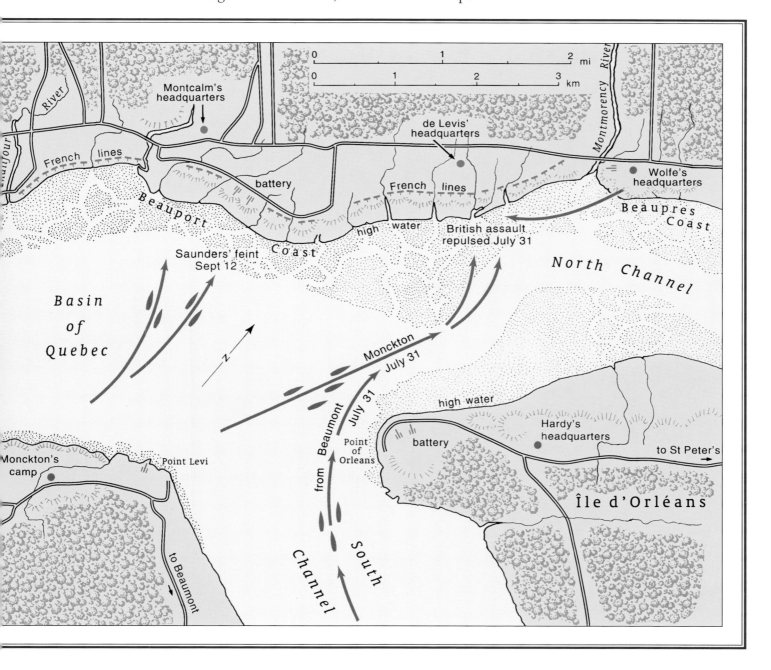

garrison numbered 486 men and 39 civilians commanded by Captain Pierre Pouchot.

Several days after the ponderous siege began, Prideaux was killed by an exploding shell and command fell to colonial officer Sir William Johnson, who forced Pouchot to surrender the fort on July 26. Meanwhile, a Canadian militia attempt to outflank Johnson's force at Fort Niagara by capturing Fort Oswego foundered due to poor leadership. The attackers retreated in disarray and manpower shortages necessitated abandoning Fort Carillon and Fort St.-Frédéric without a fight. Amherst had the opportunity to make a bold thrust on two fronts against ill-defended Montreal, but the British commander-in-chief moved so slowly that winter overtook him, ending the western campaign.

While Amherst's army achieved modest gains in the west, Wolfe moved against Quebec with 43 fighting ships and 80 transports carrying 8,600 soldiers and 13,500 sailors and marines. Wolfe's fleet arrived off Île d'Orléans' south shore on June 26. While the British reconnoitered the southern shore for suitable camps, the French attempted to burn the troop transports with fireships on the night of June 28–29. However, they lit the ships too early and the British easily evaded the flaming vessels.

On June 30, Wolfe landed 3,000 soldiers under the command of Brigadier Robert Monckton and captured Point Levi against scant resistance. This move gave Wolfe partial command of the river above Quebec and enabled construction of an artillery battery directly across the water from the fortress. Here Wolfe established a battery of massive 32-pound guns and 13-inch mortars capable of breaching Quebec's strong walls. Over the next few days, he deployed the remainder of his force in two separate camps — one under Major Hardy on the southern tip of Île d'Orléans, the other under his own command on the north shore immediately east of Montmorency River.

The French response to Wolfe's actions was sluggish. Although Montcalm had almost 15,000 defenders, many were untrained civilians either too old or too young for active service, who lacked even militia experience. A bungled attempt by 1,200 civilian troops to attack Monckton's camp on the night of July 12–13 ended in confused retreat when the attackers became disoriented in the thick forest and fired on each other. That same night, the British battery started bombarding Quebec.

While Montcalm vacillated, Wolfe appeared stymied about how to win victory. The siege dragged until July 31, when Wolfe struck the French left flank with an amphibious assault west of Montmorency River against the heavily defended ridgeline. The well-entrenched French soldiers shattered the attack with massed grapeshot and musket fire. The British suffered 210 dead and 230 wounded. Wolfe and his brigadiers quarrelled over what to do next, but finally decided to establish a bridgehead above Quebec on the north side of the river to sever the city's line of supply.

Montcalm intuited the shift of emphasis away from Montmorency and Beauport toward the Plains of Abraham, but failed to convince Vaudreuil of the threat. On September 6, Vaudreuil ordered the regiment covering the plains moved to face the nonexistent threat at Montmorency.

Wolfe's plan required close coordination with the British fleet commanded by Admiral Charles Saunders. On the night of September 12–13, while Wolfe moved a large force of infantry by flatboat to a beach beneath the Plains of Abraham, Saunders conducted a deception by massing the majority of the fleet off Beauport. The British achieved complete surprise by scaling the 175-foot cliff to reach the plains. At sunrise, 4,800 British regulars were marching toward St. Foye Road. With Vaudreuil countermanding orders that would have moved desperately needed reinforcements to face the approaching British, Montcalm hastily deployed 4,000 soldiers and just two cannon to meet the enemy. Wolfe's strategy was to force Montcalm to premature battle before the French forces could unite, and Montcalm obliged.

At ten o'clock, the French advanced briskly in line, but soon became confused as the Canadian militia put into the ranks alongside the regulars failed to maintain formation, instead dropping to the ground to reload after the first volley. Formed in facing ranks, the British hammered the approaching French with steady sustained volleys. Great holes were torn in the French line. Montcalm was mortally wounded. By half past ten the French were in full retreat. Wolfe, too, lay dead. Only fierce fire put in against the charging British soldiers enabled much of the French army to escape. British casualties numbered 68 dead and 600 wounded, versus French losses of 644 killed or wounded.

With Wolfe's death, British command passed to Brigadier George Townshend, who started cautiously digging trenches before the walls of Quebec and refused to pursue the main French body which escaped toward Montreal, leaving Quebec to its fate. On September 18, 1759, the city capitulated. The lack of aggression by Amherst in the west and Townshend at Quebec bought New France an extra year.

THE FINAL YEAR

With Montcalm's death, French command fell to Chevalier François Gaston de Lévis, who realized he must recapture Quebec to open the St. Lawrence River. Through the winter, Lévis built an ad hoc army of 7,000 men. They departed Montreal on April 12 by boat with only 12 antiquated cannon and scant supplies. Lévis hoped to capture the fortress before British reinforcements arrived by ship.

When Lévis reached Quebec, Brigadier James Murray marched with 3,000 men to meet him on the Plains of Abraham. Battle was

British troops scale the 175-foot cliffs from the beach to the Plains of Abraham on September 13, 1759.

joined on April 28, 1760, near the previous battle site. For two hours the battle raged with heavy casualties on both sides. Finally the British gave way, withdrawing behind Quebec's walls. Murray's casualties were 1,124 killed and wounded. French casualties remain disputed, with estimates of total casualties ranging from 2,000 to 833. Lévis undertook a feeble siege with his poor cannon, hoping that French ships would arrive first, but it was British sails that hove into view on May 15 and Lévis withdrew to Montreal.

Once again, Amherst undertook a three-pronged invasion that would link up on Montreal's outskirts. One column, commanded by Brigadier William Haviland, advanced up the Richelieu River, while

Amherst led another down the St. Lawrence from Fort Oswego, and a third under Murray approached from Quebec. The French could offer only token resistance, and by September the 17,000-strong British force was poised to take Montreal. On September 8, Vaudreuil capitulated. When asked for terms, Amherst stated, "I have come to take Canada and I will take nothing less." In 1763, the Treaty of Paris confirmed the loss of Canada to Britain. Spain's claim to Louisiana was confirmed, while France retained only St. Pierre and Miquelon.

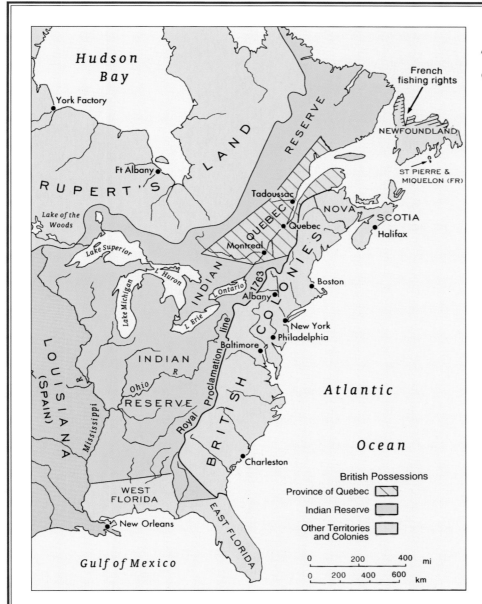

THE TREATY OF PARIS, 1763

On February 10, 1763, France signed a treaty by which it surrendered all its territory on mainland North America west of the Mississippi River to Britain, while Spain ceded Florida to Britain. In return, Spain was granted the Louisiana Territory and New Orleans from France. With several strokes of a pen, France's 150 years in North America were brought to an end and the settlers in Canada left to survive as best they could as members of a British colony.

CHAPTER THREE

War with the Thirteen Colonies

1774–1783

ANOTHER SPARK TO THE TINDER

The seeds of the next North American war were sown in the aftermath of the Seven Years War. In a bid to secure French-Canadian loyalty to the British Crown, the 1774 Quebec Act reinstated the borders of Canada to those previously held by New France, particularly in the west. It also reinforced the power of New France's traditional seigneurial and clerical ruling class. That the Quebec Act also ensured that the northernmost part of North America provided a loyal base, from which Britain might crush any rebellion by the restive Thirteen Colonies, was not lost on the Americans. As for the increasingly powerless First Nations peoples, they were relegated without consultation to a narrow boundary of land encircled by French, British, and Spanish colonial territory.

The Act also heightened American dissatisfaction with British rule. Restoring Quebec's western boundaries hampered expansion from the Thirteen Colonies. That this imposition should benefit French-speaking Catholics who were former enemies further rankled. Combined with the furore caused by colonial taxation and heavy-handed attempts to enforce British will through military might following the March 5, 1770, Boston riot, the Quebec Act helped galvanize the Thirteen Colonies to overcome traditional rivalry and unite in a bid for independence. The colonists were little impressed that the taxation initiative sought to relieve Britain of a national debt of £130 million, mostly incurred defending their colonies during the Seven Years War. The independence advocates slowly gaining a majority in the Continental Congress bridled at "taxation without representation." Protestant almost to a man, they decried the Quebec Act for surrounding them with "a Nation of papists" that would prevent America settling the continent.

Meanwhile, Congress also realized that if the Thirteen Colonies were to revolt it would be better to have French-Canadian support. So anti-Quebec propaganda was largely confined to local boundaries, while a hyperbolic show of goodwill was offered — evidenced when, on October 26, 1774, Congress extolled France's liberal tradition and invited Canadians to join in an American republic. In case rapprochement failed, the same message warned Quebec that it could have "all the rest of North America your unalterable friends, or your inveterate enemies."

On the eve of the uprising, neither Americans nor British knew how the Canadians would react. American agents cautioned that at best the Canadians would remain neutral. Quebec's leaders promised Britain loyalty and the support of the militia. Britain fervently hoped the militia would comply, because every man would be needed to crush the rebellion. In the main, American intelligence was most astute, for there was little enthusiasm among average Canadians for marching to war to defend British rule.

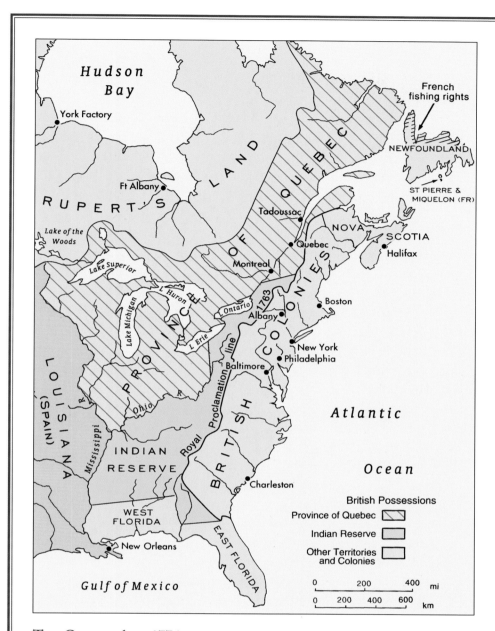

THE QUEBEC ACT, 1774

Faced with a growing rebellious population in the New England colonies, the British Parliament decided to adopt proposed legislation that removed all the territory and fur-trade operations between the Ohio River and the Mississippi, giving these to Quebec's French population. Additionally, French civil law was imposed and the Roman Catholic religion was granted prominence in the region. The Quebec Act was imposed along with three other acts that were intended to re-establish British control over its colonies in North America. Dubbed the Intolerable Acts by the American colonists, they brought the dispute between the colonists and the Crown to a head. Later in 1774, the First Continental Congress was held and open revolution soon followed.

FIRST SHOTS

The spring of 1775 brought revolution when American militiamen engaged British regulars at Lexington on April 19. Within weeks, the Americans determined to capture the British forts at Crown Point (formerly Fort St.-Frédéric) and Ticonderoga (Fort Carillon). The British garrisons were weak, with just 9 men at Crown Point and 48 at Ticonderoga. Against them marched Ethan Allen's "Green Mountain Boys," a quasi-vigilante force based in northern New York. Alongside Allen rode Benedict Arnold, recently commissioned a colonel by the Massachusetts Provincial Congress. Arnold had the commission while Allen had the troops, so Allen commanded, with Arnold providing token legal authority in the absence of a declaration of war by Congress.

On May 10, this ragtag force of about 80 men easily breached Ticonderoga's crumbling defences, guarded by only one sentry, and rousted the fort's commander from bed. The only shot fired was by the sentry and that was a misfire. Crown Point was taken soon after, again without violence. Arnold embarked days later from Ticonderoga on a sloop manned by recruits from Massachusetts to attack Fort St. Jean, even though this clearly violated Canadian sovereignty. His force insufficient to hold the fort, Arnold withdrew after burning a British sloop and pillaging some stores.

Despite the failure at Fort St. Jean, the road into Canada was now open to the Americans. On June 27, Congress authorized the invasion. Much to Arnold's chagrin, command went to New Yorker General Philip Schuyler. The general arrived at Ticonderoga on July 18 only to discover that the proposed invasion force was completely untrained. Hasty training ensued and the 1,500-strong army finally marched on August 30, arriving on Canadian soil on September 2.

Schuyler's force was one of two over which he had overall command. The Ticonderoga force, forming the left wing, was to use the Lake Champlain–Richelieu route to take Montreal. Meanwhile, a right wing of 1,200 men under Arnold would enter Canada by a little-travelled route running through Massachusetts up the Kennebec River, cross a narrow height of land, and down the Chaudière River to Quebec — a distance of about 200 miles that passed through many swamps and required the crossing of numerous ice-choked rivers. When both forces seized their objectives, the Americans would control Canada.

THE MONTREAL CAMPAIGN

Quebec Governor Sir Guy Carleton was hard pressed to stave off the Americans. He estimated that defending Canada would require 10,000 men plus supporting artillery and engineering units, yet the total regular army strength in the country numbered fewer than 1,000. The strongest garrison at Fort St. Jean was 385 strong, while only 61 soldiers protected Quebec. Officially, the Canadian militia was supposed to swell the British ranks, but Carleton's penchant for appointing

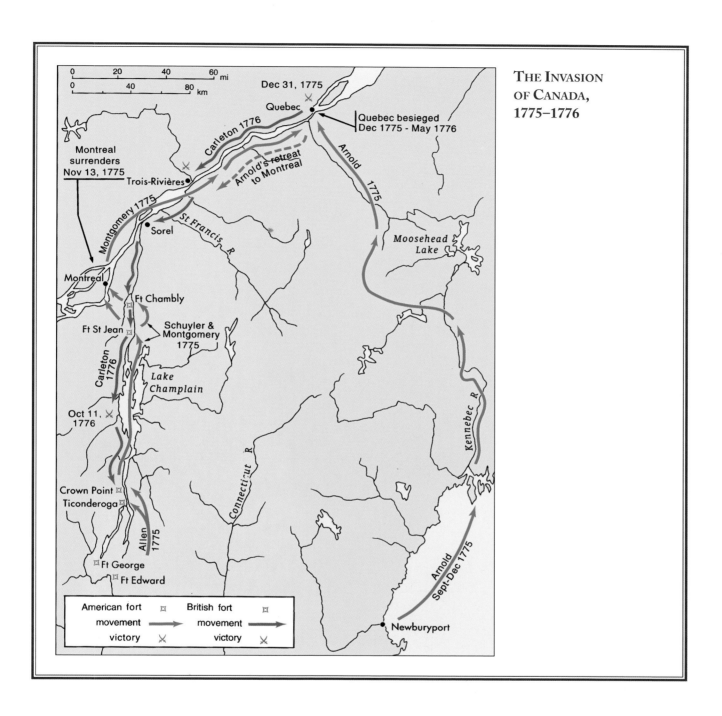

THE INVASION
OF CANADA,
1775–1776

Dec 31, 1775

Quebec

Quebec besieged
Dec 1775 - May 1776

Carleton 1776

Montreal
surrenders
Nov 13, 1775

Trois-Rivières

Arnold's retreat
to Montreal

Arnold 1775

Montgomery 1775

St Francis R

Sorel

Moosehead
Lake

Montreal

Ft Chambly

Ft St Jean

Schuyler &
Montgomery
1775

Carleton
1776

Lake
Champlain

Kennebec R

Oct 11,
1776

Connecticut R

Crown Point
Ticonderoga

Allen
1775

Arnold
Sept-Dec 1775

Ft George
Ft Edward

American fort	⌑	British fort	⌑
movement	→	movement	→
victory	✕	victory	✕

Newburyport

inexperienced and unpopular seigneurs to command, along with the wait-and-see attitude of most average Canadians, resulted in few militiamen reporting.

The American offensive meanwhile lurched into action. When Schuyler fell ill, he handed command of the left prong to his deputy, Brigadier General Richard Montgomery, who had served in the British army before joining the rebels. Although he thought the American volunteers "the worst stuff imaginable for soldiers," their ranks were growing as more ill-trained recruits arrived. By the time Montgomery set off for Fort St. Jean on August 31, 1775, the force numbered about 2,000. The first attack quickly crumbled when met with an unfounded rumour that a British warship awaited them and scant resistance was offered by a handful of British skirmishers. Montgomery followed his retreating men back to their swampy base camp at Île aux Noix, reorganized, and set out in flatboats again two weeks later. With him was a small naval flotilla consisting of a schooner, a sloop, and two row galleys each mounting a 12-pounder cannon.

By September, the Fort St. Jean garrison had grown to about 600, commanded by Major Charles Preston. Montgomery easily pushed in the British patrols attempting to prevent the fort being encircled. Two days after landing near the fort, the Americans had it surrounded and under siege. Montgomery also sent detachments north toward Montreal to foil any attempt Carleton might make to reinforce Preston.

At the head of one detachment was Ethan Allen, who decided Montreal was ripe for plucking. With only 110 men, some of whom were Canadians bribed into joining the American cause by heady promises and the payment of 30 pence per day, Allen arrived at the gates of Montreal on September 24. About 260 men, including 120 French-Canadian militiamen, marched out the next day to meet him. Despite Allen's efforts to keep his men on the field, they quickly broke and Allen was forced to surrender.

Allen's defeat and capture had a sobering effect on Montreal's pro-American elements and throughout the rest of Quebec, resulting in more militiamen reporting for duty. Carleton soon had 2,000 men in Montreal, mostly militia. But when Carleton hesitated to march to Preston's aid, many drifted off to bring in their fall harvest. An opportunity had been wasted. Fort St. Jean paid the price.

Montgomery's strength grew daily, including additional cannon and mortars, and the 1,300 men, women, and children inside the fortress walls endured ever worsening bombardments as September gave way to October. On September 20, the small garrison at Fort Chambly north of Fort St. Jean surrendered to an American assault, leaving Preston's garrison isolated. It was becoming ever more apparent that relief from Montreal was unlikely. On November 3, with food supplies virtually exhausted and winter setting in, Preston surrendered.

Combat casualties on both sides were slight, as the Americans had opted for siege over storm. The defenders had about 40 dead or wounded and the Americans 100. However, Montgomery had also had to release another 900 Americans from service due to illness.

When told that Preston had finally capitulated, Carleton immediately set about planning to evacuate Montreal and retire to Quebec. Learning that another American column was approaching Quebec via the Chaudière River, Carleton assumed Montreal was lost. If he reached Quebec, the Americans might ultimately be forced back. Illustrating his normal penchant for delay, Carleton did not sail until November 11, with 90 British regulars crammed into a few hastily gathered whaleboats. Two days later, Montreal officials surrendered the city. Montgomery, wasting no time to celebrate, sailed immediately up the St. Lawrence to link up with Arnold's column and effect Quebec's capture.

THE SIEGE OF QUEBEC

Carleton arrived in Quebec on November 19, 1775. Montgomery landed at Pointe aux Trembles 18 miles above Quebec exactly two weeks later. With him were only 300 men. But Arnold was there with the remains of his force — about 800 men. Arnold's march through the wilderness had been a gruelling experience that left several hundred dead in its wake and the rest of his men tired and poorly supplied. Montgomery's men were in little better condition. The Americans also lacked any heavy siege cannon or the engineering supplies and experts to reduce the crumbling, but still significant, fortress walls.

It is doubtful the barricade manned by fewer than 50 British troops was as stout or heavily gunned as represented in this etching of the American attack on Quebec in December 1775. The British did, however, kill Brigadier General Richard Montgomery and several others with their opening volley, prompting an American rout.

OVER:
Determined resistance by British regulars and Canadian militia at a barrier in Quebec City's St. Roch district stopped Benedict Arnold's American column, ending the day's fighting.

Inside that fort was a 1,800-man garrison that included only about 300 regulars. The rest were sailors, marines, and militia. The city was well provisioned and anti-American sentiment in the civilian populace was relatively high. If Montgomery and Arnold relied on siege, there was little probability of success. Instead they opted for attack, deciding to first capture Lower Town and from there to scale the cliffs and walls of Upper Town, the city's fortified section.

The attack went in on the early morning of December 31. Montgomery struck from the west, driving up the narrow beach below Cape Diamond. Arnold pushed through St. Roch suburb to the east and entered an equally narrow strip of ground that curved below the fortress walls to enter Lower Town, where the two forces were to join. Montgomery's men, half blinded by the blowing snow, encountered a barricade manned by fewer than 50 men. The defenders opened fire and Montgomery and several men fell dead. The rest of the Americans fled the field.

Meanwhile, Arnold's men waded through deep snow to enter the maze of St. Roch's storehouses and wharves, and overcame one defensive barricade but were stopped cold before a second. At the first barricade, Arnold was wounded and evacuated. Stymied by the stiff resistance they met, the Americans were soon attacked from the rear by reinforcements dispatched from Upper Town out of the Palace Gate. After a brief fight, most surrendered. Total American losses were about 400 captured and 100 killed or wounded. The defenders had suffered only about six casualties.

With the Americans able to muster no more than 350 men, Carleton could easily have gone on the offensive and mopped up those who remained before they could reorganize. Instead he kept his men inside Quebec's walls. Arnold quickly regrouped and dug in to endure the long winter. Congress also authorized the dispatch of major reinforcements to Quebec. These arrived in March, raising Arnold's strength to about 2,500 men, of whom only about 285 had belonged to the original offensive force of 1,775. Still, Arnold had neither the artillery nor engineers needed to reduce Quebec's walls. So he could only maintain the siege until May 6, 1776, when a relief fleet from Britain arrived. The Americans promptly withdrew. Carleton let them go unmolested.

LIBERATION OF CANADA

The American hold over the upper St. Lawrence was perilous after the siege of Quebec was lifted. To the west of Montreal, the British still controlled several forts. From these bases, Captain George Forster marched with about 140 Canadian militia and British regulars as well as several hundred native warriors to seize the Americans' western outpost, called the Cedars, at the second rapid between Lake Francis and Lake St. Louis. He easily forced the Americans to surrender, capturing some 500 prisoners and forcing an American retreat to Lachine.

Carleton now had eight regiments of regulars from Britain and four companies of artillery commanded by Major General John Burgoyne. Four thousand German mercenaries under General Friederich Riedesel, who had been enlisted by the British government, arrived later in the summer. The Americans had also been reinforced, but the new commander, General John Sullivan, had no more than 5,000 men concentrated around Montreal. An American offensive to recapture Trois-Rivières failed miserably on June 8, 1776, with the loss of 200 captured and 25 killed compared to only 17 British casualties. Once again Carleton, with more than 8,000 men at hand, failed to pursue the retreating Americans.

His lack of vigour hardly mattered for, despite the Declaration of Independence having been signed on July 4, the American army in Canada was falling apart — the victim of a smallpox epidemic, collapsing morale, and poor leadership. Arnold wrote to Sullivan that, as Canada could not be taken, "let us quit . . . and secure our own country before it is too late." Sullivan agreed and retreated from Montreal down the Richelieu to Lake Champlain.

On October 14, Carleton's troops occupied Crown Point. Now only Ticonderoga barred the British from launching a spring invasion of the Thirteen Colonies via the Richelieu–Lake Champlain corridor. Despite the protests of his generals, Carleton decided the Americans at Ticonderoga were too strong and ordered a withdrawal to Fort St. Jean, where he settled in for the winter.

NOVA SCOTIA REMAINS LOYAL

While the Americans suffered this reversal of arms in 1776, Congress also failed to incite the 14,000 New Englanders settled in Nova Scotia to take up the rebel cause. Only in November 1776 did any attempt at insurrection occur. On the Isthmus of Chignecto, a small number of New Englanders raised a motley army of only about 180 men and marched to capture Fort Cumberland, formerly the French fort of Beauséjour.

Two hundred British regulars and militia were entrenched inside Fort Cumberland's walls, formidable opponents that would have given most professional soldiers pause. The rebels, however, trusting their cause was right and God was on their side, laid siege to the fort on November 7. Learning that reinforcements were on the way to relieve the fort's garrison, they attempted two assaults that were easily beaten back. When the British reinforcements appeared, the rebels fled. The British easily overtook the rebels and, somewhat surprisingly, their commander offered clemency to those who surrendered and expressed regret for taking up arms against the King. Most did so and Nova Scotia's effort at rebellion effectively crumbled.

FINAL SHOTS

In 1777, General Burgoyne convinced the British government that he, rather than Carleton, should command an invasion from Lake Champlain that would link up with another British force under Major General Sir Henry Clinton moving north along the Hudson River from New York. When the linkage was achieved, the Thirteen Colonies would be cut in two and the rebels on either side could be eliminated at leisure. Of course, Burgoyne had first to recapture the Lake Champlain bases from which Carleton had withdrawn.

A subsidiary operation led by Brigadier General Barry St. Leger assembled at Fort Oswego and drove east toward Fort Stanwix with the aim of forcing the Americans to divide their forces to meet both this threat and that posed by Burgoyne. This strategy succeeded as General Horatio Gates was obliged to send a blocking force under Benedict Arnold to prevent the American fort being captured and his own left flank exposed to attack by St. Leger.

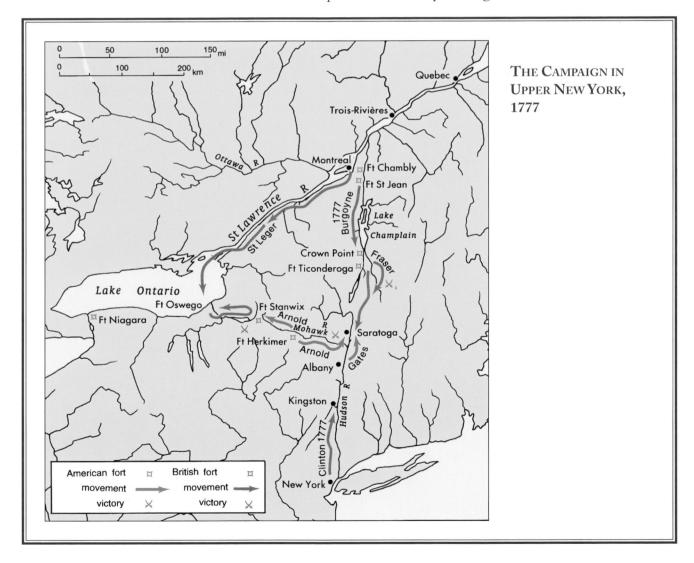

THE CAMPAIGN IN UPPER NEW YORK, 1777

Burgoyne meanwhile marched in June at the head of a combined British and German mercenary army of about 7,000 men. In the ranks was a scant Canadian element numbering barely 100 militia and only 500 native warriors. On June 20, Crown Point was occupied and on July 1, Burgoyne reached Ticonderoga, from which the Americans rapidly retreated. He set off in pursuit while Major Malcolm Fraser led a column to the left and captured Hubbardton. But the advance mired in the rough wilderness where he lost almost 2,000 men to sickness and accidents. Consequently, Burgoyne arrived before Saratoga on September 3 with only 5,000 men, many of whom were desperately weak, to find himself facing 14,000 Americans under General Gates, including Arnold's troops, which had rushed east from Fort Stanwix when St. Leger unaccountably retreated to Fort Oswego without offering battle. On October 17, blocked from advancing and unable to withdraw back the way he had come, Burgoyne surrendered his remaining 3,500 troops.

This failed invasion largely concluded Canadian involvement in the Revolutionary War. Henceforth British and Canadian militia confined themselves to the hit-and-run frontier raids that had typified New France's *la petite guerre* with the American colonies during the 17th century. The Americans reciprocated, largely attacking aboriginal nations loyal to the British. A raid by one side sparked a retaliatory raid from the other. Finally, with the second 18th-century Treaty of Paris in 1783, hostilities ceased. The Thirteen Colonies gained independence from Britain, while Quebec and Nova Scotia remained independent from the United States. Under the treaty, however, Canada lost much of its western trading territories and a vague border set on the 45th parallel pleased neither side. Another war would be necessary to settle matters.

CHAPTER FOUR

The War of 1812

1812–1814

WAR'S OUTBREAK

In early 1812, the American Congress thought the time ripe for the United States to bring all North America into the union. Congress believed that striking now, while Britain fought a war on the European continent, would assure easy victory. Neither President James Madison nor the congressmen from New England, where antiwar sentiment ran high, favoured this decision. On June 18, 1812, however, Madison bowed to Congress and declared war against Britain.

Despite the clamour for war, America was ill prepared. Its high-ranking officers were mostly elderly Revolutionary War veterans and its regular army numbered only 10,000 poorly trained men. Congress wanted to fight the war cheaply, so it authorized only modest expansion of the army to 35,000, supplemented by state militia drafts. Yet militiamen could only be required to serve for a year and could refuse service outside their state boundaries. Further, New England's opposition meant that its militias would not participate in attacks on New Brunswick and Nova Scotia.

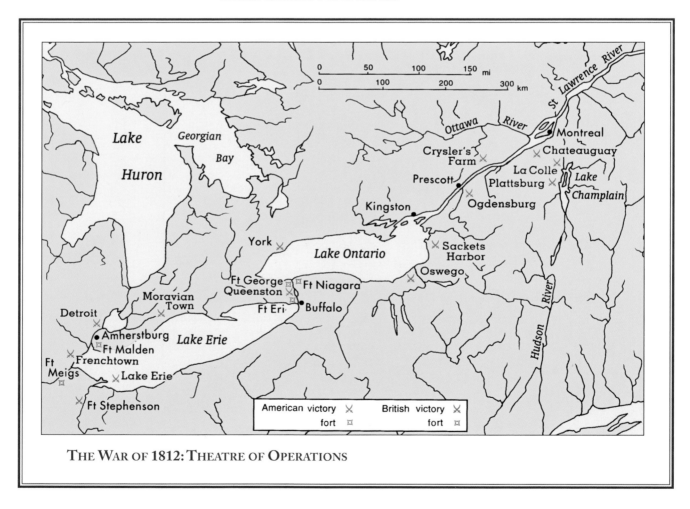

THE WAR OF 1812: THEATRE OF OPERATIONS

HULL INVADES CANADA

Even before the war proclamation, American soldiers marched against Canada. On June 12, 1812, Brigadier General William Hull led some 2,000 regular and militia troops from the Ohio Valley toward Fort Detroit. Seventeen days later, the exhausted, sickness-plagued column staggered out of the dark woods onto the shore of Lake Erie 130 kilometres from Detroit. Unaware that war had been declared and that the British would consequently be on the alert, Hull hired a ship, the *Cayahoga,* to take the ill troops and his personal papers to Fort Detroit.

On July 3, a British ship detained *Cayahoga,* the Americans on board were taken prisoner, and Hull's papers were sent to British Major General Isaac Brock. Two days later, Hull marched into Fort Detroit and was joined by several hundred Michigan militiamen. On July 12, Hull's now 2,500-strong army crossed the river into Upper Canada to occupy the small hamlet of Sandwich opposite Fort Detroit. Here he lingered rather than marching immediately against Fort Malden. Soon Hull learned that the British had captured a small American outpost, Michilimackinac, and became paralyzed by indecision. When the neighbouring Wyandot native tribe allied with the British and the Shawnee warrior Tecumseh ambushed one of his supply columns on August 5, Hull panicked, fearing an imminent massacre. He began organizing his army for a hasty retreat to, as he wrote, escape the native warriors "swarming down in every direction."

More of Hull's papers were captured during Tecumseh's ambush and Brock took decisive action in light of the mass of intelligence revealing that Hull's army was thoroughly demoralized. Although outnumbered, Brock took the offensive. Hull, rather than engage the approaching 700 British regulars and militia commanded by Brock and 600 aboriginal warriors led by Tecumseh, retreated to Fort Detroit. The British force pursued and crossed the river on the evening of August 15, attacking the next morning at dawn by firing several cannon salvoes into the stockade. Hull surrendered almost immediately. He and 582 American regulars were taken prisoner, while some 1,600 militiamen were paroled.

THE BATTLE OF QUEENSTON HEIGHTS

With the west secure, Brock planned to attack Sackets Harbor and destroy its shipbuilding capacity. Left undisturbed, the Americans would soon use this port to deploy a superior naval force on Lake Ontario. However, Brock arrived at Fort George to find an informal ceasefire in effect that benefited American Major General Henry Dearborn because his Niagara frontier army would not be ready to campaign until late autumn.

On September 9, the ceasefire ended abruptly when President Madison refused its ratification. But several weeks passed before the

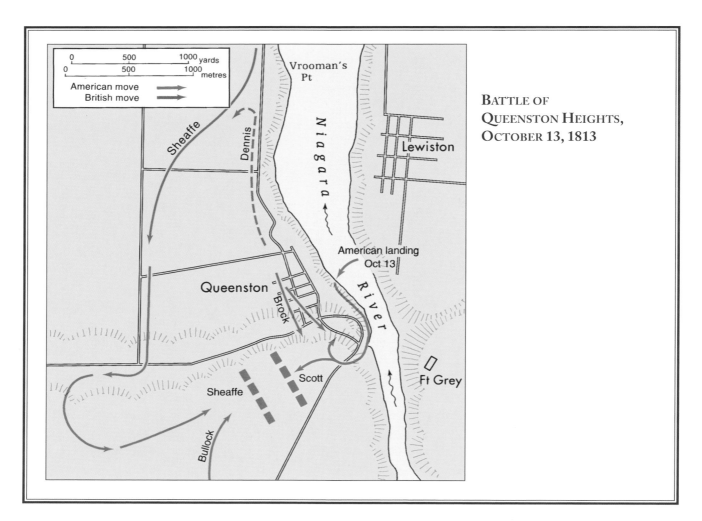

Americans sought to cross the Niagara River in front of the Upper Canadian village of Queenston at the base of the Niagara Escarpment. Facing the Americans was a detachment of regulars and militia numbering 350 men under command of Captain James B. Dennis, with a small battery dug in about halfway up the escarpment at Vrooman's Point, overlooking Queenston and facing the river crossing. The American force boasted 6,300 men, of whom 3,650 were regulars.

The Americans' first river-crossing attempt on October 12 was so bungled Brock thought it a feint. He believed Fort George was the true objective and refused to release reinforcements to bolster the Queenston garrison. The following night, however, the Americans successfully crossed the river. Realizing his mistake, Brock ordered the Fort George garrison to march to Queenston, then rode ahead to organize the defence.

Arriving to find that Dennis and the remaining 200 British soldiers had been pushed back and their battery captured, Brock unsheathed his sword and led a reckless charge up the escarpment to recapture the guns. An American sharpshooter put a bullet into Brock's chest, killing him instantly. The attack collapsed. When his aide-de-camp, Lieutenant Colonel John Macdonell, tried again, he was mortally wounded.

Having established a beachhead, American General Stephan Van Rensselaer did nothing to expand his position. He also failed to convince the New York militiamen, asserting their right not to fight outside their state, to participate in the crossing. On the opposite shore, the 1,600 American regulars on the heights waited vainly for support. Soon British reinforcements arrived and recaptured the village. Meanwhile, a main British column under command of Major General Roger Sheaffe climbed the escarpment further inland to attack the American right flank. Meanwhile, Captain Richard Bullock arrived from Chippewa with 150 men of the 41st Foot Regiment and two militia companies as reinforcements. When the British put in a charge, they quickly overwhelmed the Americans, killing and wounding about 500 and taking almost 1,000 prisoners. British and native casualties tallied only 19 killed, 77 wounded, and 21 missing.

Although a mortally wounded Major General Isaac Brock is shown here urging on the main British defence of Queenston Heights, he actually died earlier during an ill-fated attack on an entirely different flank of the American line.

WAR ON THE LAKES

Although the Americans suffered only defeat on land during 1812, in November they forced the British flagship *Royal George* to seek refuge in Kingston harbour and launched the lake's largest ship, the 24-gun corvette, *Madison*. Throughout the ensuing winter, British boat-builders at York and Kingston and Americans at Sackets Harbor worked feverishly to construct bigger, more powerful ships. With the spring, a 14-ship American squadron loaded with 1,700 infantry set out to destroy the shipbuilding facilities at York. Shortly before dawn on April 27, 1813, the soldiers landed west of the town and brushed aside meagre resistance. Meanwhile, the American ships swept into the harbour mouth and smashed the shore batteries with a fusillade of cannon fire.

Major General Sheaffe, with only 600 men, retreated rather than face inevitable surrender. He also ordered an unfinished ship, many stores, and a large ammunition magazine destroyed. When the magazine exploded, more than 250 Americans were injured or killed by the blast and falling debris. Among the 38 killed was the infantry commander, Brigadier General Zebulon Pike.

The York action came to typify operations on Lake Ontario during 1813 as each side raided opposing harbours while, fearful of

OVER:

On September 9, 1813, Captain Oliver Perry's nine warships engaged six British vessels on Lake Erie. Following a daylong battle, all of the British ships surrendered.

defeat, avoiding pitched battle. Consequently, the recently gained American superiority on Lake Ontario was reduced to a stalemate.

On Lake Erie, the American ships stationed in the sheltered harbour of Presque Isle on the south coast outgunned the British. However, the American brigs drew about ten feet while only six and a half feet covered the sandbar sheltering the harbour. As long as the British blockaded the harbour, the Americans were effectively trapped inside. The blockade was in place until July 30, when Commander Robert Barclay temporarily withdrew. American Captain Oliver Perry immediately ordered the brigs manhandled over the sandbar into open water. When the British returned on August 4, the American fleet was waiting. Outgunned and outnumbered, Barclay retreated.

Upon completion of the small frigate *Detroit,* however, Barclay sailed against the Americans on September 9 in a desperate bid to open the vital lake supply route, upon which much of the British western defence depended. The following day, his six vessels met Perry's nine ships in the southwest of the lake among the Bass Islands near Put-in-Bay. After a bloody daylong slugging match, Barclay's entire fleet was forced to strike its colours and surrender, while only one American ship was severely damaged. Casualties on both sides were heavy — 41 British killed and 94 wounded; 27 Americans killed and 96 wounded.

THE WESTERN LAND WAR

The British defeat on Lake Erie coincided with a major reversal along its shoreline as the Americans drove north up the Maumee River to liberate Fort Detroit and enter western Upper Canada. Brigadier General William Harrison launched this operation in January during the height of winter. In the vanguard of his 6,000-strong army was Brigadier General James Winchester with about 1,000 men. After easily taking Frenchtown, he settled in to await Harrison's arrival without posting pickets.

Consequently, on January 22, 1813, when Colonel William Procter counterattacked through deep snow with 600 regulars and 700 native warriors under Tecumseh, the Americans were caught still asleep. In the ensuing battle, 397 Americans were killed and 536, including Winchester, taken prisoner. British losses were only 24 killed and 158 wounded.

Exploiting this success, Procter immediately marched on Fort Meigs. Still under construction, the fort should not have posed a serious obstacle, but Procter's force was composed of 1,200 native warriors under Tecumseh and only some 900 regulars and militia. Neither the militia nor the native warriors inclined toward effective siege warfare. Procter did, however, manage to rout an American relief force, imposing 836 casualties in exchange for 101 British casualties. Then, unable to force the fort's surrender, Procter withdrew to Fort Malden to regroup and gather reinforcements.

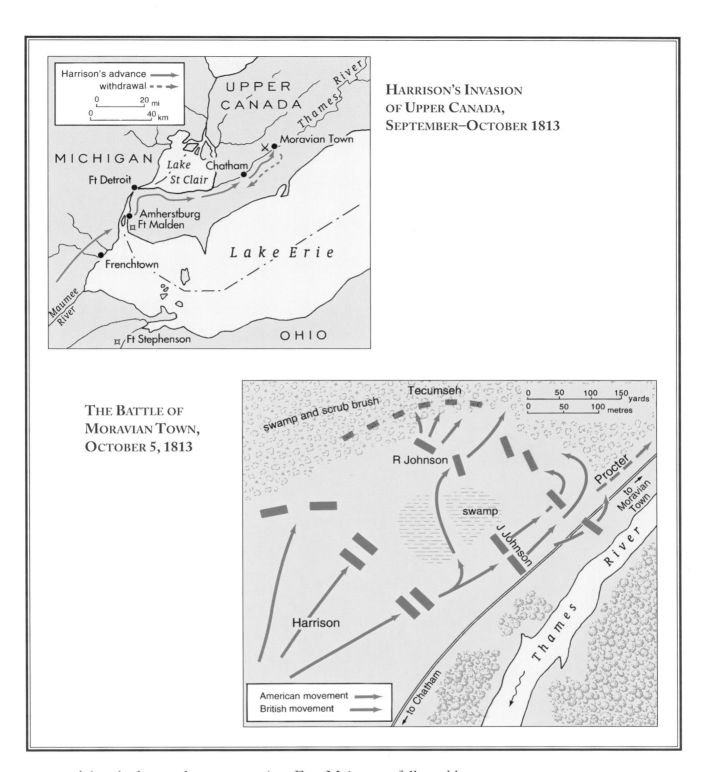

HARRISON'S INVASION
OF UPPER CANADA,
SEPTEMBER–OCTOBER 1813

THE BATTLE OF
MORAVIAN TOWN,
OCTOBER 5, 1813

A botched second attempt against Fort Meigs was followed by a failed attempt on Fort Stephenson on August 2. When control of Lake Erie was lost to the Americans, Procter lost the ability to retain the initiative or an adequate supply route to maintain the occupation of Fort Detroit. He therefore planned to withdraw to Fort George despite Tecumseh's protests that doing so betrayed his native allies.

On September 24, Procter, having convinced Tecumseh to accompany him, burned Fort Detroit and Fort Malden and withdrew overland toward Fort George. Soldiers, civilians, native warriors and their wives and children all marched eastward through rough country. On September 28, Major General Harrison landed with about 3,000 troops at Fort Malden and began a leisurely pursuit. Reinforced by 500 Kentucky cavalrymen, Harrison overtook the retreating column at Moravian Town on October 5, forcing the fight Tecumseh had wanted. Procter formed the British regulars of the 41st Foot Regiment into two open lines across the roadway fronting the little village, with the Thames River on his left and his right protected by a large swamp. Tecumseh's warriors set up inside the swamp. There was no ammunition for the cannon and no effort was made to construct any abattis in front of the infantry.

A Kentucky horseman kills Shawnee warrior Tecumseh.

When Harrison's Kentucky horsemen led by Lieutenant Colonel James Johnson charged, they quickly shattered the British defence. Procter fled the field, leaving his men and Tecumseh to their fate. The Kentucky troopers, under Colonel Richard Mentor Johnson, and the native warriors locked in hand-to-hand fighting until a cry went up that Tecumseh had fallen. The surviving warriors scattered, taking their dead with them. Only 246 British managed to escape, while 634 were either killed or wounded. Native losses were unknown. American losses were only 7 killed and 22 wounded. Having inflicted a stunning defeat on the British, Harrison did nothing to exploit his success. Instead, he burned the village, then withdrew to Detroit.

This decisive American victory, however, spelled the end of aboriginal hopes to retain control of the Ohio and Wabash valleys. It also ended any British control over the Lake Erie region.

THE NIAGARA SEESAW

Following the successful April 1813 raid on York, the Americans decided to capture Fort George and seize the Niagara frontier. In command of the 6,000-strong American force was Major General Henry Dearborn, who was so old, obese, and sickly that effective command rested with his adjutant, General Winfield Scott. Opposing the Americans was Brigadier General John Vincent and 1,500 men, of whom 1,000 were regulars.

Scott was an able soldier who emphasized proper planning and discipline. There would be no repeat of the Queenston fiasco. Instead, on May 25, 1813, he subjected Fort George to a devastating naval bombardment that soon had the fort's wooden buildings in flames. On a misty morning two days later, he landed an overwhelmingly large force out of range and view of Fort George's cannon west of Newark to encircle both Newark and the fort. Fierce fighting broke out as the Americans went head to head against the badly outnumbered defenders in a three-hour melee. Two out of three British soldiers engaged were killed or wounded — 52 killed and 306 wounded — before Vincent retreated to Beaver Dam rather than have his entire force surrounded by almost 5,000 Americans. When the Americans failed to immediately pursue, Vincent's force — numbering about 1,500 — had time to regroup.

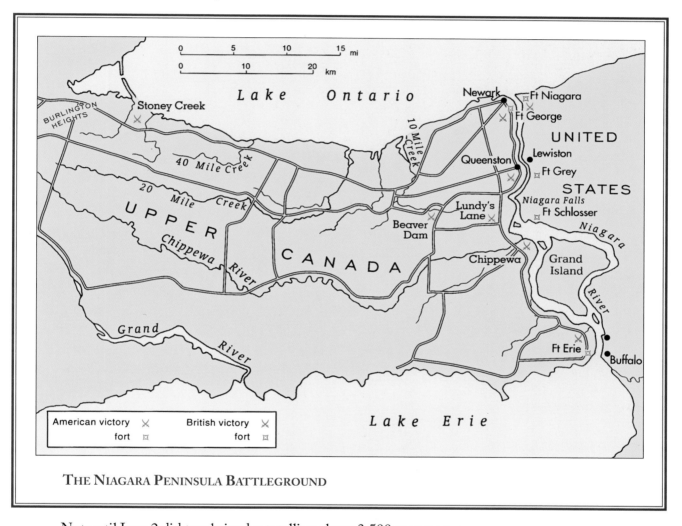

THE NIAGARA PENINSULA BATTLEGROUND

Not until June 2 did two brigades totalling about 3,500 men pursue the British. On June 5, they camped at Stoney Creek. When Vincent and his adjutant Colonel John Harvey received detailed intelligence on the American dispositions and even the security password for the night, they decided, despite being heavily outnumbered, to counter-attack. Harvey's force struck the American camp at 2:00 a.m. on June 6, using the password to close on the sentries and kill them with bayonets. Breaking into the centre of the American camp, the troops quickly captured the enemy's field guns and the two commanding brigadier generals, but then the battle deteriorated into a confused tangle. At dawn, Harvey ordered his men to retire into the woods, abandoning the guns but keeping the American commanders. Although caught by surprise, the American infantry had rallied effectively. British casualties were heavy: 23 killed, 134 wounded, and 5 missing. The Americans suffered only 55 killed or wounded and about 100 missing. The attack, however, achieved the desired effect, for the Americans promptly withdrew to Fort George.

Soon the Americans sent a raiding party of 575 cavalry and infantry under Lieutenant General Charles G. Boerstler to capture Beaver Dam, which was lightly defended by one company of regulars commanded by Lieutenant James FitzGibbon. Spending the night of June 21 at the home of James and Laura Secord, Boerstler divulged his mission to the couple. Early the next morning Laura Secord hurried almost 20 miles to Beaver Dam and warned FitzGibbon. Not knowing Boerstler's route of advance, FitzGibbon could little act on the intelligence. However, Captain Dominique Ducharne of the Indian Department, with 400 native warriors, was already tracking Boerstler's force. He soon ambushed and pinned the Americans down. When FitzGibbon arrived with 50 regulars and promised to avert a native massacre, Boerstler surrendered. The defeat before Beaver Dam resulted in the Americans hunkering down in Fort George.

THE BATTLE OF CHATEAUGUAY

Autumn brought a new American invasion effort — this time against Lower Canada, with Montreal the desired prize. The plan called for a two-pronged offensive, one against Kingston and the other using Lake Champlain. Both would link up outside Montreal to take the town. The Kingston attack, by a 7,300-strong force commanded by Major General James Wilkinson, was intended to pin down the majority of the British forces, while Major General Wade Hampton drove up the traditional Lake Champlain invasion route. Hampton's army numbered about 5,500, mostly new recruits.

The offensive was poorly executed. Wilkinson and Hampton despised each other and did little to coordinate movements. When Wilkinson fell ill, his army remained in Sackets Harbor pending his recovery. Meanwhile, Hampton found the Lake Champlain route too difficult to traverse so shifted his army 40 miles west to follow the Chateauguay River to the St. Lawrence. In late September, just short of the Canadian border, Hampton halted at Four Corners to wait for Wilkinson's army to descend the St. Lawrence by boat.

Canadian militia and native warriors started harassing Hampton's encampment, seriously deteriorating morale. Finally, on October 18, 1813, Hampton learned that Wilkinson was recovered and en route and that he should immediately march to the mouth of the Chateauguay to effect the link-up. Hampton's army, reduced to only 4,000 when some 1,500 militiamen refused to enter Canada, followed a rough

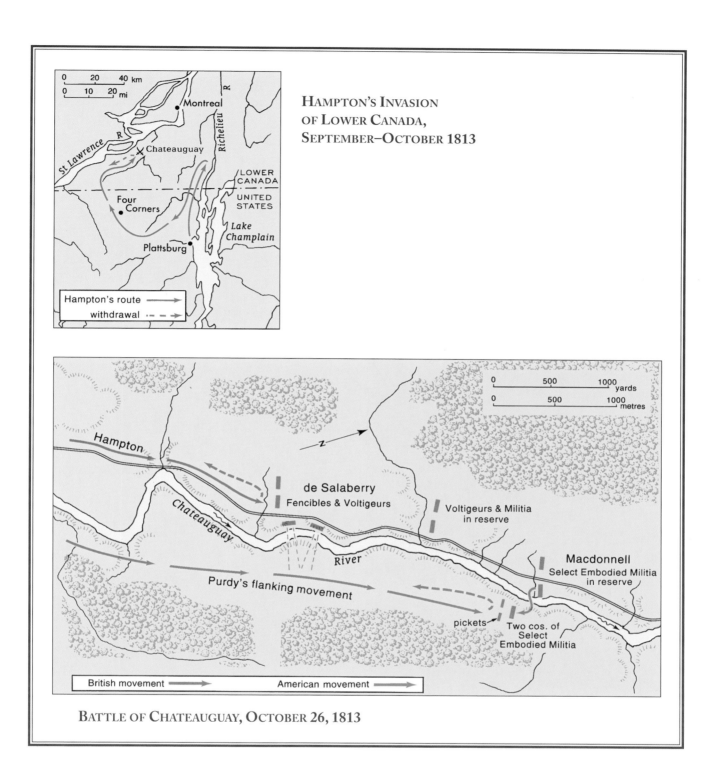

HAMPTON'S INVASION OF LOWER CANADA, SEPTEMBER–OCTOBER 1813

0 20 40 km
0 10 20 mi

Montreal

St Lawrence R

Richelieu R

Chateauguay

LOWER CANADA

UNITED STATES

Four Corners

Lake Champlain

Plattsburg

Hampton's route →
withdrawal ⇢

0 500 1000 yards
0 500 1000 metres

Hampton

de Salaberry
Fencibles & Voltigeurs

Voltigeurs & Militia
in reserve

Chateauguay

River

Macdonnell
Select Embodied Militia
in reserve

Purdy's flanking movement

pickets

Two cos. of
Select
Embodied Militia

British movement →   American movement →

BATTLE OF CHATEAUGUAY, OCTOBER 26, 1813

cart track. The moment the army crossed the border on October 21, it came under sporadic sniper fire.

Lieutenant Colonel Charles de Salaberry, commanding about 1,600 men, took up position where the river made a sharp turn and the road was cut by a ravine. De Salaberry's mixed force of French-Canadian regulars known as Fencibles and Voltigeurs, militia, and native warriors erected a stout barricade and abattis system across the narrow front flanked by the river on one side and a marshy thicket on the other. Behind this barrier he posted about 300 men. On the south bank, to the east of de Salaberry's advance force, two companies of militia numbering 160 men were positioned to cover the river ford. The rest, under Lieutenant Colonel "Red George" Macdonnell, he held in reserve.

When poor reconnaissance failed to reveal the troops guarding the ford, Hampton decided to turn the Canadian flank by sending 1,500 men commanded by Colonel Robert Purdy down the right-hand shoreline to cross the ford and strike the enemy rear. They became lost during the night amid the tangled forest, and dawn of October 26 found the Americans stumbling out on the riverbank directly across from de Salaberry's main defensive line, which promptly brought them under fire. The advance bogged down to a crawl.

By mid-morning, Hampton decided he must directly attack de Salaberry's main line, while still hoping his flanking force might get into the rear to crush the Canadians in an offensive vice. But the flankers soon bumped into the defensive line covering the ford and were subjected to a fusillade of musket fire. Taken by surprise, the Americans retreated. When Hampton's main body saw the flankers falling back, they too fled. Hampton ordered the retreat continued to Plattsburg, where he established winter quarters. The Battle of Chateauguay, as this skirmish became known, resulted in about 50 American dead or wounded and 5 Canadians killed, 16 wounded, and 4 missing.

Canadian militia and British regulars stave off a clumsily executed American attack during the Battle of Chateauguay.

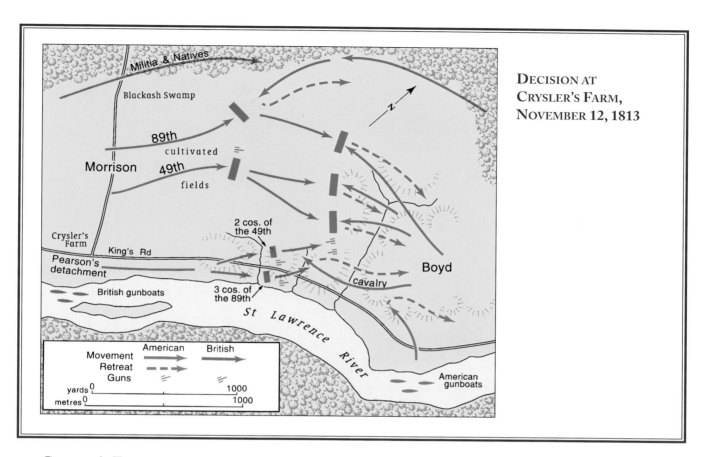

Map labels: Militia & Natives · Blackash Swamp · 89th · cultivated · Morrison · 49th · fields · Crysler's Farm · King's Rd · Pearson's detachment · British gunboats · 2 cos. of the 49th · 3 cos. of the 89th · St Lawrence River · Boyd · cavalry · American gunboats

Legend:
Movement — American · British
Retreat
Guns
yards 0 ——— 1000
metres 0 ——— 1000

CRYSLER'S FARM

Meanwhile Wilkinson, having bypassed Kingston, was advancing on Montreal with 8,000 men aboard 300 small vessels. Plagued by snowstorms and gales, the fleet struggled through the Thousand Islands until the weather cleared on November 5 and it entered the St. Lawrence River. In pursuit by boat were about 600 British regulars from Kingston. At Prescott, Fort Wellington blocked Wilkinson's passage. Wilkinson decided to bypass the fort by marching his army around it and re-embarking on the vessels, which would be floated past the fort at night. The manoeuvre was successful and the Americans were soon within sight of the Long Sault Rapids, the first of a series that ran almost unbroken to Montreal. On the night of November 10–11, the pursuing force, commanded by Lieutenant Colonel Joseph Morrison, threatened the American rear. Morrison established his headquarters in John Crysler's farmhouse. Reinforced by local militia, some natives, and men from Fort Wellington, he had about 900 soldiers, principally the 49th and 89th regiments. Morrison also had a small number of gunboats able to bring the tail of Wilkinson's armada under fire.

From Crysler's farmhouse, a road ran virtually straight from the riverbank across an open field to Blackash Swamp, about half a mile inland. Log fences bordering the road provided stout cover for Morrison's troops. Covering his left flank in the woods bordering the swamp, Morrison deployed a screen of natives and militia. Beyond the fence line, a large wheat field gave way to a ploughed field followed by two gullies and a ravine. Between the two gullies, a small British force composed of two companies of the 49th Regiment and three 89th Regiment companies under Lieutenant Colonel Thomas Pearson cut the road and served to funnel the Americans into the fields fronting Morrison's main defensive line.

Wilkinson had no choice on November 12 but to meet Morrison's threat to his rear. At the same time, he remained intent on continuing the move downstream toward Montreal. So he split his force, assigning Major General John Boyd with 2,000 regulars to stave Morrison off. After waiting in vain for a British attack, Boyd sent one brigade supported by another forward in three columns. The first brigade slogged across the open, muddy field under rainy skies. They easily pushed in the screen of British skirmishers until the main line raked the advancing Americans with musket fire. Boyd moved the second brigade up with one supporting cannon to reinforce the wavering first brigade. The cannon ripped holes in the British line, but it held, and the two sides locked in a brisk musketry exchange.

Soon Morrison sensed that the inexperienced Americans were tiring and ordered Pearson to mount a bayonet charge against the guns. The veteran soldiers surged forward, and as the companies of the 89th fought off a cavalry attempt to block them, the 49th captured the cannon, and forced Boyd's brigades from the field. Morrison's casualties were 22 killed, 148 wounded, and 9 missing — approximately a fifth of his entire force. The Americans lost 102 killed, 237 wounded, and more than 100 taken prisoner.

The Battle of Crysler's Farm did not prevent Wilkinson's advance on Montreal, but he soon learned that Hampton had retreated to winter quarters. Wilkinson knew that a large army faced him. Lacking Hampton's men, he decided the offensive must be abandoned and retreated across the border.

The failed Montreal offensive adversely affected the Niagara frontier, which had been stripped of troops to bolster Wilkinson's army. When the British marched a small force toward Fort George, the Americans retired across the border to Fort Niagara. Before doing so on December 10, however, they evicted Newark's 400 residents and burned the town. This wanton destruction embittered Canadians, who demanded retribution.

After reoccupying Fort George, 550 British regulars led by Colonel John Murray crossed the Niagara River on December 19 and surprised the garrison at Fort Niagara. The fort fell quickly, with 67 Americans killed and 11 wounded, in exchange for only 5 British killed and 3 wounded. Another 344 Americans were taken prisoner. Only 20 managed to escape. Meanwhile, another British and aboriginal force commanded by Major General Phineas Riall crossed the river at Five Mile Meadows to destroy Lewiston and then, proceeding southwards, burned Manchester, Fort Schlosser, and Buffalo.

STALEMATE IN THE NIAGARA

In January 1814, President Madison agreed to peace negotiations in Ghent, Belgium, more because of a Royal Navy blockade of American ports than the military misfortunes. While the talks proceeded at a leisurely pace, the war continued.

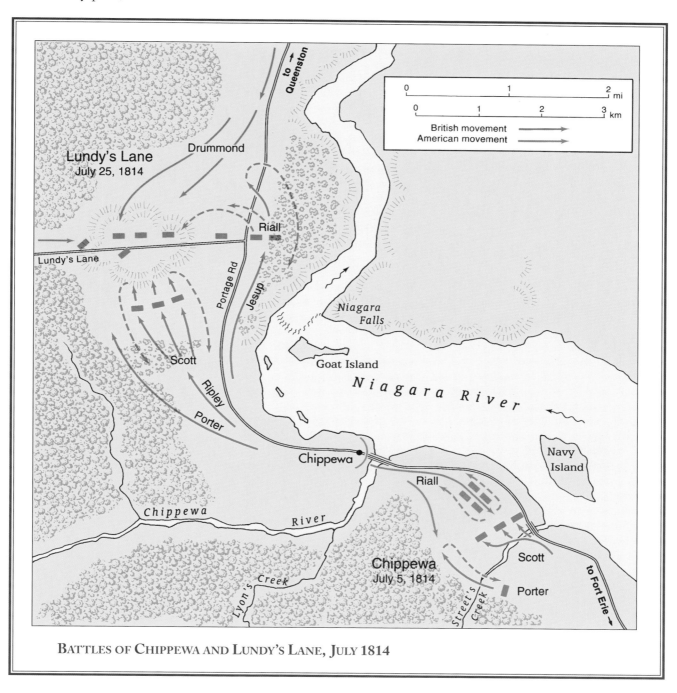

BATTLES OF CHIPPEWA AND LUNDY'S LANE, JULY 1814

Major General Jacob Brown commenced American operations against Upper Canada, supported by the Lake Ontario fleet commanded by Commodore Isaac Chauncey. Previously noted for his aggressiveness, Chauncey had become increasingly cautious. In Kingston Harbour, the British had a 10-ship fleet commanded by Commodore James Yeo, including the new 44-gun *Princess Charlotte* and 60-gun *Prince Regent*. Although Chauncey had the same number of ships, these latter two seriously outgunned anything the Americans had afloat. He therefore had little interest in assisting the army to attack Kingston.

Brown was equally reluctant to attack Kingston, so when he received two contradictory sets of orders from the U.S. Secretary of War he disregarded those demanding an attack on Kingston in favour of ones advocating the liberation of Fort Niagara. Whether Brown realized that the latter orders were only a feint intended to fool the British is unknown. He marched from Sackets Harbor toward the Niagara frontier with 3,500 men.

The new British commander, Lieutenant General Gordon Drummond, and Yeo had been unsure whether Kingston could withstand a combined marine and land attack. Now that danger was gone. Furthermore, Brown had left relatively few men to defend Sackets Harbor or Oswego, which provided the supply link to Lake Erie via the Hudson and Mohawk valleys. Unfortunately for the British, neither Drummond nor Yeo realized this paucity of strength. Believing Sackets Harbor still strongly defended, they opted to attack Oswego.

On May 4, 1,000 infantrymen boarded Yeo's ships and sailed for Oswego. Protecting Oswego was Fort Ontario, garrisoned by about 300 men. Drummond wanted to strike quickly but Yeo vacillated for 24 hours to ensure a safe landing spot. By the time Drummond's men landed, the American garrison numbered 600 and easily repulsed the attack.

Meanwhile, Brown planned to bypass Fort George, capture Fort Erie, and then march diagonally across the Niagara Peninsula to capture Burlington. This would effectively cut the supply line to the two forts, leaving their defenders to starve. With Burlington in hand, Chauncey's fleet could pick up Brown's men at the head of the lake and finally sail against Kingston.

On July 3, 1814, this plan was put into action, proceeding well at first as the Americans crossed the Niagara River and forced the surrender of Fort Erie's small garrison by day's end. The next day, they advanced toward Chippewa with Brigadier General Winfield Scott's brigade leading. The British Niagara frontier commander, Major General Phineas Riall, realizing his supply line was imperilled, met Brown's main force with 1,500 regulars, 300 militia, and about 300 native warriors.

Riall crossed the Chippewa on July 5 and threw back a thin line of Pennsylvanian militia. Driving the militia before him, Riall was stunned to suddenly confront Scott's fully prepared regiments, who had turned out that morning for a dress parade and were now deployed in two lines with muskets raised. As Riall's men were advancing in columns, only the front ranks could fire, while all the American troops enjoyed a clear field of fire. Although the British musketry was deadly accurate, the heavier American volleys shredded the British ranks. British losses were 500 men killed, wounded, or missing, while the Americans suffered about 275 casualties.

Riall fell back to Fort George. According to plan, Brown should now bypass the fort and march on Burlington. But to do so would leave Riall free to cut his supply line. Brown looked to Chauncey to bring up his fleet to provide both supplies and the firepower to take Fort George. Chauncey, however, refused for fear of exposing Sackets Harbor to attack.

Uncertain what to do next, Brown camped at Queenston, while Riall moved his men to Twenty Mile Creek where he could move to protect either Fort George or Burlington. Brown's militiamen set about pillaging the nearby Canadian villages in revenge for the devastation wrought the previous winter. Finally realizing that Chauncey would never sail to his support, Brown withdrew to the Chippewa on July 24. Riall followed with about 1,000 regulars and militia, taking up position on a westward-running track called Lundy's Lane that branched off Portage Road. To Riall's rear, another 1,000 regulars were at Ten Mile Creek preparing to march south to join him.

Nor was this the only British force in the area. Drummond was coming down Queenston Road with a strong force, intending to find Riall and then bring Brown to battle. Learning of this force and unaware that Riall's men held Lundy's Lane, Brown sent Scott's brigade of 1,072 officers and men toward Queenston on July 25 along with approximately 1,300 militia and native troops under General Peter Buel Porter. Early in the day, Porter advanced ahead of Scott along a line bordering the woods on the western flank where he was ambushed by a combined militia-native force preceding Riall's main body. After several volleys were exchanged, Porter's force fled just as Scott arrived. Scott, seeing Riall's troops, deployed his men for a frontal assault. Just then, Drummond rode up and moved his 1,600 soldiers into a line on the northern slope of the hill where Lundy's Lane crossed it. He also positioned several guns and rocket units on the heights.

Scott attacked at 6:00 p.m., with his right flanking force under Major Thomas Jesup driving back the British left to reach the lane. Riall, commanding this flank, was wounded and captured. The surviving elements of his force fell back upon Drummond's strong position on the hill. Scott's main force struck Drummond's defensive bastion,

The American defeat at Lundy's Lane marked the end of efforts by the U.S. to conquer Canada.

but repeated charges against the British centre failed to break through or to silence their cannon. At nine o'clock, Scott's badly thinned ranks were reinforced by two brigades, one led by Brigadier General Eleazor Ripley and the other by Porter. The Americans started to push the weary defenders back, managing to capture the British guns on the crest. Just as the British line seemed ready to crack entirely, however, 1,200 more redcoats and militia arrived to steady the defence.

From ten o'clock to midnight, the two sides remained locked in a vicious, confused tangle that saw knots of soldiers exchanging musketry at ranges of only 10 to 15 yards. Drummond, Brown, and Scott were all severely wounded. Shortly after midnight, the Americans disengaged. The Americans lost 171 killed, 572 wounded, and 110 missing. British losses were 84 killed, 559 wounded, 193 missing, and 42 taken prisoner.

At dawn, Ripley — now commanding the Americans — realized he would soon be hopelessly outnumbered. Ripley withdrew to Fort Erie. Drummond besieged the fort on August 3. A British attack on August 15 ended disastrously with 57 dead, 309 wounded, and 539 missing or prisoners, in exchange for only 84 American casualties. The siege continued until September 16 when the Americans attacked a British battery. American losses in the ensuing melee were 79 killed, 432 wounded or missing. British losses were 115 killed, 176 wounded, and 315 missing, along with three of six siege guns destroyed. On September 22, Drummond retreated to Chippewa.

BRITISH OFFENSIVES

Elsewhere, British and Canadian forces moved decisively to the offensive as more than 16,000 British regulars from Europe poured into Quebec harbour. Most were victorious veterans of the Spanish Peninsula Campaign. On September 1, Governor General George Prevost marched with 10,000 men to seize Plattsburg. On September 6, he halted inside the town on Saranac River's northern shore. Facing him on the opposite shore were only 3,000 Americans, but in Plattsburg Bay a squadron of four ships and ten gunboats commanded by Captain Thomas Macdonough stood in support. Prevost decided that an attack would only be possible if these ships were beaten off.

On the morning of September 11, four British ships commanded by Captain George Downie met the American fleet in a fierce naval battle. Downie was killed in the opening moments but the battle raged for two hours, ending with one British ship aground on Crab Island and the other three forced to surrender. Witnessing this defeat, Prevost ordered a retreat to Lower Canada, which was unmolested by the Americans.

Meanwhile, British troops under Lieutenant General John Sherbrooke invaded northern Maine from New Brunswick and annexed all territory north of the Penobscot River to shorten the lines of communication on British territory. On August 24, the British captured Washington after defeating a 5,000-strong American force and set fire to the Capitol, the White House, and several other buildings. Failed assaults against Baltimore and New Orleans followed. The latter battle was fought on January 8, 1815, the result of slow communications. News of the Ghent Treaty that ended the war on December 24, 1814, did not reach North America before the British suffered a major defeat trying to capture the strategic port of New Orleans. The treaty returned boundaries to prewar status and ensured Canada's survival.

CHAPTER FIVE

Years of Rebellion
1837–1885

THE 1837–1838 REBELLIONS

By the spring of 1837, inhabitants of Upper and Lower Canada had become dangerously polarized over the issue of responsible government versus the existing oligarchic system. In Lower Canada, unrest was heightened by ethnic divisions between French Canadians and Anglo Canadians. Leading the Lower Canada reformers was Patriote Party leader Louis-Joseph Papineau. In Upper Canada, radical reformers rallied around William Lyon Mackenzie.

Mackenzie and Papineau believed that the threat of armed insurrection alone would force a transfer to the colonial assemblies of decision-making powers held by the appointed Executive Council to the Governor General. Mackenzie and Papineau were wrong. Although willing to implement modest reforms, Britain was unprepared to grant the colonies political independence based on majority rule.

On September 5, 1837, about 800 Patriote Party members formed the paramilitary association Fils de la Liberté. Pro-government elements responded with the Doric Club. On November 6, a street fight started outside the Doric Club headquarters in Montreal. Six days later, a government proclamation forbade all public assembly and authorized formation of a volunteer corps of infantry, artillery, and cavalry to maintain order. Lower Canada's British military commander,

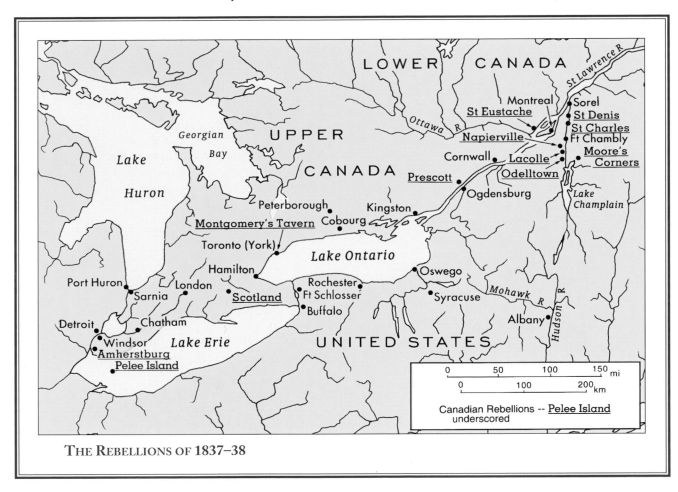

THE REBELLIONS OF 1837–38

John Colborne, quickly filled out this corps with Doric Club members. The proclamation also ordered pro-reform leaders, including Papineau, arrested. When a detachment of Montreal Volunteer Cavalry sought to carry out this task, they were ambushed and routed by about 40 reformers.

The arrest attempt led several hundred armed *habitants,* wearing their trademark long, homespun grey coats known as *capotes* and bright toques and sashes, to gather at St. Charles and St. Denis, east of Montreal. On November 18, British Lieutenant Colonel G. A. Wetherall marched from Montreal with four infantry companies and two field guns to Fort Chambly on the Richelieu River, south of St. Charles. Four days later, Colonel Charles Gore embarked by steamer with five infantry companies, a 24-pounder gun, and a troop of Montreal Volunteer Cavalry to Sorel at the mouth of the Richelieu, to the north of St. Denis. The two forces were to crush the insurrectionists between them.

Gore decided to cover the 18 miles to St. Denis at night for a surprise dawn attack. Struggling along roads transformed into quagmire by heavy rain that turned to snow just before dawn, Gore's 300 sodden and exhausted men emerged from the woods north of St. Denis to find the defence centred on a stone-walled mansion that dominated the surrounding fields. Gore's cannon fire proved ineffective in this situation. Three times, the attackers attempted to storm the mansion before nightfall forced Gore to break off the action and undertake a gruelling retreat. Casualties were light, with only 6 dead, 10 wounded, and 6 missing. The rebels lost 12 dead and 7 wounded.

Two days after Gore's defeat, Wetherall approached St. Charles with 350 men. He believed more than a thousand rebels awaited his attack, but in fact, only about 80 poorly armed *habitants* were dug in behind a log barricade that could easily be turned. A fierce battle ensued, with British soldiers and *habitants* locked repeatedly in hand-to-hand fighting. In less than an hour, the hopelessly outnumbered and outgunned rebels were routed. British casualties were 3 dead and 18 wounded; rebel casualties remain disputed but were likely less than Wetherall's claim of 56 killed.

On November 30, Gore returned to Sorel with eight infantry companies and a four-gun battery. After retracing their earlier march to St. Denis, the British soldiers found the town abandoned. Demoralized by the St. Charles defeat, most rebels had fled to their farms. Leaving a garrison in St. Denis, Gore pursued Papineau southward but the rebel leader and his compatriots escaped into Vermont.

When about 200 rebels attempted to invade Canada from Vermont on December 6, well-armed local loyalist volunteers blocked them at Moore's Corners. After a short firefight, the rebels fled.

One rebel bastion remained — Two Mountains County northwest of Montreal. On December 14, Colborne approached St. Eustache

With 2,000 men supported by six cannons, British regulars easily routed the last habitant rebels at St. Eustache on December 14, 1837.

on a bitter-cold winter day with an overwhelmingly superior force of almost 2,000 men, six field guns, and a rocket troop. Wading through waist-deep snow, the British regulars surrounded the town and slowly pushed the approximately 400 rebels back until their leader, Dr. Jean-Olivier Chénier, barricaded the survivors inside the St. Eustache church, convent, and presbytery. After Colborne's field guns battered the church, a bayonet charge seized the presbytery, which was then set alight. Soldiers used the resulting smoke screen's cover to creep up on the church and set it on fire. When the insurgents fled the burning building, many were shot down or bayoneted while trying to surrender. Among the dead was Chénier. About 70 rebels died and another 120 were taken prisoner.

Early in 1838, Robert Nelson and Dr. Cyrille-Hector Octave Côte proclaimed the provisional government of the Republic of Lower Canada and fomented rebellion in the Richelieu River district. In the autumn, they gathered 2,500 poorly armed supporters at Napierville. Côte and a small band of men marched south to acquire weapons in the United States. On their return trek, they encountered a blocking force of loyalists and militia at Lacolle that easily scattered the rebel column. With Côte's men went any prospect of Nelson being able to arm his force, so Nelson and about 1,000 rebels retreated toward the border. At Odelltown, 200 militia barred their path. After failing to break the militia line, the rebels could only return to Napierville where British regulars soon dispersed them. The Lower Canada Rebellion was ended.

In Upper Canada, December 7, 1837, had been set as the date for Mackenzie's rebellion. The rebels were to assemble at Montgomery's Tavern and proceed down Yonge Street to seize the House of Assembly in York. Learning that the authorities knew of the plan, the date was advanced to December 4. Although almost 200 men gathered outside the tavern, they lacked sufficient provisions or arms to undertake an armed insurrection. While Mackenzie's commanders dithered for a day trying to find weapons, loyalists prepared to defend York. Finally, with night rapidly approaching on December 5, the rebels advanced down Yonge Street. Those with firearms led, followed by pikemen and then by rebels armed only with sticks and cudgels.

At Maitland Street, a thin 27-man picket met them with one volley before retiring. The rebels in front fired back and dropped to the ground so their comrades behind could put in a volley. Instead, those in the rear thought their front line had been killed or wounded and fled to the tavern.

After many orders and counter orders, the authorities attacked the rebels at Montgomery's Tavern on December 7 with about 1,000 men and two 6-pounder cannon. About 150 rebels were in woods half a mile south of the tavern on the road's west side, 60 more were to the east behind a rail fence fronting Paul Pry Inn, and the unarmed remainder of about 300 waited back at the tavern.

Seeing the rebels behind the fence, Colonel Allan MacNab drew up his cannon and fired on the inn. When the infantry advanced, the rebels on both sides of the road reeled back to the tavern, which

It is doubtful that the rebels making a stand before Montgomery's Tavern were as numerous or well organized as depicted in this contemporary wood engraving. Nor was the tavern set on fire.

MacNab quickly brought under artillery fire. The advance lost all cohesion, but the rebels were by now in full flight. The entire battle lasted only 20 minutes. One rebel was killed outright and several died of wounds, while the government force had only five men with minor wounds. Mackenzie fled to the United States, several other leaders were imprisoned, and two were executed.

In the London district west of York, Dr. Charles Duncombe raised a force of about 400 insurgents east of Oakland at Scotland on December 13. MacNab dispersed the rebels the following day by marching against them with a vastly superior force. Duncombe sought refuge in the United States.

December 14 marked the day Mackenzie returned to Canada with about 25 men, occupied Navy Island on the Niagara River, and proclaimed a provisional government. Gaining some American support, Mackenzie slowly built up his island force. Meanwhile, MacNab assembled about 2,500 militiamen at nearby Chippewa. By December 28, the American steamer *Caroline* was in Mackenzie's service, shunting supplies and men from Buffalo to Navy Island. On the evening of December 29, about 50 Canadian loyalists crossed into New York State, boarded *Caroline* at Fort Schlosser, and burned her.

The destruction of the American ship strained Anglo-American relations and spawned an influx of American volunteers to Navy Island, just east of Chippewa. Still Mackenzie's force numbered only about 450, while the government forces at Chippewa grew daily. On January 13, 1838, the rebels, now calling themselves republicans because so many were Americans, abandoned the island, effectively bringing to an end Mackenzie's attempts to organize a rebellion from south of the border.

Five days earlier, another republican force aboard several small vessels sailed against Amherstburg, where they tried to incite a local uprising. The schooner *Anne* attempted to shell Amherstburg but was instead boarded and captured by Canadian militia. Other disorganized attempts to strike across the border at Canadian targets followed, but all were ineffectual and easily repelled, although the Canadian vessel *Sir Robert Peel* was captured and burned in revenge for *Caroline*'s destruction.

The rebels' last gasp came on November 12 with an attempted amphibious invasion of Canada from Oswego on the town of Prescott. Two schooners initially formed the backbone of the small flotilla, but one ran aground en route at Ogdensburg. The remaining vessel then drifted past Prescott, finally managing to land at Windmill Point a short way downstream. Here about 200 republicans established a bridgehead centred on the hamlet of New Jerusalem and its six-storey-high stone windmill. Shortly after the landing, the small Canadian vessel *Experiment* cut the invasion force off from resupply. The following day, a combined force of almost 800 militia and British marines besieged the position. After four days of sporadic fighting, four infantry companies and three field guns were brought up and three hours later the vastly outnumbered republicans surrendered. About 80 were killed and the remaining 137 taken prisoner, compared to 16 government dead and 60 wounded. Of those involved in the invasion, only 29 were British subjects. Following the Battle of the Windmill, the U.S. government prevented organization of further invasion forces behind its borders and hostilities in Upper Canada ceased.

THE FENIAN RAIDS

After the American Civil War, many Irish veterans were mobilized by the Fenian Brotherhood to seize Britain's North American colonies and release them only in return for Ireland's freedom. Once they invaded the colonies, the Fenians believed the local populace would rise against British rule.

On April 17, 1866, the schooner *Ocean Spray* sailed into Eastport harbour in Maine bearing some 500 Springfield rifles to arm about 1,000 Fenians secretly gathered there. Once armed, they were to launch an amphibious invasion against Campobello Island, New Brunswick. British and American authorities knew of the Fenian plot. Five thousand New Brunswick militia supported by British regulars established a chain of posts along the St. Croix River and several British warships were deployed in local waters. On April 19, American soldiers seized the *Ocean Spray* arms and warned the Fenians that neutrality laws would be enforced. Most of the Fenians dispersed back to New York City. A small band, however, raided Indian Island on April 22 and burned a customs warehouse and three stores before being chased off. Another 50 Fenians pirated a schooner, sailed into New Brunswick waters, and were promptly chased back to Maine by a British warship.

After the Campobello fiasco, Canadian and British authorities dismissed the Fenian threat. This enabled a 1,500-man force commanded by John O'Neill to cross the Niagara River into Canada from Buffalo on May 31. The border here was undefended for a 25-mile stretch. O'Neill occupied Fort Erie, tore up some railway, and marched about five miles toward Black Creek before setting up camp. Here he awaited Fenian reinforcements while his men looted surrounding settlements for horses and food.

Meanwhile, the Canadian militia under Major General George Napier secured Welland Canal — the strategic objective nearest the Fenians. On June 1, Colonel George Peacocke marched to Chippewa with 1,700 men and the following day started toward Stevensville, where he planned to join another 850-strong militia unit coming by train from Port Colborne to Ridgeway and then by forced march north to Stevensville. The combined force was then to attack the Fenians. Peacocke, however, set out late and took a roundabout route. The

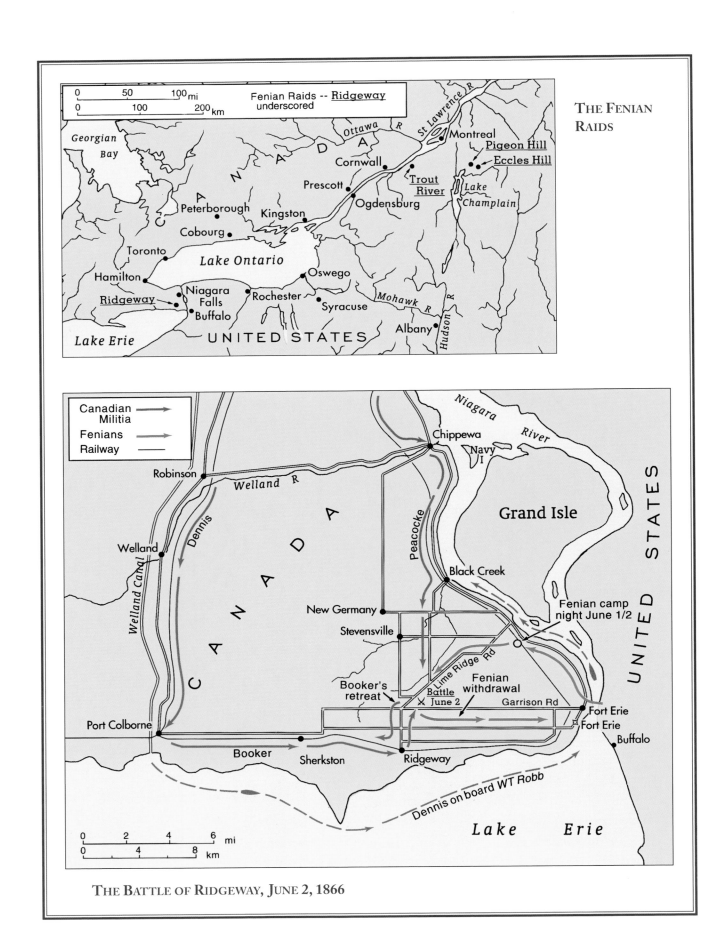

THE FENIAN
RAIDS

Fenian Raids -- Ridgeway
underscored

Georgian Bay

CANADA

Ottawa R

St Lawrence R

Montreal

Pigeon Hill

Eccles Hill

Cornwall

Trout River

Prescott

Ogdensburg

Lake Champlain

Peterborough

Kingston

Cobourg

Toronto

Lake Ontario

Hamilton

Niagara Falls

Ridgeway

Buffalo

Rochester

Oswego

Syracuse

Mohawk R

Hudson R

Albany

UNITED STATES

Lake Erie

Canadian Militia

Fenians

Railway

Niagara River

Chippewa

Navy I

Grand Isle

Robinson

Welland R

Dennis

Welland

Welland Canal

CANADA

Peacocke

Black Creek

UNITED STATES

Fenian camp night June 1/2

New Germany

Stevensville

Lime Ridge Rd

Booker's retreat

Battle June 2

Fenian withdrawal

Garrison Rd

Fort Erie

Fort Erie

Buffalo

Port Colborne

Booker

Sherkston

Ridgeway

Dennis on board WT Robb

Lake Erie

THE BATTLE OF RIDGEWAY, JUNE 2, 1866

Port Colborne column, commanded by Lieutenant Colonel Alfred Booker, detrained at Ridgeway and marched toward Stevensville along a route that would intersect Lime Ridge Road.

The Fenians had reached Lime Ridge Road in the meantime, dug in on a formidable ridge position overlooking the road, and were able to ambush Booker's column from behind a hastily erected fence-rail barricade. Despite their fire, Booker's militia advanced steadily until a false report of approaching Fenian cavalry resulted in confused and contradictory orders. Some militia units retreated, while others continued the advance, and a few formed into squares to repel cavalry. Soon a general retreat was ordered. During the two-hour engagement, the Canadians lost 10 killed and 57 wounded; the Fenians lost 10 killed and several wounded.

While the Battle of Ridgeway raged, Lieutenant Colonel John Stoughton Dennis and the Dunnville Naval Brigade requisitioned the tugboat *W. T. Robb* and sailed from Port Colbourne to Black Creek only to find the Fenians had decamped. Dennis then returned to Fort Erie. After seizing the fort, the brigade was quickly beaten off when O'Neill pulled back to meet this threat to his rear lines. Six Canadians were wounded and 54 taken prisoner. The tugboat escaped with the survivors and 59 Fenian prisoners to Port Colborne. Peacocke, on learning that the Ridgeway engagement was concluded, had marched his troops directly to Fort Erie, hoping to intercept O'Neill's retreating force. However, he arrived too late to prevent the Fenians' escape to Buffalo, where American authorities arrested O'Neill and 600 followers.

The Niagara raid was only part of a grander Fenian plan, which called for simultaneous frontier raids. Most never materialized because Canadian militia blocked designated border entry points. On June 7, however, 1,800 Fenians under Samuel B. Spiers used the Lake Champlain invasion route to enter Quebec and hole up on Pigeon Hill to await 1,200 men who never arrived — and probably had never existed. On June 9, Spiers withdrew to Vermont, leaving behind 200 zealots quickly driven off by militia without casualties to either side.

No more Fenian raids followed until 1870, when about 200 Fenians led by O'Neill struck on May 25 near where Spiers had launched his failed effort. Barely across the border, the force came under fire from about 80 men positioned at Eccles Hill. Finding themselves suddenly leaderless when O'Neill was arrested by U.S. police at the border crossing, the Fenians wavered. By the time O'Neill's compatriot Spiers arrived to take charge, the Canadians had been reinforced by a strong force of infantry and cavalry. The Fenians, having suffered three killed and several wounded, fled. There were no Canadian casualties.

Two days later, about 200 more Fenians crossed the Quebec frontier at Trout River, advanced half a mile, and erected a barricade on a slight rise of ground. A superior militia force soon arrived and, following a 30-minute rifle exchange, the Fenians withdrew, having been inside

OVER:
In reality, the Fenians at Ridgeway were well positioned behind a fence-rail barricade and confusion reigned in the Canadian ranks to such a degree that the attack turned into a general retreat, which is only hinted at in this 1869 illustration.

Canada no more than 90 minutes. One Fenian was killed, one wounded, and one taken prisoner, while one Canadian was wounded.

The final Fenian raid was a fiasco aimed at inciting a Métis uprising in the Red River Valley. Crossing at Pembina on October 4, about 70 Fenians seized a Hudson's Bay Company trading post and marched about 20 prisoners back into the United States. The local American military commander, however, quickly deployed 30 men to free the prisoners and dispersed the Fenians without firing a shot.

THE RED RIVER EXPEDITION

In 1869, the Hudson's Bay Company agreed to transfer sovereignty of the Red River Colony to Canada. Aboriginal and Métis concerns that this would jeopardize their land rights and culture were heightened by a Canadian-sponsored resurvey that showed no regard for current occupancy and the appointment to Lieutenant-Governor of pro-annexationist William McDougall. On December 1, when the transfer to Canada stalled, Louis Riel immediately declared a provisional government, which in January 1870 undertook negotiations with Canada for entry into Confederation.

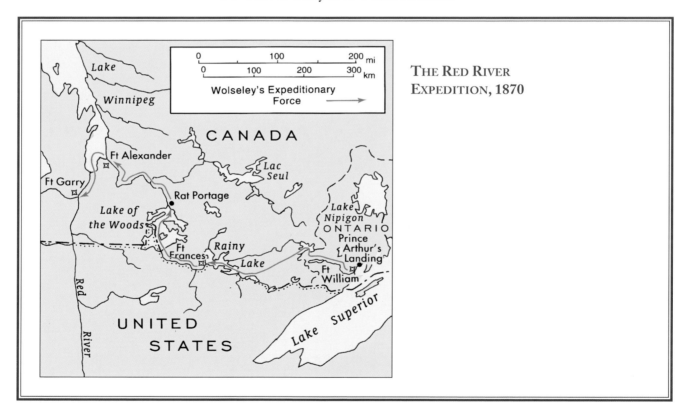

THE RED RIVER
EXPEDITION, 1870

The subsequent Manitoba Act created a new province with very limited boundaries and the guarantee of one million acres of land for Métis settlement. However, because Riel had earlier court-martialled and executed Ontario Orangeman and adventurer Thomas Scott, Canada refused to grant amnesty to Métis leaders.

As the political negotiations were being concluded, an expeditionary force of 400 British regulars and 800 Ontario and Quebec militiamen commanded by Colonel Garnet Wolseley embarked on May 25 from Prince Arthur's Landing to follow the old North West Company fur-trade route to Fort Garry. Their mission was to establish Canada's authority in the newly formed province. After an arduous trek, they reached Fort Garry on August 24. Fearing arrest, Riel fled. For the next few years, a small militia garrison was retained in Manitoba.

THE START OF THE NORTH-WEST REBELLION

By 1884, Métis and aboriginal peoples throughout the Canadian prairies were in dire straits. Virtual extinction of the bison, coupled with inadequate distribution of alternative rations by the federal Indian Department, caused near starvation among many aboriginal peoples. For their part, the Métis found the transition from an economy based on hunting and trapping to one based on agriculture difficult. While Cree chief Big Bear sought to unite prairie First Nations into a confederacy, a Métis delegation convinced Louis Riel to return from exile in the United States and provide desperately needed political leadership.

At a public meeting on July 8, Riel urged everyone in the Northwest to unite and press Ottawa for reforms. Métis, aboriginal, and white settler support for Riel was strong. Riel spent the rest of the summer and fall organizing and developing a petition to Ottawa regarding the various grievances, which was delivered to the federal government late in 1884. When Ottawa offered no response at all to the petition, he organized a meeting in St. Laurent, Saskatchewan, on March 8, 1885. The gathering ratified a 10-point "Revolutionary Bill of Rights." The bill demanded provincial legislatures for Alberta and Saskatchewan, land grants for Métis in these provinces similar to those won in Manitoba, better provisions for aboriginal peoples, and rights for settlers to prevent speculator exploitation.

A provisional government was proclaimed on March 18, but the proclamation clearly stated it would disband if Ottawa appointed a commission to deal with Métis claims and address the concerns of white settlers. Riel was appointed the government's leader and Gabriel Dumont its military commander. The government's first act was to begin prudently stockpiling supplies against "the emergency of war." By the following day, an armed force had gathered at Batoche, the centre of the Métis community, on the south branch of the Saskatchewan River.

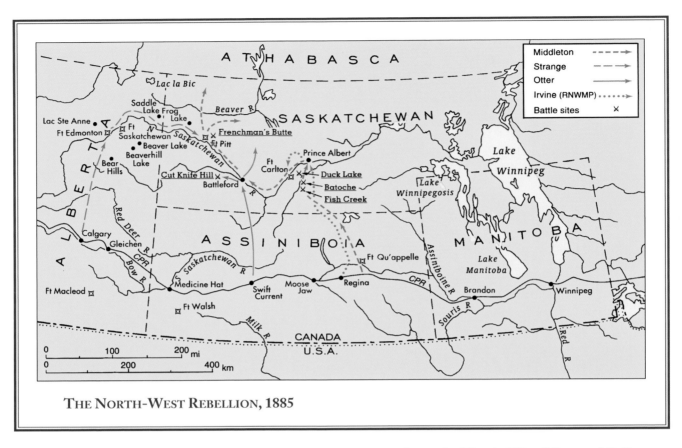

THE NORTH-WEST REBELLION, 1885

While the Métis organized, nearby North-West Mounted Police (NWMP) reinforced Fort Carlton. On March 18, NWMP Commissioner A. G. Irvine marched from Regina to quash any rebellion. To meet the two-front threat posed by the NWMP, Dumont shifted the majority of the Métis fighters to Duck Lake on March 25, severing the road between Prince Albert and Fort Carlton.

The next day, NWMP Superintendent Leif Crozier moved from Fort Carlton toward Duck Lake with 56 policemen, 43 volunteers, and a 7-pounder cannon. As the police column drew near, Dumont and 25 Métis chased away its scouts. Crozier scattered his men in a small cluster of trees and behind the column's few sleighs, positioned broadside across the road. Dumont's men took cover around a hut facing the police. Neither side fired a shot; both realized that to do so would mean war. Crozier and interpreter John McKay approached Dumont's brother Isidore and the native warrior Asiyiwin to discuss the standoff. When a scuffle broke out between Asiyiwin and McKay, the latter suddenly drew a revolver and, after killing Isidore, mortally wounded Asiyiwin. Crozier ordered his men to open fire. The North-West Rebellion had begun.

While the police remained in the woods and behind the sleighs, the inexperienced volunteers spontaneously tried to rush the house. Bogged down in waist-deep snow, they were easy prey for the Métis riflemen. Nine were killed, as were three policemen, before Crozier ordered a general retreat. Eleven others were wounded. Of the five Métis and one native man who died, four were related to Gabriel Dumont.

While the 30-minute Battle of Duck Lake was underway, Irvine's column reached Fort Carlton by an alternate route from Prince Albert. The next day, Irvine ordered the fort abandoned. Before leaving Fort Carlton, Irvine telegraphed Ottawa for 1,500 soldiers to crush the rebellion. Ottawa, however, was already mobilizing and a 90th Winnipeg Rifles company had entrained to Fort Qu'Appelle the day before the Duck Lake battle.

Meanwhile, the Duck Lake victory brought many native people into the rebellion. Assiniboine and Cree warriors moved from reserves to the west against Battleford, forcing the white settlers there to seek refuge inside the police fort. On April 2, a band of Big Bear's warriors, acting against his wishes, attacked the small community of Frog Lake. Nine white settlers were killed and most of the village burned. Seeing no alternative now but to join the rebellion, Big Bear led his warriors to pillage stores at Lac La Biche, Saddle Lake, Beaverhill Lake, Lac Ste. Anne, Bear Hills, and Beaver Lake. They also drove the NWMP detachment from Fort Pitt on April 15, killing one constable.

While Riel's forces were successful at every turn, Ottawa had mobilized with surprising speed and efficiency. An advance force of one company of the 90th Winnipeg Rifles arrived at Qu'Appelle on April 10. By the end of the month, 3,000 militiamen drawn from Nova Scotia, Quebec, Ontario, Manitoba, and the Northwest Territories had arrived in several drafts at Qu'Appelle. Major General Frederick Middleton was in overall command. Because the unrest was widespread, he divided the North-West Field Force into three columns. Under Middleton's command, 900 men and two artillery batteries advanced on Batoche from Fort Qu'Appelle. A second 300-strong column commanded by Lieutenant Colonel William Otter embarked at Swift Current and proceeded overland to relieve Battleford. Meanwhile, a 700-man third column commanded by Major General Thomas Strange mobilized in Calgary to march north to Fort Edmonton and on to Fort Pitt.

THE BATTLE OF BATOCHE

On April 23, Middleton advanced from Clarke's Crossing, about 35 miles upstream from Batoche, with his column split evenly on either side of the South Saskatchewan. Dumont and 200 Métis lay in ambush at Fish Creek. On April 24, Middleton's force came into sight and the rebels fired an opening fusillade before confining themselves to sniping at sure targets to conserve ammunition. The Métis position inside a coulee proved largely impervious to the militia's rifle and artillery fire. With half his men on the opposite side of the South Saskatchewan, Middleton's numerical superiority was nullified.

As the day wore on, the Métis situation worsened as ammunition ran low, thirst and hunger plagued the fighters, and artillery fire succeeded in driving off their Cree allies, who had been positioned in brush close to the river shore. The coulee became as much a trap as a defensive redoubt, because a retreat would expose them to militia fire. Consequently, the rebels were surprised when the militia unexpectedly withdrew. Middleton's men had taken heavy casualties — 10 dead and 45 wounded out of about 400 engaged. The Métis suffered only four killed.

The Fish Creek defeat convinced Middleton he needed more men and a new plan. This belief was further reinforced when Otter, having reached Battleford on April 24, moved against Chief Poundmaker on May 1 with 300 men, two cannon, and a Gatling gun. On May 2, they crossed Cutknife Creek and started up its steep western bank. On the opposite side of the slope, Poundmaker's tribe was encamped. Taken by surprise, only a few native warriors reached the crest in time to fire on the force's advance elements. This proved sufficient, however, to stall the militia advance as Otter's men paused to engage the skirmishers. Caught on the exposed slope, the militia presented good targets to the increasing native force, which sniped at them from the cover of trees on the reverse slope. After six hours of fighting, Otter's men retreated. They suffered 8 dead and 14 wounded, but believed they had inflicted hundreds of native casualties, particularly with the Gatling gun. In reality, only six native men were killed and three wounded.

On May 5, the steamer *Northcote* landed at Middleton's Fish Creek encampment. The *Northcote,* whose open decks were fortified the next day with sandbags, sacks of oats, boxes of meat, and timbers, was essential to Middleton's plan to capture Batoche. At the same time as his 886-strong Field Force attacked the Métis defensive line, the *Northcote* was to sail past Batoche. While Middleton's artillery reduced the Métis defences, *Northcote* would unload 50 soldiers in the enemy rear. On May 7, the *Northcote* and Middleton's contingent advanced 13 miles from Fish Creek to Gabriel's Crossing, and the following day the land force moved to a position eight miles from Batoche. At 5:30 a.m. on May 9, the Field Force advanced against Batoche and *Northcote* sailed from Gabriel's Crossing, towing two barges loaded with fuel and supplies.

Middleton's column fell behind schedule, so *Northcote* steamed adjacent to Batoche alone at 8:00 a.m., to the consternation of the defenders. Métis and native warriors rallied quickly, abandoning their gun pit defences to bring the ship under fire. At 8:15 a.m., the steamer approached the ferry cable the Métis had lowered just minutes before. Although insufficiently low to stop *Northcote,* the cable sheared off her smokestacks, spars, and masts. Her boilers crippled by the loss of the smokestacks, *Northcote* drifted virtually powerless through some rapids and three miles downstream before successfully anchoring. The steamer and soldiers on board played no further role in the fighting.

At 9:00 a.m., Middleton's column approached Mission Ridge, immediately south of the main settlement. Here the church and rectory stood with two hastily fortified houses 400 yards to the front. After setting both houses on fire with Gatling gun and artillery fire, the militiamen advanced toward the church and rectory and accepted the surrender of the neutral priests, who were sheltering there. From the church, Middleton pushed his entire force forward, intending to take Batoche in an all-out attack. He was unaware that the Métis were well concealed in deep gun pits positioned in surrounding scrub bush.

The artillery were drawn up on the edge of Mission Ridge and both 9-pounder guns started shelling Batoche, while the Gatling gun opened up on the river's western shore. Instantly, the artillery battery and its supporting infantry were fired upon from the concealed positions. Middleton ordered a withdrawal while the Gatling gun suppressed the Métis fire. When Middleton attempted to drive to the right from a starting position at the church, with the Gatling gun in support, he was quickly checked by Métis fire. Despite the heavy fire, none of Middleton's men were killed in either advance and only a few were wounded.

With photography in its infancy at the time of the North-West Rebellion, this image by militiaman James Peters shows militia troops engaging the Métis at Fish Creek.

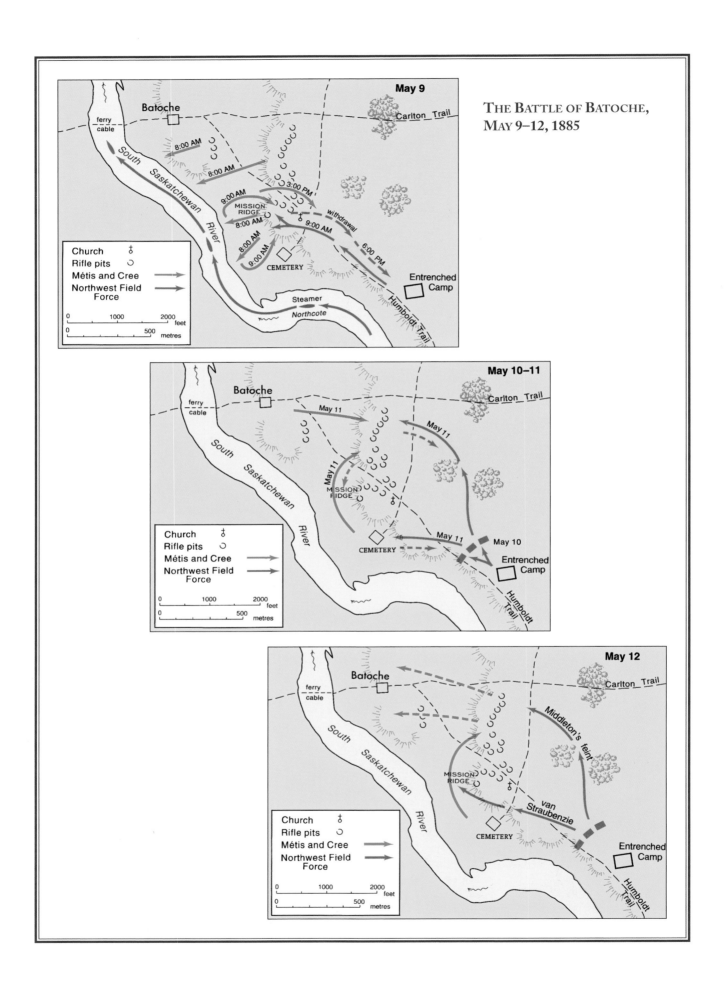

THE BATTLE OF BATOCHE,
MAY 9–12, 1885

Realizing the danger the Gatling gun posed, Dumont attempted to capture it, but was driven back. Another militia advance was also blocked and one soldier was killed. The Métis then attempted to encircle the Field Force from the north, starting a prairie fire to screen their advance. When the fire fizzled out, however, they withdrew. By 3:00 p.m. both sides hunkered down and gunfire became desultory.

With night approaching, Middleton had to either withdraw to the camp eight miles back or move it forward to maintain the link between his soldiers and supplies. The decision was made to advance the camp to a quarter-mile south of the church and fortify it by circling the wagons and filling in the space between with makeshift walls constructed from supply boxes, sacks, personal trunks, and hastily dug earthworks. When the fortification was ready, Middleton withdrew to its protection.

The next day, Middleton established gun pits to the front and left of this forward base of operations and heavily shelled Batoche and the Métis positions to demoralize the defenders. Attempted militia advances were checked throughout the day by heavy Métis fire. On May 11, Middleton conducted a small northward reconnaissance, hoping to outflank the Métis positions. To meet this threat, the defenders had to draw men from the positions facing the Field Force's front. This enabled the soldiers there to advance as far as the cemetery, confirming that the Métis were thinly spread.

The militia artillery battery is firing on Batoche minutes before Métis fighters attempt to capture the guns, but are driven off by the artillerymen.

Accordingly, on May 12 Middleton ordered a two-pronged attack, with a feint first to the north to draw off some of the Métis before the head-on attack at Mission Ridge. The feint by Middleton had the desired effect, but a strong west wind prevented the main force hearing the gunfire intended to signal success and so it remained in position. Disgusted, Middleton returned to camp and gave a vague order to Lieutenant Colonel Bowen van Straubenzie to advance as "far as he pleased." He then retired to his tent.

By now, the Métis were desperately short of ammunition and men. Of the original force of 250 to 300 defenders, only 50 to 60 had not fled or been wounded and these were widely scattered, some still facing the site of Middleton's feint, others holding positions on the ridge, and others inside Batoche.

Van Straubenzie led the Field Force forward in the mid-afternoon, and within minutes the militia spontaneously charged forward. The men lunged down the slope despite heavy fire and soon drove the last Métis fighters out of Batoche. In the wake of this defeat, the rebellion quickly crumbled. Casualties during the four-day battle were surprisingly light — 8 Field Force killed and 22 wounded, while Métis casualties were never recorded but were undoubtedly less than Middleton's estimate of 51 killed.

Riel surrendered three days later and Dumont fled to the United States. On May 24, Middleton marched into Battleford and

Militiamen sleeping inside the fortification they erected on the outskirts of Batoche

accepted Poundmaker's surrender two days later. On May 27, Strange engaged Big Bear's Cree in an inconclusive battle at Frenchman's Butte. After several weeks evading pursuit, Big Bear gave himself up on July 2 at Fort Carlton. Riel was tried and hanged for treason on November 16, 1885. Poundmaker and Big Bear were each sentenced to three years' imprisonment. After living in exile in the U.S. until 1888, Dumont returned to a general amnesty and settled again in Batoche in 1893. Like so many of the prairie Métis and native peoples, he proved incapable of adapting to the agrarian culture and economy imposed by the Canadian government and yet there was little room for the hunting and trapping society that had previously existed. Dumont died in 1906 of heart failure.

CHAPTER SIX

The South African War

1899–1902

Deploying the First Contingent

On November 29, 1899, Canada's first contingent of 1,039 men and 4 nursing sisters disembarked from *Sardinian*'s cramped confines at Cape Town to serve in the British Empire's war against two Afrikaner republics: the Republic of South Africa (Transvaal) and the Orange Free State. Although support for the war, which had broken out on October 11, was mainly confined to outspoken Ontario-based pro-imperialists, the government reluctantly agreed the following day to raise a Canadian contingent. The 2nd (Special Service) Battalion, Royal Canadian Regiment (RCR), was quickly recruited and thousands cheered its departure from Quebec City on October 30.

In order to deploy a force abroad in just 18 days, the Department of Militia drew heavily on urban-based militia units. Ten of 96 militias provided about 35 percent of First Contingent volunteers; a further 13 percent were drawn from the Permanent Force and the North-West

SOUTH AFRICA, 1899

Mounted Police. Of its 40 officers, 12 were professional soldiers. Six of these, including its commander Lieutenant Colonel William Otter, had served in the North-West Rebellion.

Apart from the militia and Permanent Force volunteers, the battalion left Canada largely untrained, for even the Mounties had no real military training. Thirty days at sea aboard a hastily outfitted, crowded, and poorly provisioned ship little rectified matters. In Cape Town, the battalion joined a British army reeling from a Boer invasion of northern and central Cape Colony and northwestern Natal. Mafeking, Ladysmith, and Kimberley were besieged. Between December 10 and 15, British troops suffered three major defeats, largely because the Boers enjoyed numerical superiority over Britain's South African forces. The Canadian arrival was part of a massive buildup that would field almost 500,000 British Empire troops against only 88,000 Boers. It would, however, be months before the reinforced and reorganized British army was ready to move to the relief of the besieged towns.

During this period, the RCR trained at Belmont Station, where typhoid fever and other illnesses afflicted about one-third of the battalion. While only three men died, fully one-tenth were hospitalized when the battalion joined Major-General Horace Smith-Dorrien's 19th Brigade at Gras Pan, preparatory to a British offensive against the capitals of both republics on February 12, 1900.

BATTLE OF PAARDEBERG

On February 13, the RCR marched as part of a column consisting of 30,000 soldiers, 7,000 non-combatants, 14,000 horses, and 22,000 mules and oxen hauling 600 wagons. Raising red dust clouds, they travelled under a remorseless desert sun from Ramdam toward the Modder River. The column's advance toward Bloemfontein forced Boer General Piet Cronje to lift the Kimberley siege and attempt to stop it with only 12,000 men at Paardeberg Drift.

The British, however, won the race to the ford (called a drift by the Afrikans) and cut Cronje off on February 18. While Cronje's men entrenched in the centre of a crook in the river east of the drift, the RCR and the British battalions of the 19th Brigade crossed to the northern shoreline to prevent the Boers from escaping the trap. Except for two battalions from the Highland Brigade that remained on Signal Hill, on the south side of the river, to block any Boer attempt to retreat southward, the remaining British battalions, along with several artillery pieces, took up position on a height immediately dubbed Gun Hill. Once these units were in position, the Canadians spearheaded the advance against the Boers.

Descending from a ridge onto a plain, the Canadians came under fire from Boer snipers dug in on the opposite shore about 1,800 yards off. After advancing another 200 yards, the Canadian formation took

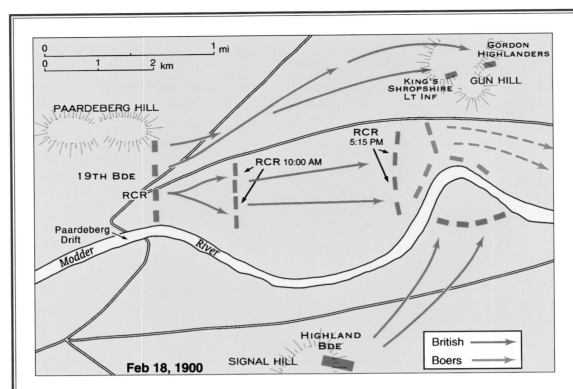

FIRST PHASE

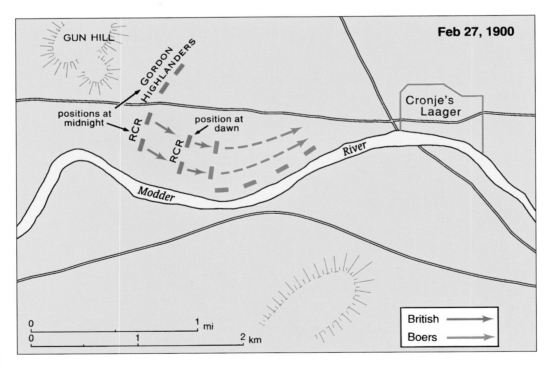

SECOND PHASE

THE BATTLE OF PAARDEBURG, FEBRUARY 18–27, 1900

cover at about 10:00 a.m. to avoid the increasing fire. For the next hour, the men advanced in short rushes of 20 to 30 yards at a time or by crawling forward. The scattered sections in the Canadian centre made little forward progress in the ensuing confusion, but the left flank managed to get within 800 yards while the right flank closed to within 400 yards before both were completely stalled by Boer gunfire. For hours the men lay under a burning sun, the slightest movement drawing fire, until mid-afternoon when a brief rainstorm drenched them.

Soon three companies of the Duke of Cornwall's Light Infantry arrived, commanded by Lieutenant Colonel William Aldworth. Telling Otter he had been sent to "finish the business" with a bayonet charge if necessary, Aldworth ordered his men to charge at 5:15 p.m. Many Canadians joined the wild charge, which was greeted immediately by a withering Boer fusillade. In minutes, the attack collapsed. Aldworth, his adjutant, and many men lay dead or wounded in the open. More casualties followed as Cornwall and RCR troops sought to recover them.

With darkness, the survivors withdrew to the main drift, while the Boers slipped back to their main encampment two miles east of the river crook. "Bloody Sunday," as this day that marked the worst fighting Canadians saw during the war was thereafter known, accounted for 21 of 39 RCR men killed in South Africa and 60 of 123 wounded. Three-quarters of the casualties occurred during the charge. For their part, the Cornwalls lost 56 men, almost all killed in the charge.

The failed frontal assault convinced the British to resort to a siege, which lasted until February 26. At that time, believing the Boers were sufficiently low on supplies and morale, the Canadians were ordered to conduct a night attack against Cronje's Laager — a rough fortress created out of the Boer supply wagons, supply crates, and hastily dug trenches. Accordingly, the RCR advanced at 2:00 a.m. on February 27 in two lines that drew within 100 yards of the Boers before drawing sporadic fire. The men hit the ground and hastily dug trenches. For 15 minutes, a fierce firefight ensued until inexplicably four of six Canadian companies suddenly withdrew in disarray to the start line, now held by the Gordon Highlanders. 'G' and 'H' companies remained in position, largely holding their fire until dawn presented them with viable Boer targets.

After an hour of intense gunfire exchange, the Boers raised a white flag. Within an hour, Cronje surrendered and led about 4,000 Boers into captivity. Canadian casualties for the day were 13 killed and 21 wounded. The Battle of Paardeberg was the first major overseas engagement in which soldiers served officially as Canadian rather than British troops. It was also Britain's first major victory in South Africa and it enabled the capture of Bloemfontein, the Orange Free State capital.

OVER:
Men of the Royal Canadian Regiment during the February 1900 march to the Modder River

A rare turn-of-the-century action shot of a Canadian soldier firing his Lee Enfield rifle during the Battle of Paardeberg.

RAISING THE SECOND CONTINGENT AND LORD STRATHCONA'S HORSE

Even as the RCR marched toward Paardeberg, a second contingent gathered in Halifax preparatory to shipping out. Unlike the first contingent, these men were organized into either mounted infantry or mounted artillery battalions — initially designated the 1st Canadian Mounted Rifles (which became the Royal Canadian Dragoons* in August 1900), the 2nd Canadian Mounted Rifles (CMR), and Royal Canadian Field Artillery (RCFA). The contingent numbered 1,289 men, of whom 750 were mounted infantry and 539 were artillerymen. Most of the 2nd Canadian Mounted Rifles were westerners, with many North-West Mounted Police officers, while the Dragoons were largely Permanent Force or militia cavalrymen. The artillerymen were primarily Permanent Force or recruited in eastern urban centres from militia units.

* For the purpose of clarity, 1CMR is henceforth referred to as the Royal Canadian Dragoons (RCD).

Deployed in three ships that sailed at varying times, the first Second Contingent troops arrived at Cape Town on February 16 and the last on March 21. The ships had left Halifax with 1,172 horses on board. Many horses died en route and those that survived were too emaciated, ill, or weak for immediate service. To make up the deficiency, Canadians had to accept small Argentine ponies for mounts, and mules were used for hauling guns and wagons.

It soon became clear that Second Contingent would seldom all serve together. This was particularly true for the RCFA, where even batteries were broken up among various British columns fighting Boer commandos. After their defeat at Paardeberg, Boer generals largely

Marches and Battles of Canadian Forces, February 1900–March 1902

avoided set-piece battles where British superiority in manpower and firepower ensured defeat. Instead they formed roving commandos ranging in size from a few men to several thousand. Drawing on an extensive network of resupply depots and sympathetic Boer inhabitants, the commandos travelled light, hit hard and fast against static British communication networks, and melted away before the British could respond. This guerilla warfare frustrated British efforts to capture and secure Afrikaner territory. It also required thousands of men to protect vital road and rail networks upon which the British depended for supplies and reinforcement.

First assigned to "rebel chasing" was the RCD and the RCFA's 'D' and 'E' batteries. From March 4 to April 14, sections of these two units trekked in company with hundreds of British soldiers over 700 miles of harsh terrain from Victoria West to Upington without engaging any Boers.

Twelve days after the RCD and RCFA section set out on its long trek, Canada's third contingent, Lord Strathcona's Horse, sailed from Halifax for Cape Town. Although recruited similarly to other contingents and organized as a mounted rifle company, all the unit's costs were paid by Lord Strathcona, Canada's High Commissioner to London. The regiment was also attached directly to the British army and hence not formally a Canadian contingent. Raised in western Canada, the regiment numbered 540 men and was commanded by former NWMP superintendent Sam Steele. En route to Cape Town, 27 percent of its horses died from disease, mostly pneumonia. Those that lived were in poor condition upon arrival on April 10. The men were scarcely better off, with 63 reporting sick within the first two weeks of deployment.

MARCHING TO PRETORIA

Meanwhile, on March 7 the RCR had joined a major British advance on Bloemfontein. The RCR was spared from small engagements at Poplar Grove and Dreifontein prior to the column's arrival in the Orange Free State capital on March 15, after a gruelling, sweltering march during which the men averaged 15 miles a day. A typhoid epidemic broke out shortly thereafter, killing six men. On April 20, when the regiment left Bloemfontein to clear a Boer commando to the city's east, it left 4 officers and 150 men in hospital.

On April 25, the Canadians advanced across an open plain in extended order under protection of British artillery shelling to seize the small village of Thaba 'Nchu and two adjacent kopjes. Withering Boer rifle fire that killed one man and wounded two others stopped the line cold. While trying to organize his men, Otter suffered a slight bullet wound to the chin and neck that removed him from command for a month. The Battle of Israel's Poort raged for three hours until the Boers withdrew, but there were no further Canadian casualties.

The next day, another attack was mounted against the Boers, who had again occupied the village to block the road to Pretoria. A confused four-day battle culminated in the Canadians and Gordon Highlanders scaling the steep face of the table-topped mountain of

The Gloucesters charging a Kopje and facing death, near Norvals Pont (Feb. 3rd), S. Africa.
Copyright 1900 by Underwood & Underwood.

Thaba 'Nchu itself and clearing the Boers from this vital stronghold. Despite the ferocity of the Boer rifle and artillery fire, the Canadians suffered only one man killed. This victory opened the way for the British march on Pretoria.

Fortunately for the illness-reduced RCR, a draft of 103 volunteers arrived just before the battalion joined the advance. There was, however, no time to train or integrate them into the unit. On May 10, the RCR reached the Zand River, where a battle for the ford was underway. Four Canadian companies tried to seize a rise on the extreme right of the British line overlooking the river, while the remaining companies supported a brigade engaged on the left. No sooner did the companies reach the rise than they came under heavy fire from about 800 Boers. Due to the small hill's confined space, only one company could form a firing line, while a second moved into reserve, and the other two were returned to the main brigade to minimize exposure to enemy fire. Eventually an artillery section came up and broke the stalemate, scattering the Boers. Two Canadians were killed and two wounded.

On May 26, Otter resumed command and the RCR, now numbering only 443 men, crossed the Vaal River — the first British infantry battalion to enter the Transvaal. Three days later, they reached Klip River and discovered Boers entrenched on Doornkop Hill. At 1:45 p.m., the RCR and other 19th Brigade battalions advanced, with the Canadians and Gordon Highlanders leading. The facing Boers set fire to the veldt and the clothes and hair of some troopers were singed

A popular form of journalistic and travel photography in the latter part of the 19th century is demonstrated in this photographic plate of a carefully staged shot of troops storming a kopje. Using a special double lens camera, the photographer captured the same image simultaneously but from two slightly different angles. When viewed through a device known as a stereoscope the two photos were presented, one frame to each eye, through separate lenses inclined toward each other. This caused the photos to blend together and resulted in a three-dimensional image.

as they skirted the flames. When the front line was 1,800 yards from the defensive line, inaccurate Boer artillery fire came in. As the Canadians entered a fire-blackened stretch fronting the hill, the Boers, entrenched a thousand yards uphill, caught them in crossfire. The Canadians took cover, but the Gordons pressed on. Just before nightfall, they charged the Boer position with bayonets. The Gordons lost 20 killed and 70 wounded, but cleared the hill, supported by the Canadians. Canadian casualties were 7 wounded and no dead.

On June 5, the remaining 436 men of RCR entered Pretoria, which the Boers did not defend. After Pretoria, the RCR took up garrison duty at various railroad stations until the regiment's duty tour was complete. On October 1, eleven months after arriving in Cape Town, the RCR departed for Canada.

The RCR was not the only Canadian regiment that participated in the march to Pretoria. In a separate column, three CMR squadrons and the RCD rode in the 1st Mounted Infantry Brigade. Their 33-day march took a different route than that of the RCR column. They fought several sharp actions, particularly at Coetzee's Drift on May 5, participated in the Zand River and Doornkop battles, and entered Pretoria on June 6. Remarkably, during these engagements only two Canadians were wounded.

RELIEF OF MAFEKING

While the RCR and mounted infantry regiments marched to Pretoria, Royal Canadian Field Artillery batteries joined the effort to relieve Mafeking, where Colonel Robert Baden-Powell's men were withstanding a Boer siege of the town. The British plan was to advance on Mafeking from both north and south. To the north, only one British regiment existed, the 800-strong Rhodesian Regiment, which was too weak to challenge the Boers. 'C' Battery RCFA therefore sailed as reinforcement, along with the 5,000-strong Rhodesian Field Force, to Beira in Portuguese East Africa. From there, a 1,000-mile arduous journey partially by train and the rest by march brought the column to Mafeking from the north. On May 15, the Field Force married with a column approaching from the south at Jan Massibi and encountered the Boer siege force about noon of May 16.

The Canadian battery soon engaged in an artillery duel with Boer gunners at Sanie Station that raged for three hours, with the Canadian guns firing off 106 rounds. The fire succeeded in clearing the road and at 4:00 a.m. on May 17, forward elements entered Mafeking to a warm welcome from Baden-Powell and the other British defenders. 'C' Battery remained in northwestern Transvaal, including participation in a skirmish at Jericho on October 24, until ordered back to Cape Town on November 20 for a December 13 sailing to Canada. During this time, it slogged from one small engagement to another, chasing elusive Boer commandos that occupied towns and destroyed rail tracks with near impunity. Although deployed in other parts of South Africa and the Afrikaner states, the same unrewarding task fell to the other Canadian artillery units.

LELIEFONTEIN

After Pretoria, the CMR and RCD cavalry participated in many fighting patrols chasing Boer commandos. Resulting skirmishes proved costly, with several men killed or wounded. The worst skirmish occurred near Honing Spruit, when 400 Boers attacked 9 CMR riders. Two men were severely wounded during the escape and four were captured. Four other troopers, all from Pincher Creek, Alberta, lay concealed behind a railroad bed's scanty cover and attempted to cover the men's flight. They soon drew the fire of about 50 Boers. In the ensuing firefight, two were killed and two wounded.

Eventually, both Canadian mounted regiments moved to north-eastern Transvaal and were dragooned into Major General Horatio Herbert Kitchener's scorched-earth strategy, intended to deny the commandos succour and support by burning farms and imprisoning the civilian Boer populace. On November 6, a column commanded by Smith-Dorrien set out to break up Boer commandos in the Carolina area. The CMR, RCD, and 'D' Battery participated. After a series of skirmishes that failed to quell the Boers, Smith-Dorrien decided at Leliefontein to withdraw and return to Belfast. The rearguard fell to the Royal Dragoons.

No sooner had the withdrawal begun on November 7 than two commandos, numbering about 200 men, attacked. The Dragoons quickly deployed and, supported by 'D' Battery's two guns, held off the Boers while conducting an initial orderly withdrawal of the guns behind a screening force maintained by the mounted infantrymen. As the Boers pressed harder, however, the situation became increasingly desperate and it seemed likely the guns would be captured. Only a hasty ambush sprung by Dragoons' Lieutenant Richard Turner and 12 men prevented Boer success. The entire action cost the Dragoons 3 dead and 11 wounded. Turner and two other men were awarded Victoria Crosses. Leliefontein was Second Contingent's last major action. Most of its soldiers returned to Halifax on January 8, 1901.

SERVICE AS BULLER'S SCOUTS

The men in Lord Strathcona's Horse were, like other Canadian mounted infantry battalions, assigned to carrying out Kitchener's scorched-earth policy. They did so as part of General Sir Redvers Buller's Natal Field Force. Rather than weakening Boer resolve, the strategy only hardened their determination to resist. On September 1, 1900, the Strathconas marched with Buller toward Lydenburg in pursuit of Louis Botha's 2,000-strong commando. Soon the Natal Field Force and Botha's commando locked in a sporadic running battle, with

Men of the 2nd Canadian Mounted Rifles wearing their trademark American-style Stetsons that the Canadians introduced to South Africa

Botha withdrawing and Buller trying to block his retreat. After a month, Buller abandoned the chase. By mid-October, Buller's force broke up and the Strathconas prepared to return to Canada.

A sudden rekindling of Boer action under General Christiaan De Wet caught the British by surprise, however, and Kitchener redrafted the Strathconas on October 24. Three days later, Steele and his tired, increasingly dispirited force set off again. The chase persisted as the Strathconas marched and counter-marched across the Orange Free State and Transvaal districts that the RCR and Second Contingent had previously fought over. Although several battles were fought, De Wet eluded capture and the pursuit was abandoned on January 9, 1901. By month's end, the Strathconas sailed home. Twenty-three had died in South Africa.

Although a further 1,248 Canadians served with the South African Constabulary, this unit was a police force rather than a military

one. Drawn from across the country, the constables sailed from Halifax on March 29, 1901. Upon arrival in South Africa, they were scattered throughout the constabulary and soon engaged in counter-guerilla patrolling that entailed the implementation of scorched-earth tactics and short, usually futile firefights with Boer commandos such as that at Boschbuilt on March 13, 1902. On May 31, 1902, the Boers reached a peace agreement with the British and shortly thereafter most constabulary agreed to be discharged and returned to Canada.

In all, 242 of the 7,368 Canadians who served in South Africa died there. Their service set an important precedent because most served in distinct units commanded by Canadian officers. Henceforth, this would be the standard organizational structure for Canadian units serving as part of Commonwealth forces.

CHAPTER SEVEN

World War I

1914–1918

HASTENING TO WAR

On August 3, 1914, Germany invaded Belgium as part of its overall invasion of France. The next day, Britain declared war — an act that automatically included Canada and other Commonwealth nations. Not that this troubled Canadians, who almost unanimously supported Britain.

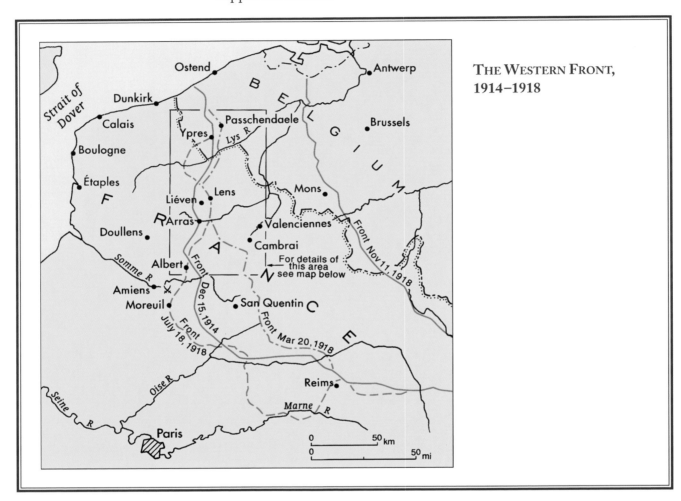

THE WESTERN FRONT, 1914–1918

Canada, however, was unprepared for the daunting four-year military task that followed. Its permanent army was just 3,110 strong and the navy had only 393 sailors and officers. Both were equipped with outdated weapons — and the navy possessed only two ships. Canada did have a 64,000-man militia and from this immediate pool a European expeditionary force was quickly cobbled together. Fearing the war might end before Canadians could see action, Parliament rammed through a bill to raise a 25,000-man contingent financed by a $50 million appropriation. Response to Minister of Militia Sam Hughes's call for militia recruits was overwhelming and 35,000 men soon jammed into a hastily constructed camp at Valcartier, Quebec, to undergo rudimentary training.

On October 3, 1914, the 33,000-man Canadian Expeditionary Force (CEF) and 7,000 horses were crammed aboard 32 transports.

Escorted by 10 British warships, the then largest armed force ever to cross the Atlantic sailed for England and landed 11 days later. More training followed on Salisbury Plain as the war dragged into winter with no quick battlefield or diplomatic resolution emerging.

By the end of 1914, the CEF in England numbered 56,584 men. Five months to the day from Britain's war declaration, the Princess Patricia's Canadian Light Infantry (PPCLI), privately raised and funded by Montreal millionaire Hamilton Gault, was the first Canadian battalion to enter the front line. The PPCLI, composed almost entirely of British ex-soldiers who had immigrated to Canada, joined the British 27th Division at St. Eloi. In February 1915, it carried out the war's first trench raid when '4' Company sent a group of men across no man's land against the German trenches. The PPCLI would serve with the 27th until becoming part of 3rd Division of the Canadian Corps in early 1916.

Approximately one month after the PPCLI's battlefield debut, the CEF, essentially the Canadian 1st Division organized into three

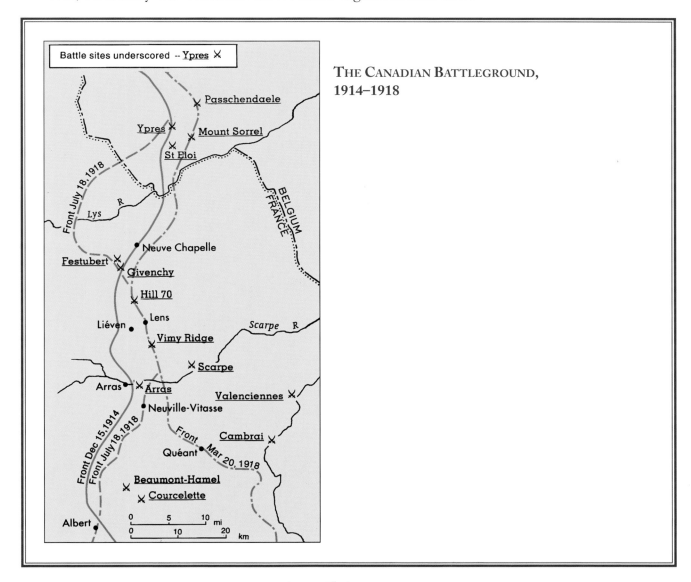

THE CANADIAN BATTLEGROUND, 1914–1918

infantry brigades and one brigade of artillery, deployed to France. British General Edwin Alderson held divisional command, but Canadians commanded the brigades.

YPRES SALIENT

On April 17, 1915, the 18,000-strong 1st Division entered the Ypres Salient in Belgium. A French Algerian division was on the left and the British 28th Division flanked the Canadian trenches on the right. It was expected the Canadians would hone their battlefield skill in what British intelligence expected to remain a quiet sector despite the fact that German artillery had started pounding rear areas two days previously and the bombardment had continued. Soon Ypres itself was reduced to a ruin.

The artillery remained relentless until, at 4:00 p.m. on April 22, the German guns concentrated on the Algerian line and then swung to include the Canadian 3rd Brigade's lines. At 5:00 p.m., greenish-yellow clouds of chlorine gas released from 6,000 cylinders floated out of the German lines on the salient's northern edge and rolled like mist over the Algerians. Behind the war's first gas attack advanced German infantry.

The Algerians fled or died in place, rendering a four-mile-wide swath of trench line defenceless. The Canadians were also caught by the gas cloud, suffering many casualties, but managed to hold when they realized its effects could be partially mitigated by urinating into a cloth and pressing it to their faces. At 11:30 p.m., Alderson ordered a Canadian counterattack against Kitchener's Wood to destabilize the Germans and recover captured British artillery. Fifteen hundred men went into the attack, which soon broke in the face of heavy machine-gun fire. By dawn, only 500 withdrew; the rest had been killed or captured.

Throughout April 23, the Canadians grimly held their sections and attempted to recapture ground to the left while British regiments poured in piecemeal to plug the ragged four-mile gap. The next day, the Germans engulfed the Canadian line in another gas attack and slowly the Prussian Guard pushed the defending battalions back to a new line on the crest of Gravenstafel Ridge to the left of St. Julien village. Confusion reigned over the battlefield, with individual brigades, battalions, and even companies fighting in isolated pockets against bitter odds. On April 27, 1st Canadian Division withdrew to reorganize. On May 8, the Germans attempted a last desperate breakthrough at Frezenberg Ridge. The PPCLI were among those who broke this attack. When the Germans withdrew, 678 PPCLI were dead or wounded and only 150 remained in the trenches. Casualties in 1st Division totalled 6,036 — well over half the division. Four Canadians won the Victoria Cross for gallantry.

1st Canadian Division's respite was short, as it moved almost

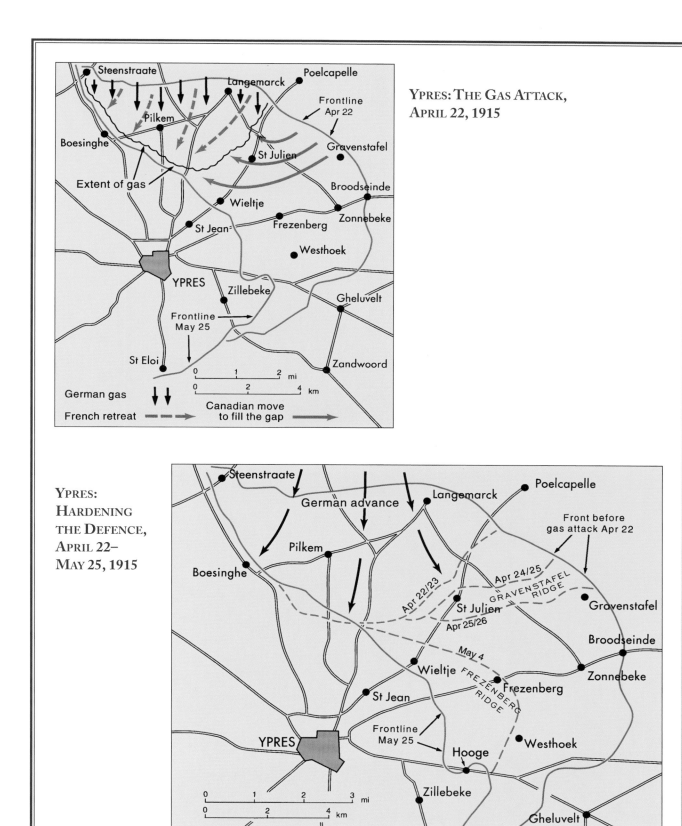

YPRES: THE GAS ATTACK,
APRIL 22, 1915

Steenstraate
Poelcapelle
Langemarck
Frontline
Apr 22
Pilkem
Boesinghe
Gravenstafel
St Julien
Extent of gas
Broodseinde
Wieltje
St Jean
Frezenberg
Zonnebeke
Westhoek
YPRES
Zillebeke
Gheluvelt
Frontline
May 25
St Eloi
Zandwoord

0   1   2   mi
0   2   4   km

German gas

French retreat   Canadian move
                        to fill the gap

YPRES:
HARDENING
THE DEFENCE,
APRIL 22–
MAY 25, 1915

Steenstraate
Poelcapelle
German advance
Langemarck
Front before
gas attack Apr 22
Pilkem
Apr 24/25
Boesinghe
Apr 22/23
"GRAVENSTAFEL
RIDGE"
St Julien
Gravenstafel
Apr 25/26
Broodseinde
May 4
Wieltje
FREZENBERG
RIDGE
Frezenberg
Zonnebeke
St Jean
Frontline
May 25
YPRES
Hooge
Westhoek
Zillebeke
Gheluvelt

0   1   2   3   mi
0   2   4   km

immediately south to Festubert, where the British hoped to shatter the German line. On May 23, 2nd and 3rd Brigades assaulted the German line, only to be caught in the barbed wire and subjected to withering machine-gun fire. The failed attack resulted in 2,468 Canadian dead and wounded. A month later, an attack by 1st Brigade at Givenchy-lex-la-Bassée was completely disrupted when a large British mine meant to destroy German emplacements exploded prematurely and caused 366 Canadian casualties.

CANADIAN CORPS

When 2nd Canadian Division joined the 1st on September 13, 1915, the Canadian Corps was formed, with Alderson commanding and Canadian brigadiers Arthur Currie and Richard Turner becoming

Canadian soldiers go over the top in one of all too many futile attacks.

divisional commanders. The corps spent the winter facing Messines Ridge. Here they endured sleet, snow, bitter winds, drenching rains, and the day-to-day terror of static warfare punctuated by enemy artillery harassment and small trench raids either launched or staved off. They also learned the awful reality of living in the trenches, where dysentery and trench foot were rampant, sleeping quarters poor, rats ever present, and the din caused by the guns almost constant. By year's end, the corps had suffered an additional 2,692 casualties, of whom 688 died holding this "quiet sector."

It was not quiet much longer, however, for the British had been patiently tunnelling since August at nearby St. Eloi, about three miles south of Ypres and adjacent to the Canadian trenches. Throughout the winter, the tunnelling crept ever closer to a dominant German-held feature dubbed "The Mound." When the tunnels were completed in early March, tons of explosive were emplaced in six locations and on March 27, 1916, at 4:14 a.m. the charges were set off. Two German companies were wiped out and large sections of the German trenches were destroyed, but the British 9th Brigade's attack faltered and became a bloody close-quarters slugging match, with the last bomb crater captured only on April 3.

Second Canadian Division was sent in the next day to shore up the new defensive line. Until April 19, it held out against repeated infiltration attacks, but was hard pressed to maintain cohesion amid the mud- and water-choked craters and shattered trenches created by the mines and continuous artillery fire. On April 19, the survivors withdrew after the division had 1,373 casualties and the Germans largely recaptured all the ground initially taken.

In the battle's aftermath, accusations of corps command incompetence arose, so on May 28 Lieutenant General Sir Julian Byng replaced Alderson despite the former's protestation that he knew not a single Canadian. With the arrival of 3rd Canadian Division in early 1916, the Canadians assumed responsibility for a major Ypres Salient section, enabling General Sir Douglas Haig, overall British commander, to concentrate British divisions in the Somme.

In the last week of May, 3rd Division, commanded by General M. S. Mercer, took up position along a two-and-a-half-mile front south and east of Zillebeke running right to left from Hill 60 past Mount Sorrel, Hill 61, Hill 62, Sanctuary Wood and on to "The Gap," as the ruin that had been Hooge village was now called. Soon 3rd Division was alerted by aerial reconnaissance that the Germans were rehearsing an attack. On June 2, the assault began with the worst barrage so far experienced by Commonwealth troops. The fire decimated the Canadian line from Mount Sorrel to Sanctuary Wood. Among those killed almost instantly was Mercer, who had come forward to visit the 4th Canadian Mounted Rifles. The Rifles were virtually eliminated in minutes, suffering 626 casualties out of 702 men. The PPCLI lost 400 men. The Germans advanced easily into the gap torn in the Canadian line to take Mount Sorrel and Hills 61 and 62, but after advancing only 1,200 yards unaccountably dug in.

Byng ordered a counterattack that night, but poor communications resulted in a delay until 7:30 a.m., when 3rd Division's remaining reserves and two brigades from 1st Division went forward. In minutes, the leading troops were being slaughtered by machine-gun and artillery fire and the attack collapsed. Currie's 1st Division was now ordered up.

Although urged to make haste, Currie spent nine days developing a detailed battle plan, to allow reconnaissance operations to familiarize the troops with their objectives, and to rehearse the operation prior to its launch. His approach foreshadowed Canadian operations at Vimy Ridge. Currie also massed artillery and set down a detailed firing plan that called for five successive phases of barrage over the course of one day. For the first four phases, the firing would rise to a crescendo, stop, and then begin again after a short interlude. This was intended both to draw the defenders out of their protective shelters and to confuse them as to when the infantry assault would actually come.

The fifth phase reached crescendo at 8:30 a.m. on June 12 and the Canadians poured into the German lines immediately after the guns fell suddenly silent. They met little resistance and took 200 prisoners. The Battle of Sorrel was over. Canadian casualties were approximately 8,000 men, while the Germans suffered 5,765 casualties. Despite losing more men, the Allies claimed victory because the Canadians ultimately regained all lost ground.

THE SOMME

On July 1, 1916, British forces once again tried to decisively break the German lines, this time at the juncture where the French and British trenches met near the Somme River. Among the attacking regiments was the Royal Newfoundland Regiment. In 30 minutes at

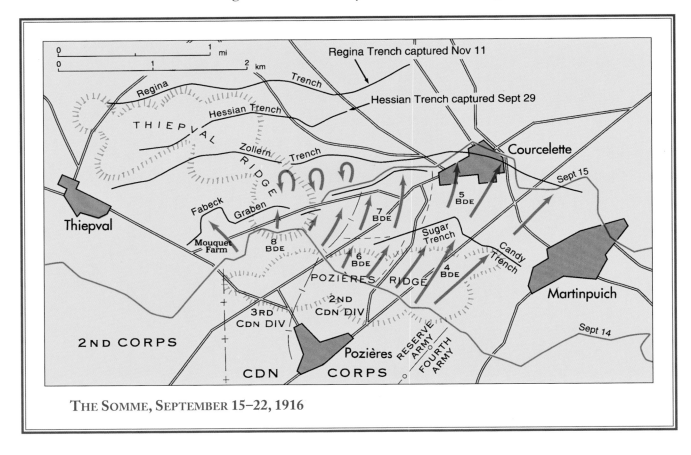

THE SOMME, SEPTEMBER 15–22, 1916

Beaumont-Hamel it was shredded by enemy machine-gun fire, suffering 684 casualties out of 801 men. The Newfoundlanders' experience typified the day's action, which ended with 57,470 British casualties — the highest casualty rate in any single day of the war.

Haig, however, was determined to break through. Fruitless attacks ground up one division after another throughout the summer. On August 31, Canadian Corps moved from the Ypres Salient to face Pozières Ridge, a long limestone feature overlooking the British line. Byng was ordered to take the ridge and the town of Courcelette behind it.

At 6:20 a.m. on September 15, a massive rolling barrage pounded the German lines and the Canadians went into the attack, with 2nd Division on the right moving on Courcelette and 3rd Division on the left striking at Mouquet Farm and the vital German trench Fabeck Graben. Supporting the Canadians were seven tanks, the weapon's battlefield premiere. Two failed to start and four were quickly knocked out by German artillery, but the lone survivor, lurching across rough terrain at one mile per hour, reached its objective and was credited with suppressing enemy machine-gun nests along the way. Whether because of the tank or not, 2nd Division fought its way into Courcelette at dusk. Meanwhile, 3rd Division was locked in a fierce firefight at Mouquet Farm and inside the German trenches.

The first battalion into Courcelette was Royal 22nd Regiment, followed closely by a Nova Scotia regiment. These drove through the town and into the fields beyond, but were almost cut off when German defenders hidden inside the town's basements emerged to engage the following New Brunswick Regiment in house-to-house fighting. The two forward battalions assumed defensive positions and fought off 11 determined counterattacks over the next two days, also taking about 1,000 prisoners.

When heavy rain set in, the Canadian attack mired in the muck. Between September 15 and 22, the Canadians suffered 7,230 casualties, but Canadian Corps was ordered to carry on. Accordingly, 1st Canadian Division fought its way through two trench lines on September 26 toward Regina Trench, set immediately behind Thiepval Ridge. Although a remnant of one battalion won the ridge and reached Regina, it was quickly thrown back by a German counterattack. Continued attacks over the next few days enabled the Canadians to clear Hessian Trench on September 29, leaving the Canadians well poised to finally take Regina Trench. On October 1, seizing Regina Trench fell to 2nd Division. The attack foundered in the face of driving rain, deep mud, and murderous machine-gun fire. The week of rain that followed brought the entire Somme front to a standstill, broken by Currie's 1st Division attacking Regina on October 8. As before, the position proved impregnable even with support from 3rd Division battalions. The day's casualties tallied 1,364.

A tank makes its ponderous way across no man's land during the vicious fighting at the Somme in November 1916.

On October 10, a fourth Canadian division joined Canadian Corps. Soon the inexperienced 4th Division was trying to batter its way into Regina Trench. One battalion got into the trench on October 21 but was thrown back. The next day, however, Brigadier General Victor Odlum's 11th Brigade captured a fragment of the line. Again rain precluded further operations and the Canadians could only grimly hang on to their gains. A November 9 artillery barrage presaged the division's next major assault on Regina Trench. Precisely at midnight on November 10, the attack went in and the trench fell shortly before dawn on November 11.

Beyond this trench, however, stood Desire Trench. A week later, Odlum's 11th Brigade advanced through driving snow and won a short section. Supporting attacks by other British and Canadian brigades failed and the 11th was isolated. Soon it retreated to Regina Trench and the final Canadian Corps divisions here were withdrawn.

The Somme was winding down, as Haig finally accepted defeat. Total Allied losses were 623,907, opposed to 465,525 German. Canadian casualties were 24,029. Nothing but a few thousand yards of strategically meaningless ground had been won, but a large percentage of one British generation had perished. British morale bottomed out. In Canada and throughout the Commonwealth, talk of an early end to the war ceased.

THE AIR WAR

While most Canadians served in the army during World War I, about 24,000 joined either the Royal Flying Corps or the Royal Naval Air Service. In 1918, these services combined as the Royal Air Force (RAF). Although Canada did not establish its own air arm, its contribution to the British air service was significant. By 1918, one-third of RAF airmen were Canadian, as were 11 of the 27 RAF aces to have shot down 30 planes or more. Billy Bishop alone was credited with downing 72 planes, more than any other RAF pilot.

Most of 1915 had been spent developing this innovative and little understood military service. Not until late 1916 would the air war significantly impact the ground fighting. This took the form of providing aerial reconnaissance of enemy dispositions and bombing and strafing enemy concentrations. The dogfights that so captured civilian imagination on both sides resulted mainly from attempts to prevent completion of ground-support tasks.

Canadian pilots also guarded Great Britain from Zeppelin bomber attacks and attempted to locate and sink submarines. Poor submarine detection equipment and the crudity of bomb systems rendered anti-submarine operations largely futile. The high altitudes at which Zeppelins drifted over Britain also frustrated most attempts to shoot down the dirigibles. However, Canadian Robert Leckie managed to both down two Zeppelins and to severely damage a German submarine.

A rare photo capturing RAF and German planes in a dogfight

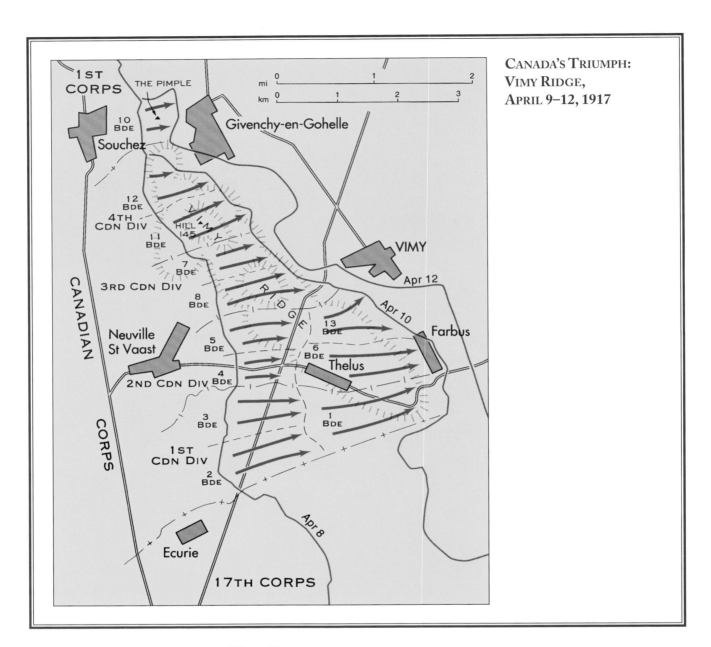

Map labels: 1ST CORPS, THE PIMPLE, 10 BDE, Souchez, Givenchy-en-Gohelle, 12 BDE, 4TH CDN DIV, HILL 145, 11 BDE, 7 BDE, 3RD CDN DIV, 8 BDE, VIMY, Apr 12, Apr 10, 13 BDE, Farbus, Neuville St Vaast, 5 BDE, 6 BDE, Thelus, CANADIAN, 2ND CDN DIV, 4 BDE, 3 BDE, 1 BDE, CORPS, 1ST CDN DIV, 2 BDE, Apr 8, Ecurie, 17TH CORPS, RIDGE

VIMY RIDGE

The winter of 1916–17 found Canadian Corps facing Vimy Ridge, one of the Western Front's most disputed positions. At its highest point, the five-mile-long ridge northeast of Arras reached 475 feet. Since its capture in 1914, the Germans had transformed the ridge into their most heavily fortified sector in France. Into the ridge's western slope and along the ridgeline, deep underground caverns capable of housing entire battalions had been carved in the chalk. The trench network ran three lines deep and was designed to oppose the heaviest assault until reinforcements could arrive to repel any Allied gains. From its heights, the Germans could easily observe all Allied rear area activity, rendering a surprise attack hopeless. This contributed greatly to German confidence that the position was impregnable.

Byng was advised in November 1916 to plan on capturing Vimy Ridge in early spring with virtually no support from other units, as these would be engaged in a general British offensive across the entire Arras front. To succeed, Byng and his trusted subordinate Currie, 1st Division commander, knew they must develop a new tactical approach or the Canadians would be slaughtered to no avail. Both recognized that previous Allied strategy had failed to adapt to the unique circumstances imposed by trench warfare. The French relied largely on their troops' fighting élan and the British on massed artillery barrages to pound the German defenders senseless prior to a ponderous infantry assault. Both approaches had proven badly wanting. For the British, the Somme symbolized the ultimate charnel house; for the French it had been Verdun.

British and French doctrine treated the common soldier as cannon fodder not to be trusted with personal initiative. Currie convinced Byng this approach was wrong, particularly given the independent nature of Canadians. What Currie envisioned were platoons that could lose commanders and still function. He also reorganized the platoons so that riflemen, bombers, and machine gunners were incorporated in one body rather than isolated in separate platoons that were not trained to work together.

The two generals also improved the creeping barrage technique developed during the Somme, where artillery fire progressed a short distance ahead of the advancing infantry. If the artillery adjusted fire forward in accordance to carefully timed lifts, it could walk the infantry right into the enemy trenches behind a curtain of protective fire. New explosives and concentration plans were developed to enable the artillery to rip holes in German barbed wire. Lieutenant Colonel Andrew McNaughton invented a means to presight German gun positions so that the Canadian artillery could destroy them quickly in the attack's opening moments. Another Canadian, Brigadier General Raymond Brutinel, promoted the use of machine guns for indirect fire by spraying repeated and concentrated bursts over the heads of the enemy rather than firing at specific targets. The intent was to deny the Germans easy movement inside their own lines.

The final requirement Currie and Byng sought before approving the attack was that the RFC gain air superiority over the battlefront. Throughout April 1917, an air war raged overhead as almost 400 Allied fighters tangled daily with a German force that was only about 150 strong but equipped with better planes and arguably more skilled pilots. The attack was set for Easter Sunday, April 8, but was soon pushed back to April 9.

For two preceding weeks, the Germans were subjected to a ceaseless barrage by 480 18-pounders and 250 howitzers and heavy guns supplied with 50,000 tons of shells — more than a million rounds. On the last day, most guns turned against the massive tangles of barbed wire

OVER:
The 29th Infantry Battalion advances through German barbed wire and heavy fire during the assault on Vimy Ridge.

fronting the German line. At dusk on April 8 when the firing slowed, the Germans rushed to their defences, but no attack materialized. The Germans stood down.

At 5:30 a.m. on April 9, 983 guns and mortars rained explosives down on the German line for three minutes with Brutinel's machine guns adding to the storm. All four Canadian divisions advanced behind this wall of fire. The leading elements swept through large gaps in the barbed wire and into the forward trenches before the defenders emerged from their protective shelters. This first wave had been instructed to immediately move on to the second trench system and leave mopping up to the second wave, which took thousands of dazed prisoners still stumbling from their shelters. Meanwhile, McNaughton's artillery-spotting technique proved itself as the Canadian gunners managed to eliminate 176 of 212 German batteries. Unable to direct artillery against the Canadians, the Germans could do little to stem the advance.

By 7:00 a.m., 1st Division was on its objective; the 3rd, with a British brigade attached, was on Vimy's crest 30 minutes later; and the 2nd arrived there 30 minutes after that. Fully three-quarters of the ridge was taken. On the left flank, however, 4th Division had been tasked with seizing Hill 145 — Vimy's highest point — and a prominent knoll on the far left flank dubbed "the Pimple." Although the division got through the first trench line relatively quickly, the Germans rallied and subjected the Canadians to devastating machine-gun fire. Many battalions were shredded and the survivors were pinned down

Powerful naval guns added the weight of their fire to the barrage on Vimy Ridge that preceded the Canadian attack.

well short of Hill 145. Reinforcements were chewed up until the only reserve left was the 85th Nova Scotia Battalion, a work battalion virtually untrained for combat. The 85th attacked Hill 145 at 5:45 p.m. and an hour later drove the Germans off in vicious hand-to-hand fighting.

After three days' reorganization, Byng sent 10th Brigade against "The Pimple." Attacking through sleet and snow, this western Canadian brigade cleared the knoll, but half its troops were killed or wounded.

Vimy Ridge's capture marked the deepest Commonwealth advance in two and a half years. The victory came at a grim price. About 40,000 Canadians were involved in the attack; of those, 3,598 were killed and 7,004 wounded. It was also a relatively hollow victory, as the German line resolidified well back on the Douai Plain and no exploitation beyond the ridge proved possible because the overall Battle of Arras ended in another stalemate. The war of attrition continued, while at home Canadians faced a conscription crisis that tested the nation's resolve to reinforce the divisions fighting in the trenches.

After the victory at Vimy Ridge, the line soon stalemated and Canadians returned to the grim life of static trench warfare.

Little time was given Canadian Corps to rest and integrate fresh reserves. On June 6, Currie assumed corps command and two days later 3rd and 4th Divisions successfully attacked south of Lens. At dawn on August 15, Canadian Corps attacked Hill 70 just north of Lens, taking it in just 20 minutes. The Germans immediately counterattacked and for three days the Canadians repulsed repeated counterattacks. Finally the Germans, having suffered 20,000 casualties, broke off the engagement. Canadian Corps had 5,843 dead or wounded.

PASSCHENDAELE

While the Canadians fought at Lens, most of the British army was involved in Haig's latest massive offensive in Belgium, designed to bring about the long-dreamed-of war of movement. Heavy rains accompanied its start on July 31 and soon the 100,000-strong British Third Army was hopelessly bogged down in an ever deepening quagmire. After a third of the army had become casualties, the Second Army replaced it. This force got within a short distance of Passchendaele Ridge on October 4 but, wallowing in thick mud and decimated by prolonged fighting, could go no further. By this time, almost 250,000 men had been killed or wounded for virtually no gain.

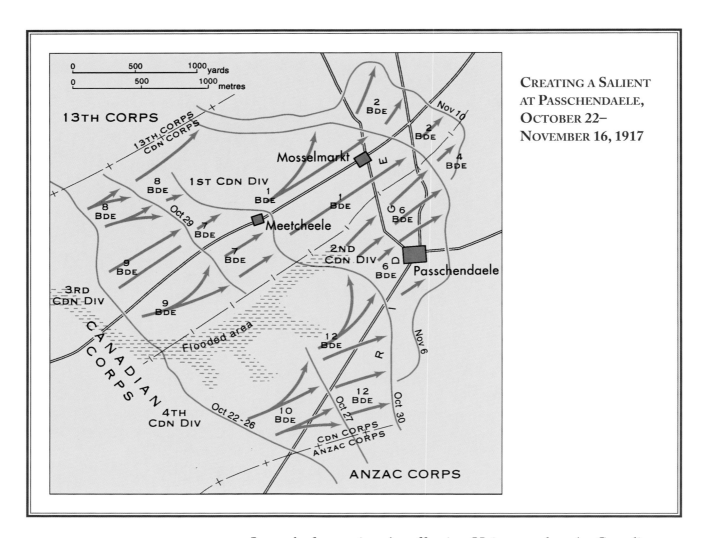

Instead of scrapping the offensive, Haig turned to the Canadian Corps. Currie initially balked at the assignment, but in the end the Canadians marched into the muddy moonscape of Passchendaele with orders to seize the ridge and the town of Passchendaele itself. Ever methodical Currie delayed until October 25 so he could design an attack that had a modicum of hope. His plan called for a three-stage advance with intervals between to allow fresh forces and supplies to come up through the virtually impassable landscape. Supporting the attack on the Canadian left flank was the British XIII Corps and on the right flank the Anzac Corps, comprised of Australian and New Zealand divisions.

At 5:40 a.m. on October 26, 1917, 3rd and 4th Divisions wallowed into a sea of mud and shell craters transformed into small lakes, only to be cut up by heavy machine-gun fire coming from nearly impregnable cement pillboxes. For two days, the attacking battalions tried repeatedly to crack the German line, at a cost of 2,481 men.

On October 30, fresh battalions joined the fray. They advanced 1,000 yards to gain the main ridge positions at a price of 1,321 dead or wounded. The dead had to be left where they fell and it took 12 men to carry each stretcher case back through the mud and slop. Canadian Corps' remaining two divisions relieved the worn-out 3rd and 4th and prepared to attack on November 6. By noon, they seized the pillboxes, which were nearly all that marked what had once been the village of Passchendaele. Four days later, they cleared the remaining section of ridge in vicious fighting. Although the ridge position was like a finger thrust into the German line, the Canadians managed to stave off the inevitable counterattacks that hit them from three sides.

On November 14, Currie led his men past a relieving force to regroup in the Lens-Vimy sector. Passchendaele cost the Canadians 15,654 dead or wounded. More than 1,000 dead were never recovered from the mud.

THE GERMAN OFFENSIVE

At 6:40 a.m. on March 21, 1918, the Germans went on the offensive, striking with devastating force along a 50-mile-long front held by British Fifth Army that stretched from Arras to the Oise River. The British line crumbled and there were insufficient reserves to mount a counterattack. Ninety thousand British soldiers were captured, along with 1,000 artillery pieces. In one day, the Germans advanced 10 miles. Within three days, all the ground captured during the Battle of the Somme was lost. The German ground effort was strongly supported by air power as the Germans compensated for their numerical inferiority by creating 30-plane squadrons that fought in disciplined, mutually supporting packs.

With the entire British front in jeopardy, Haig scrambled to find reserves to plug the holes and stem the German tide. Haig wanted to

Men of the 16th Canadian Machine Gun Company hunker in shell holes amid the mud and carnage of Passchendaele.

break Canadian Corps up and commit it to battle piecemeal, but Currie objected vigorously and the breakup was only temporary. Still, during this time, Brutinel's Mobile Machine Gun Corps was scattered in sections to points in dire need of motorized machine-gun troops. Second Division fought for several weeks with the British Third Army. At Moreuil Wood on March 30, all three regiments of the previously little utilized Canadian Cavalry Brigade used their rapid mobility to establish a key blocking position that faced the Germans advancing on Amiens. Despite heavy casualties, the cavalrymen held and stopped the Germans cold, although they were left in possession of a deep salient that reached Villers-Bretonneux to the north and Moreuil to the south.

By April 29, the offensive ran out of steam across the entire front, as the Germans proved to have insufficient manpower and mobility to decisively sever the British line. They had merely shoved the line back. The cost for the Germans was 56,639 dead and 181,338 wounded. These were losses the German Army could scarcely afford and, so weakened, was hard pressed to hold its gains.

AMIENS

Meanwhile, Canadian Corps, comparatively unscathed by its minimal involvement in the British attempts to stop the offensive and refreshed by a May to mid-July respite from battle, readied for future action. That opportunity came when Haig approved an Australian infantry-cum-tank attempt to wipe out the German salient created by the spring offensive at Amiens, France, which followed their successful implementation of a combined arms assault on the village of Hamel. The Australians wanted a dependable force on their flank and asked Haig for the Canadians. Haig agreed.

Moving with great secrecy to the Amiens sector to avoid alerting the Germans of the forthcoming attack, the Canadians settled in on the Australian right with French divisions on their own right. At 4:20 a.m. on August 8, 1918, a 20-minute barrage preceded the Canadian advance, which depended, like the Australian attack, on tanks rather than artillery fire to clear the wire. A heavy mist blanketed the ground as the infantry and tanks advanced in Currie's favoured three-wave form of attack. Three divisions went forward in line: 2nd Division on the left, 1st Division in the centre, and 3rd Division on the right. When the French lagged on the right flank, the Royal Canadian Regiment slipped into the French sector and captured Mézières to maintain the momentum. This could have opened up a gap between 3rd Division and 1st Division, but Currie quickly inserted the British 3rd Cavalry Division — including the Canadian Cavalry Brigade — to keep the line solid. With its flank exposed by the still lagging French, 3rd Division's casualties mounted, causing Currie to leapfrog 4th Division through them to keep the

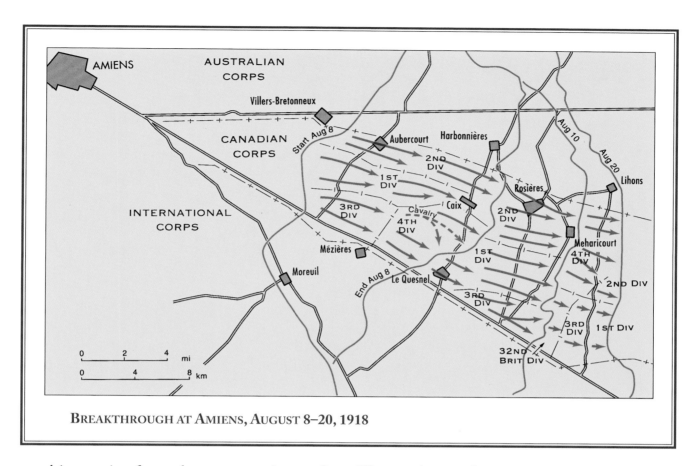

BREAKTHROUGH AT AMIENS, AUGUST 8–20, 1918

drive moving forward across a continuous front. The attack proved a stunning success, with the Germans thrown back eight miles by the Canadians, seven miles by the Australians, and about four miles by the French.

However, by the next day the advance slowed before stiffening German resistance. At dusk, the Canadians were well ahead of the Australians and the French were stalled before old German defence positions developed during the Battle of the Somme. The following day, the Canadians too came up against a section of the old fortifications and for three days the battle raged on with only modest gains. Finally, after having advanced a total distance of 14 miles, Haig called the offensive off. Losses were once again heavy, with 4,000 Canadians killed or wounded out of 9,000 total Commonwealth casualties. But the Germans lost 27,000 men and 400 guns. Canadians captured 5,000 prisoners and 160 guns. On the night of August 19–20, the Canadians withdrew from the Amiens line, five days after the Kaiser ordered his foreign minister to initiate peace negotiations.

DRIVE TO VICTORY

The Allied commanders realized that continued pressure must be maintained on the German Army or it would soon recover from its recent losses. Limited offensives were undertaken all along the line, with Canadian Corps leading British Fourth Army in a drive through the German Drocourt-Quéant Line into the open country behind Cambrai, France. This was the same battlefield where the Newfoundland Regiment had been butchered during the Somme. Facing the Canadians were five, heavily fortified defensive lines about a mile deep.

Currie's plan called for three divisions — 2nd, 3rd, and the Scottish 51st Highland Division — to lead for three days, then give way to the 1st and 4th Divisions. In support were 50 tanks. The attack proceeded at 3:00 a.m. on August 26 and initially went well, with the rapid fall of Monchy-le-Prieux. Beyond Monchy-le-Prieux, however, the Canadians stalled against the heavily fortified Hindenburg Line. The next day brought rain and the inevitable mud. The Canadians and Highlanders slogged on. Gains were slow, but they managed to get close enough to the Drocourt-Quéant Line to enable the relieving divisions to undertake an assault against it. Doing so cost the two Canadian Corps divisions 5,801 casualties.

On September 2, 1st and 4th Canadian, accompanied by 4th British Division, attacked. Despite heavy close-quarters fighting, the divisions reached their objectives about two miles beyond the Drocourt-Quéant Line. The day cost the Canadians another 5,622 dead or wounded. This modest victory, however, forced the Germans to undertake large-scale withdrawals all along the Western Front in anticipation of a breakthrough. Dawn found the trenches forward of the Canal du Nord abandoned. Allied high command was elated and realized that one more massive push might end the war before the year

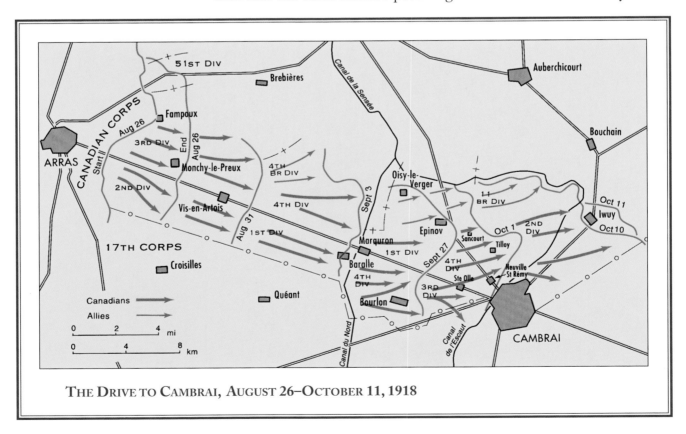

THE DRIVE TO CAMBRAI, AUGUST 26–OCTOBER 11, 1918

was out. The Canadians were immediately ordered to renew the advance, easily securing the ground to the front of the Canal du Nord by the end of September 3. German reaction to this massive setback was despondent. The Kaiser wrote: "Now we have lost the war!"

His despair was only increased by the Allied ability to replace both aircraft and personnel more quickly than the Germans, which served to overcome the squadron-pack tactics so effectively employed by German airmen during the early months of 1918. During the war's last months, Allied planes completely dominated the skies over front lines and were largely unopposed when conducting bombing raids against rear area targets.

On September 12, the Allies attacked along the entire Western Front, regaining almost all ground that had been lost to the German offensive. Currie made plans to attack Canal du Nord by concentrating his divisions in a narrow bridgehead, rather than attempting to storm the heavily fortified canal defences on a broad front. The unconventional attack went in at 5:20 a.m. on September 27 behind a heavy barrage. Initially, it was a complete success and within three hours of the infantry securing positions on the opposite side, Canadian engineers had erected crossings over the dry but deep canal to move supplies, men, and tanks forward. The Germans could only fall back to the Marcoing Line. It seemed Cambrai, the hoped-for prize, must soon fall.

But German resistance again stiffened, with counterattacks forcing the Canadians to desperately defend ground won the previous day. September 29 was little better, although some battalions managed short advances to take Ste. Olle, enter the suburb of Neuville St. Rémy, and to capture Sancourt in some of the bitterest fighting Canadians had ever seen. The next day, the PPCLI took Tilloy but little else was achieved. By October 1, the exhausted Corps was

Canadian Corps heavy artillery provide supporting fire for the advance east of Arras in September 1918

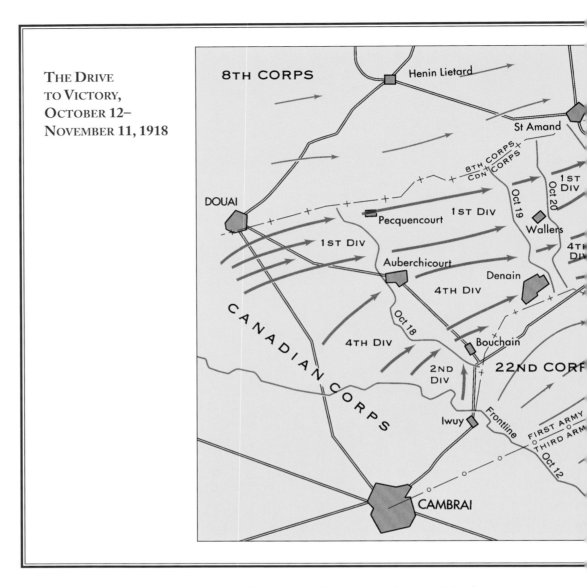

ordered to pause and regroup. Corps casualties since August 8 had mounted to 30,000.

After a short reorganization, the Corps was back on the offensive on October 8 when 2nd Division approached Cambrai against only light resistance. The German Army was collapsing all along the front as the Allies continued to press forward against every conceivable weak point. On October 10, 3rd Division cleared Cambrai and discovered the Germans in full retreat. The infantry marched after them, fighting occasional skirmishes as they crossed into Belgium.

The advance took on a stunning momentum unheard of since the opening months of the war in 1914, with infantry averaging gains of three miles an hour against barely any resistance. While German fire had little deterring effect, the advance was slowed by problems maintaining adequate supply lines to keep the front line soldiers fed. So, too, did destroyed bridges and railroads, and mined sections of roads. Cheering throngs of Belgian civilians in every village also distracted the foot-weary infantry from the march.

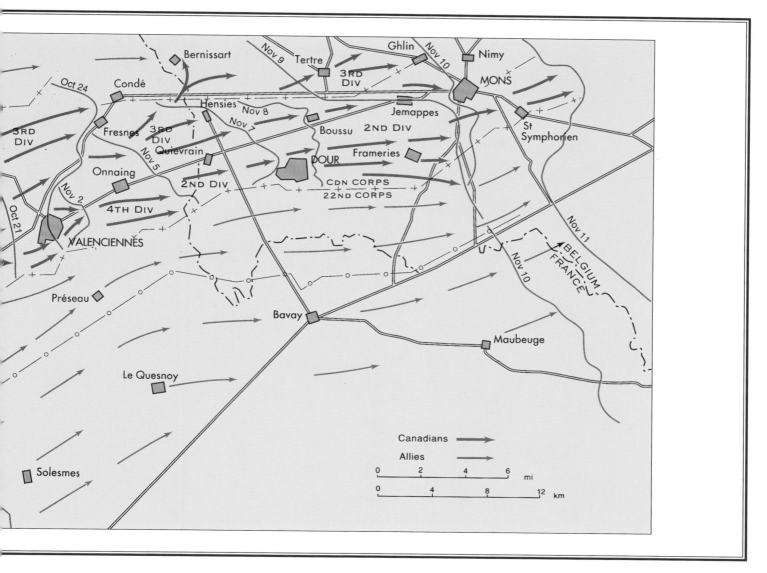

Bernissart
Nov 9 Tertre Ghlin Nov 10 Nimy
Oct 24 Condé 3RD DIV MONS
Hensies Nov 8 Jemappes St Symphorien
3RD DIV Nov 7 Boussu 2ND DIV
Fresnes 3RD DIV Quievrain
Nov 5
Onnaing DOUR Frameries
2ND DIV CDN CORPS
Nov 2 22ND CORPS
4TH DIV

Oct 21
VALENCIENNES

Préseau

Bavay
Nov 11
BELGIUM
Nov 10 FRANCE

Maubeuge

Le Quesnoy

Canadians →
Allies →

0   2   4   6
|_____|_____|_____| mi
0   4   8   12
|_____|_____|_____| km

Solesmes

By November 9, Canadian Corps was on the outskirts of Mons, the city where the British Army had begun its 1914 retreat. Here resistance stiffened even as only hours remained until an armistice was certain. On November 10, 2nd and 3rd Divisions fought a battle that many veterans later condemned as a prestige engagement aimed at wresting the city from German hands before the armistice. In the coalfields outside the town, they met heavy resistance from machine-gun posts positioned in the slagheaps. Most of Mons fell, but the price was 350 casualties. The following morning at 10:58 a.m. Private George Price — the day's only Canadian casualty — was shot dead by a sniper. Two minutes later the war officially ended.

In all, 619,636 men had been mobilized for army service, of whom 424,589 went overseas. More than 5,000 men joined the Royal Canadian Navy, most serving on ships engaged in coastal patrol duties. At war's end, 59,544 of those who served overseas in all branches of the service were dead or missing and presumed dead, and 172,950 had been wounded.

CHAPTER EIGHT

World War II

1939–1945

THE LIMITED WAR

On September 9, 1939, Canada declared war on Germany in retaliation for its invasion of Poland on September 1. Typically, Canada had allowed its military to decay in the inter-war years. The Canadian Army numbered only 4,261 soldiers of all ranks and was poorly armed. The Royal Canadian Navy had 2,000 sailors serving on four modern destroyers, two antique destroyers, and four minesweepers. The Royal Canadian Air Force fielded little more than 3,000 men and had only 35 planes deemed combat worthy. Reserve strengths numbered 51,000 militia, and about 1,000 navy reserves and 1,000 air force auxiliary.

Prime Minister Mackenzie King's government agreed to field an expeditionary army of two divisions, with one transferring as soon as possible to Britain and the second following only if the war were protracted. King also allocated $353 million for the British Commonwealth Air Training Program (BCATP), which would recruit about 20,000 pilots and 30,000 aircrew drawn from throughout the Commonwealth for training at Canadian bases.

Mobilizing three military arms from scratch proved so difficult that at year's end only about 65,000 of the 100,000 approved army allotment were enrolled. Still, by February 1940, about 23,000 Canadians were deployed in Britain as part of 1st Canadian Infantry Division.

Spring brought the German invasions first of Denmark and Norway, then on May 10 of France. Within 11 days, the Germans reached the English Channel near Abbeville, trapping the British Expeditionary Force in a pocket from which it was soon rescued by the Dunkirk evacuation. On June 12 and 13, a 5,000-strong Canadian contingent landed at Brest, France, and started inland to build an Anglo-French fortified redoubt on the Breton peninsula. When the Germans entered Paris on June 14, however, the Canadians were brought back to Britain. With France's surrender, Canada, with a population of only 11 million, became Britain's single largest ally.

LIFELINE TO BRITAIN

In July 1940, German submarines — U-boats — sank 38 ships, then another 56 in August, and 63 in October, against a same-period loss of 28 U-boats. To help defend the convoys, the Royal Canadian Navy increased its manpower to 1,500 officers and 15,000 men by 1941 and expanded the fleet to 26 corvettes.

As the Battle of the Atlantic heated up, a more decisive battle was being fought in Britain's skies. On August 13, 1940, 2,422 Luftwaffe fighters and bombers challenged Britain's meagre 579 fighters. While the unofficial "Canadian" squadron of RAF 242 was engaged from the outset, No. 1 RCAF Squadron deployed on August 20. During its first sortie on August 26, No. 1 Squadron downed three Dornier

215 bombers but had one pilot killed. It remained in near continuous action for the battle's duration and, when withdrawn on October 9, claimed 38 enemy kills, with 3 Canadians dead and 10 wounded. The RAF and RCAF victory forced Germany to cancel a planned amphibious invasion of Britain.

Germany next concentrated on strangling Britain's supply lifeline to North America. Despite U-boat shortages, the Germans seriously disrupted Allied shipping, sinking more than 200,000 tons in March 1941 alone. On May 11, U-boats sank two merchant ships in the Gulf of St. Lawrence.

Throughout 1941, about 5,000 merchant ships departed Canadian ports for Britain. The naval ships leaving Canada would escort the merchants to a Mid-Ocean Meeting Point, where they would hand off to escorts out of Iceland. These, in turn, would pass the merchants into the safekeeping of escorts based in Great Britain at an Eastern Ocean Meeting Point about 400 miles west of Eire (see map, p. 154). Most of the merchants got through. Some convoys, though, were decimated. On September 9, Convoy SC-42, protected by one destroyer and three corvettes, was attacked by eight U-boats southeast of Greenland. Until it came under air protection from Iceland and was reinforced by nine more warships two days later, SC-42 lost 16 merchant ships out of 56. Although new tactics and equipment would eventually redress the Allied inability to protect the convoys, at the end of 1941 things looked bleak.

BATTLE OF HONG KONG

On December 7, 1941, Japan attacked British, American, and Dutch possessions in the Pacific, including Pearl Harbor, which incited the United States to join the war. To bolster British defences in the Pacific, Canada had earlier sent 1,973 men serving in the Royal Rifles of Canada and the Winnipeg Grenadiers to join Hong Kong's weak 20,000-man garrison. The Canadians arrived on November 16.

On December 8, three Japanese regiments attacked the British defensive line on the mainland. In five days, the defenders were forced back to the island for a last-ditch stand. On December 18, Japanese attackers successfully established a beachhead and soon pushed inland. That night, the Royal Rifles launched several counterattacks, suffering heavy casualties in hard fighting. Bloody fighting continued until December 23, when the Royal Rifles were withdrawn to Stanley Fort.

Meanwhile, the Winnipeg Grenadiers were fighting on the western part of the island under command of Canadian Brigadier J. K. Lawson. The Japanese soon pushed in the Canadian line and, on December 19, Lawson's headquarters was surrounded and he and his men were killed. The remaining companies continued fighting, particularly 'D' Company, which stubbornly denied the Japanese the only

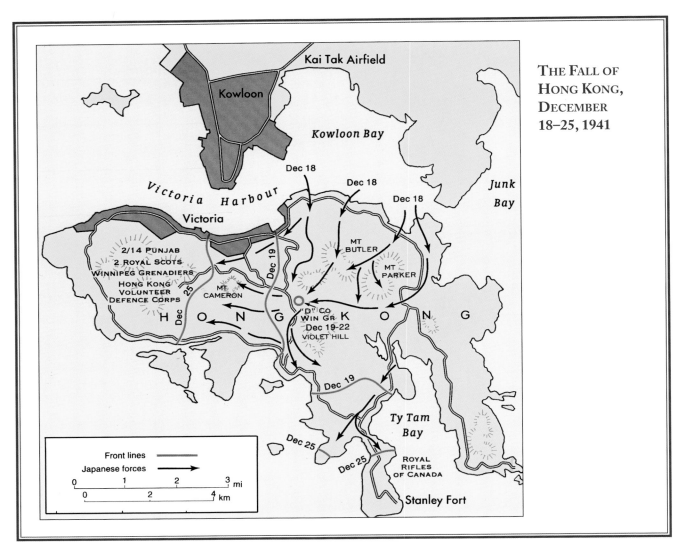

THE FALL OF
HONG KONG,
DECEMBER
18–25, 1941

Kai Tak Airfield

Kowloon

Kowloon Bay

Victoria Harbour

Victoria

Junk Bay

2/14 PUNJAB
2 ROYAL SCOTS
WINNIPEG GRENADIERS
HONG KONG
VOLUNTEER
DEFENCE CORPS

MT BUTLER

MT PARKER

MT CAMERON

"D" CO
WIN GR
Dec 19-22
VIOLET HILL

H O N G   K O N G

Dec 18
Dec 18
Dec 18
Dec 19
Dec 25
Dec 19

Ty Tam Bay

Dec 25
Dec 25

ROYAL RIFLES OF CANADA

Stanley Fort

Front lines
Japanese forces

0   1   2   3 mi
0   2   4 km

decent north-south road crossing the island until December 22. On that day, the company, numbering only 38 wounded men, surrendered.

The previous day, surviving elements of the battalion had occupied Mount Cameron, which they held tenaciously until being forced off on the night of December 22–23. On December 25, Stanley Fort surrendered, followed by a general surrender the following day. Canadian losses were 300 killed and 493 wounded. During a long, brutal imprisonment, which ended only with Japan's surrender in 1945, another 257 men died.

AIR WAR OVER EUROPE

British strategy in 1942 was to regain the initiative by strategically bombing German targets. In July 1942, Bomber Command set out to destroy both German transportation systems and civilian morale. The offensive proved that high-level, nighttime bombing techniques were wildly inaccurate, with only one out of every five bombers coming within even five miles of assigned targets. Still, Air Marshall Arthur

Harris argued that even inaccurate area bombing yielded positive results if enough planes were committed.

The Royal Canadian Air Force played a key role in Bomber Command. In April 1941, No. 405 Squadron arrived equipped with twin-engine Wellingtons. The following year, seven more Halifax- or Lancaster-equipped RCAF bomber squadrons undertook operations. Eight Canadian squadrons were organized into No. 6 Group on January 1, 1943. Eventually, No. 6 Group grew to 15 squadrons. Twenty percent of Bomber Command personnel were Canadians.

No. 6 Group flew 41,000 operations in total, dropping 126,000 tons of bombs. In 30 months of operation, No. 6 Group lost 3,500 crewmen, while another 4,700 Canadians died flying in other Bomber Command squadrons. How horrific these losses were is best understood by looking at the average fate of 100 aircrew. On average, 9 died in training, 51 died in operations, 12 became prisoners of war, 3 suffered wounds, and only 25 survived uninjured.

Whether nighttime bombing seriously reduced German industrial and transportation ability or profoundly eroded civilian and military

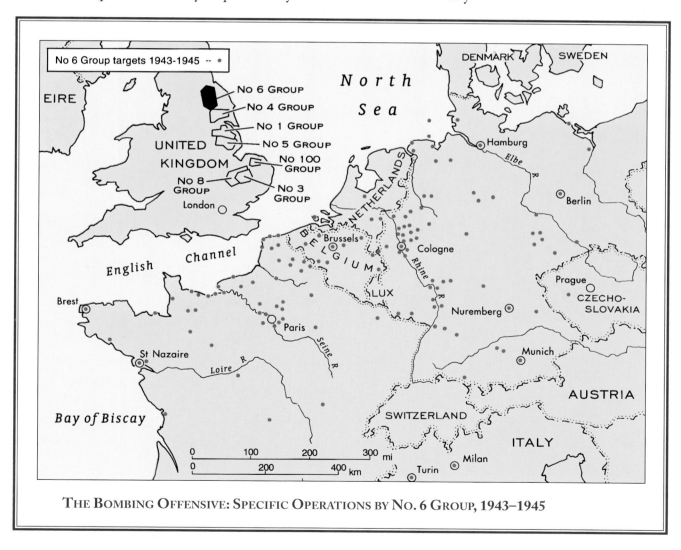

THE BOMBING OFFENSIVE: SPECIFIC OPERATIONS BY NO. 6 GROUP, 1943–1945

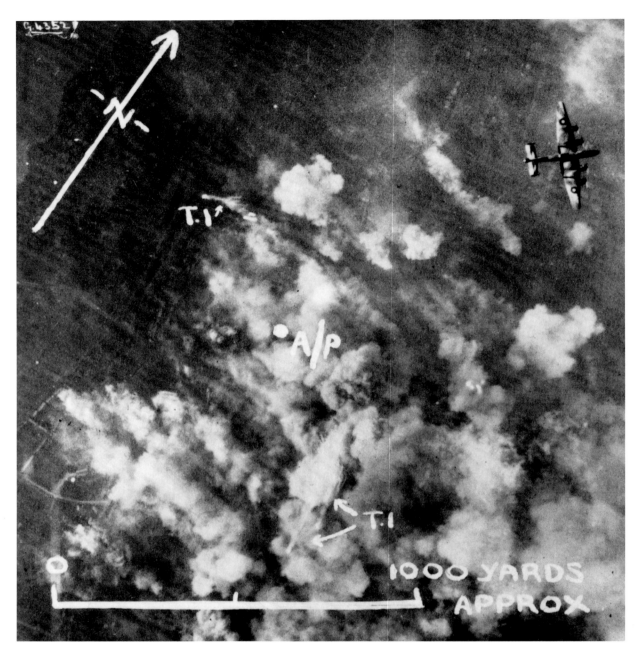

This No. 6 Group Halifax bomber was photographed during a daylight raid on the German city of Julich, but most RCAF and RAF bombing was carried out at night.

morale is much debated. That the bombing caused much loss of life is indisputable. It is estimated that bombs dropped from Canadian aircraft killed about 560,000 Germans and wounded a further 675,000. Throughout the escalating bombing campaign, German war production paradoxically continued to rise. It is probable, however, that without the bombing damage this production would have been far greater, possibly delaying or even altering the war's final outcome.

DIEPPE

Air power alone could not defeat Germany. An extended ground campaign would have to be fought, involving first a massive amphibious invasion of mainland Europe. In October 1941, Lord Louis Mountbatten began developing techniques, equipment, and policy to effect an opposed, combined arms-amphibious landing. Mountbatten's staff believed that securing a large port to enable follow-on reinforcement and supply of the initial landing force was essential. Any port would, of course, be heavily defended. To test whether a port-based invasion was practicable, Mountbatten planned a strong raid against the small port of Dieppe, well within flying range for Allied fighters based in Britain.

Canada provided 2nd Canadian Division and Calgary Armoured Regiment as the primary attack force. In all, 4,963 of the 6,000 men tasked with carrying out operation "Jubilee" were Canadians.

After a false start on July 2, 1942, due to bad weather, the force of 237 ships and landing craft sailed across the English Channel on the night of August 18–19. En route, it encountered a German coastal convoy and gunfire between escort ships was exchanged. Any chance of surprise was now lost, as the German coastal defences were undoubtedly alerted.

The complex plan called for five separate assaults. Two commando forces were to attack German coastal batteries that protected the main beaches while the Canadians would attack three beaches: Blue Beach at Puys just east of Dieppe, White Beach facing Dieppe itself, and Green Beach west of Dieppe at Pourville. At Blue Beach, the Royal Regiment landed at 5:10 a.m. It was immediately met by heavy small-arms fire and was soon pinned beneath the facing cliff, well short of its objective of a gun battery on the eastern headland. Unable to advance or withdraw, the men were slaughtered. By 8:30 a.m., 199 of 554 men ashore were dead. Only 67 managed to escape back to the landing craft. The rest surrendered.

At Green Beach, the South Saskatchewan Regiment also landed at 5:10 a.m. and quickly managed to capture Pourville, but a blocking force holding a bridge prevented it reaching the radar station objective. When the Cameron Highlanders of Canada came up in support, heavy mortar and machine-gun fire checked their advance. Lacking heavy weapons, the two battalions could only retreat to the ships for evacuation. The 1,026-strong force suffered 154 killed, 269 wounded, and 256 taken prisoner.

Three Canadian battalions, one British commando unit, and the Calgary Regiment's tanks landed exactly on time at 5:20 a.m. at White Beach, disembarking 29 Churchill tanks. Two tanks sank and 15 were immobilized when the beach chert broke their tracks. The remaining tanks got over the seawall but their armour-piercing shot proved ineffective against light infantry targets. Infantry and tanks were soon pinned down. The Essex Scottish, Royal Hamilton Light Infantry, and Fusiliers Mont-Royal all were ashore by 7:00 a.m. Two hours later, the attack was falling apart. It took a subsequent two hours for an evacuation to be ordered. By 2:00 p.m., those who were going to escape had and the ships withdrew.

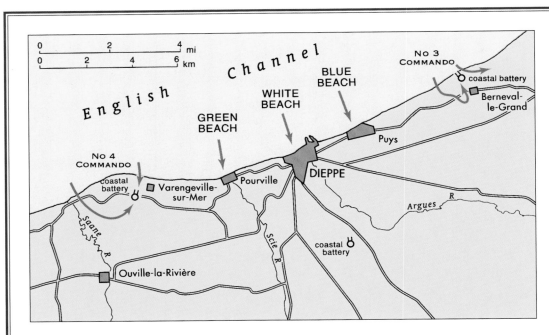

DIEPPE LANDING ZONES, AUGUST 1942

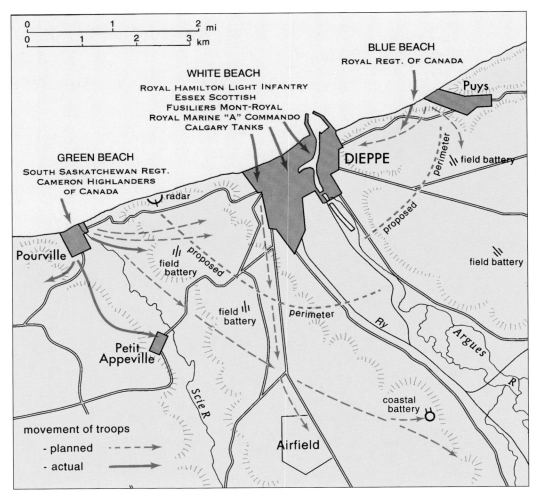

THE DISASTER OF DIEPPE, AUGUST 19, 1942

Of the 4,963 Canadians, 2,211 returned to Britain. About half had never landed during the attack. Total casualties were 3,367, including 901 dead and 1,946 prisoners. The merits of the Dieppe raid remain disputed.

In the aftermath of Dieppe, Churchill tanks of the Calgary Armoured Regiment, dead infantrymen, and wrecked landing craft are scattered across White Beach.

BATTLE OF THE ATLANTIC

During 1942, Germany's U-boat war escalated, with actual submarine strength increasing from 91 operational boats to 212 by year's end. In November, 119 Allied ships were sunk, followed in March 1943 by another 108. Such losses could not be immediately replaced. But by late 1942, the tide was beginning to turn and favour the Allies, as support groups, often including aircraft carriers to provide air coverage along the shipping routes, were deployed. Whereas in 1941, for example, air cover from Iceland only extended in an arc of about 450 miles west of the island, by early 1943 this protection extended 600 miles westward to a point where less than 200 miles of ocean were unprotected by air cover. A further major factor contributing to the support groups' success was the British ability to crack German naval codes, following the removal of a code-encryption system on May 8, 1941, by a British boarding party put onto a sinking German ship. Code-named Ultra, this codebreaking operation enabled the support groups to launch pre-emptive strikes against U-boats gathering to attack Allied convoys.

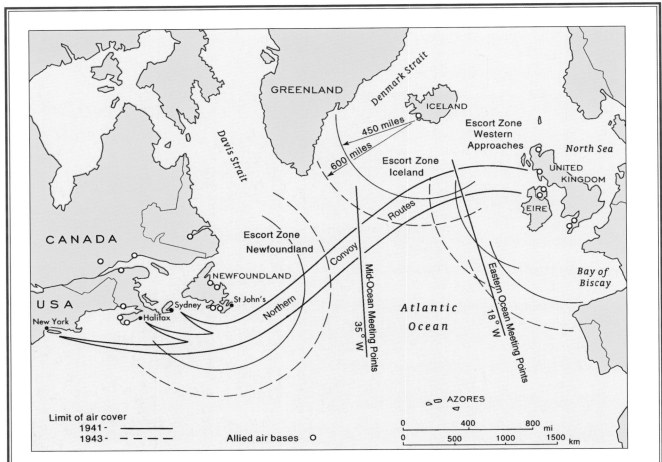

BATTLE OF THE NORTH ATLANTIC

As the range of defensive air coverage extended outward from the Maritime coast, Iceland, and the United Kingdom, the protection provided to convoys maintaining a supply and personnel pipeline to Britain increased dramatically and the threat posed by Germany's U-boat fleet gradually decreased.

In May 1943, 41 U-boats were sunk. An aged RCAF Catalina bomber, protecting one convoy, sank U-630. During the convoy's Atlantic transit, six more submarines were intercepted and sunk by warships and aircraft and two others were lost in a collision. The next convoy suffered no losses and the escorts claimed five submarine kills.

German Admiral Karl Dönitz subsequently abandoned the U-boat offensive, privately declaring the Battle of the Atlantic lost as Allied technology, tactics, and, unknown to the Germans, Ultra intelligence eliminated the U-boat ability to seriously cut shipping volumes. In addition, the Allies were simply too numerous by the end of 1943, with Canada providing 306 operational warships and 71,549 officers and men, and 4,553 female personnel known as Wrens. Losses, of course, continued, particularly among the merchant marine. The Canadian Merchant Navy — by war's end the world's fourth-largest fleet, with 12,000 men — paid a terrible price of 1,578 killed. Statistically, this casualty rate exceeded that of the RCN, which enrolled 99,688 men and 6,500 women during the war and lost 2,024 killed.

INVASION OF SICILY

Germany's Sixth Army surrendered at Stalingrad in February 1943, followed by the May surrender of 275,000 Germans and Italians in North Africa — a defeat that made further Allied operations in the Mediterranean Theatre possible. Having earlier decided that Sicily would provide a launch pad for an invasion of Italy, the Allies moved immediately to planning Operation Husky, with Canada's 1st Infantry Division and 1st Army Tank Brigade participating. The invasion of Sicily was to be undertaken by the U.S. Seventh Army and Britain's Eighth Army, with the Canadians serving in the latter. Major General Guy Simonds, at 39 Canada's youngest general, commanded the Canadians. The Allies landed on July 10, with the Canadian beaches situated on the extreme tip of the Pachino peninsula, Sicily's southernmost point. Their initial objective was Pachino airport. Resistance by Italian troops was weak and the airport was secured within a few hours. Soon the Allies moved northward, with the Canadians taking an inland route.

On July 15, the Canadians reached a hastily but well-deployed German defensive line. German tactics, entailing a well-entrenched defence using ridges, mountains, and river crossings to block the Allied advance and force a full deployment, foreshadowed those used throughout the Italian Campaign. Once the Canadians deployed to launch a decisive attack, the Germans withdrew to another nearby defensive line. This tactic threw the Allied advance well behind schedule.

At Valguarnera, 1st Canadian Infantry Brigade met the fiercest resistance yet offered. In the confused battle's aftermath, the Canadians counted 200 enemy dead and wounded and 280 prisoners, compared to 40 Canadians killed and 105 wounded. For the next 17 days, the Canadians were hotly engaged. At Leonforte, 2nd Canadian Infantry Brigade spent a night of tough house-to-house fighting. Agira fell only when the Loyal Edmonton Regiment and Seaforth Highlanders of Canada scaled the peaks overlooking the town. The fight for Agira cost 462 casualties — the most for a single Sicilian campaign engagement.

By the first week of August, the Germans were being pressed toward the northeastern coast of Sicily in such a way that the Americans, British, and Canadians were starting to trip over each other. The Canadians drove toward the town of Adrano on the western flank of Mount Etna, but so, too, did the British 78th Division. A race ensued

HMCS Pictou *struggles in the all too common rough seas during the Battle of the Atlantic in March 1942.*

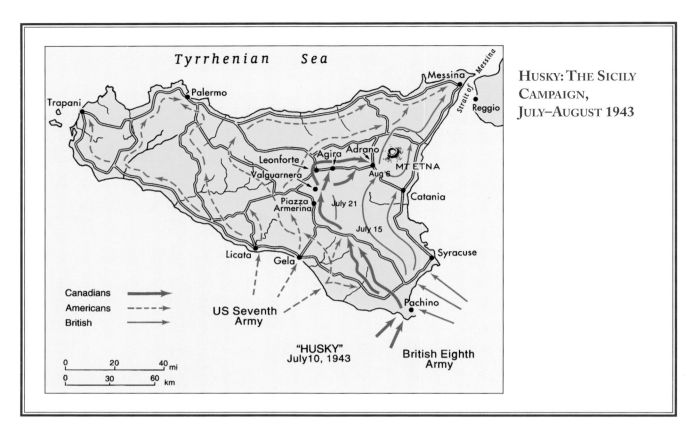

which was called off when the Canadians were ordered to stand down on the outskirts on August 6 to allow the 78th Division unrestricted access to the town. On August 17, the Germans evacuated Sicily. By then, the Canadians had marched 130 miles and suffered 2,310 casualties, including 562 dead.

THE ITALIAN CAMPAIGN

The relatively easy Sicily invasion convinced the Allies they could drive up Italy's boot and capture Rome before Christmas. Accordingly, Eighth Army crossed the Strait of Messina on September 3 and the U.S. Fifth Army landed at Salerno on September 9, the day after Italy unconditionally surrendered to the Allies. While Eighth Army met little resistance, Fifth Army bogged down before determined German counterattacks. To enable Eighth Army to link up with the embattled Americans, the Canadians were ordered to seize Potenza, a road junction 50 miles east of Salerno. Moving out on September 17, they captured Potenza on September 20, only to find the Americans had broken out of the Salerno beachhead. They were now advancing on Naples, which fell on October 1.

Stiffening German resistance at Salerno signalled a shift in Germany's Italian strategy. At first, the plan had been to withdraw north of Florence to the Gothic Line. But the Germans soon recognized the defensive advantage presented by Italy's rugged southern countryside and decided a more advanced defensive line could check the Allies before Rome for the winter of 1943–44. Dubbed the Gustav

Line, it hinged on Monte Cassino, a 1,700-foot-high mountain looming over the town of Cassino, in the west and the Sangro River in the east. Stubborn resistance up the length of the boot bought time for constructing the line, which was divided into the Winter Line to the west and the Bernhard Line to the east. It took, for example, from October 1–14 for the Canadians to advance 25 miles from Lucera to Campobasso. Surprisingly, the Germans chose not to defend the foothill town and it served for several months as a rear-area base for future Canadian operations.

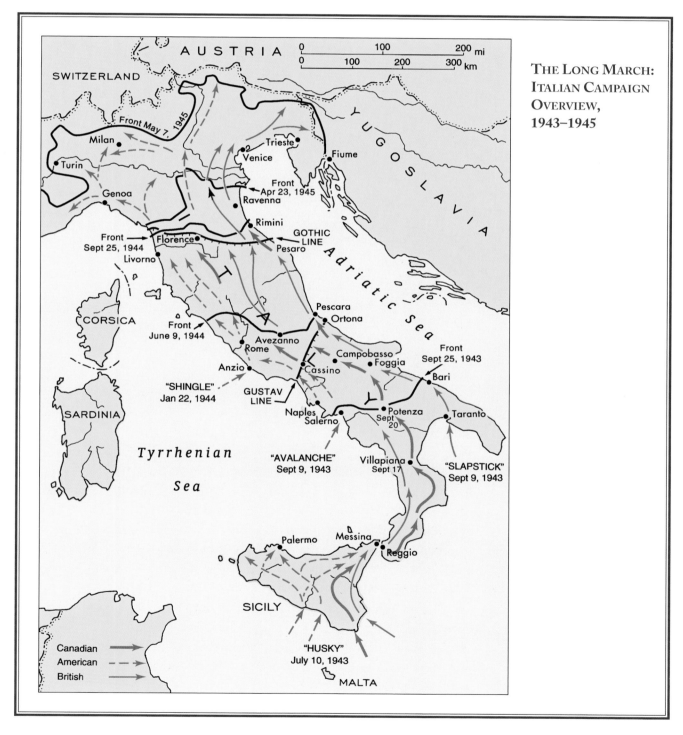

THE LONG MARCH: ITALIAN CAMPAIGN OVERVIEW, 1943–1945

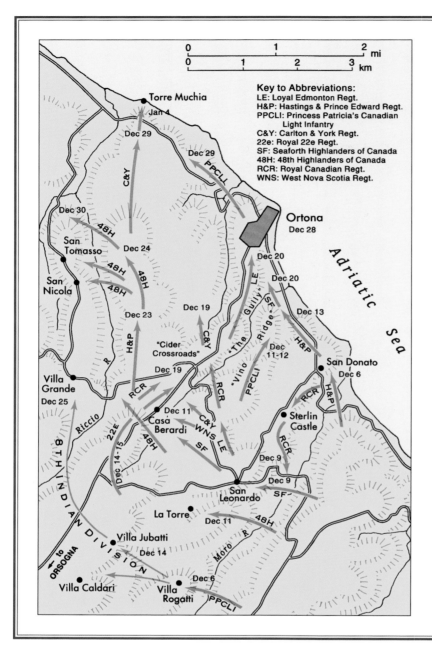

BLOODY DECEMBER:
THE MORO RIVER
AND ORTONA,
DECEMBER 6, 1943–
JANUARY 6, 1944

Key to Abbreviations:
LE: Loyal Edmonton Regt.
H&P: Hastings & Prince Edward Regt.
PPCLI: Princess Patricia's Canadian
Light Infantry
C&Y: Carlton & York Regt.
22e: Royal 22e Regt.
SF: Seaforth Highlanders of Canada
48H: 48th Highlanders of Canada
RCR: Royal Canadian Regt.
WNS: West Nova Scotia Regt.

The slow advance toward the main German defensive lines convinced Allied Field Marshal Harold Alexander, Deputy Supreme Commander, Mediterranean, that he should shift most of Eighth Army from the Adriatic coast to support a Fifth Army breakthrough at Monte Cassino. Eighth Army commander General Bernard Montgomery vetoed that plan in favour of a bold advance by his divisions through the Bernhard Line to Pescara, for a hook across the Apennines along Route 5 to Avezanno, about 50 miles east of Rome. Such an attack would force the Germans to shift divisions away from Monte Cassino, enabling a Fifth Army breakthrough. Failing that, Eighth Army could continue its advance into Rome. Alexander agreed, and on November 28 the British began forcing a crossing of the Sangro River. Casualties were high; the Germans withdrew only grudgingly to a new line behind the Moro River. The Canadians took over on the night of December 5–6.

Heavy rains had turned the landscape into a boggy quagmire and the rugged terrain, thick olive groves, and vineyard wires rendered support of infantry by tanks virtually impossible. The Canadians kicked off on December 6 with an assault across the Moro River on three fronts. Only the Princess Patricia's Canadian Light Infantry made any headway, capturing Villa Rogatti. This attack, however, was supposed to have been a diversionary effort and, when the Royal Canadian Engineers determined that it would be impossible to construct a bridge across the river below Villa Rogatti, the PPCLI were withdrawn. A firm bridgehead was finally established across the river at San Leonardo by December 9. A quick advance to the Ortona-Orsogna lateral road, forcing a withdrawal from Ortona, was expected, but 1st Division became bogged down in front of a deep, narrow defile soon respectfully nicknamed The Gully.

Repeated frontal assaults by battalion after battalion were cut to pieces. Only when the Royal 22e Regiment managed to outflank The Gully to its west on the night of December 14–15 and drive down the road to a farm called Casa Berardi was the position turned. It took another four days, however, for the badly depleted Canadian battalions to finally seize the vital Cider Crossroads junction, after which

An antitank gun fires up a street on the outskirts of Ortona.

the Germans grudgingly withdrew from The Gully into the streets of Ortona.

Finally, on December 20, the Loyal Edmontons and Seaforth Highlanders fought their way into the outskirts of Ortona and became locked in a vicious house-to-house battle which the German 1st Parachute Division refused to break off. Attempts by other battalions to flank Ortona were unsuccessful until the street battle concluded with an orderly German withdrawal on the night of December 28.

The December fighting cost 2,339 Canadian casualties, including 502 killed. There were also 3,956 evacuations for battle exhaustion and 1,617 for sickness, out of a total Canadian strength at the beginning of December of about 20,000. First Canadian Infantry Division required a long period of rebuilding after Ortona. It had, however, mauled two German divisions — 90th Panzer Grenadiers and 1st Parachute Division — and achieved its objective. Montgomery's offensive, however, lay in tatters. There would be no overland thrust to Avezanno.

With the New Year, Alexander implemented his original plan and most of Eighth Army moved to the Monte Cassino front. During the winter, the Canadians in Italy had been joined by another division, 5th Canadian Armoured Division, and all were organized into 1st Canadian Corps, commanded by Lieutenant General E. L. M. Burns. By late April 1944, the Canadians were on the Monte Cassino front.

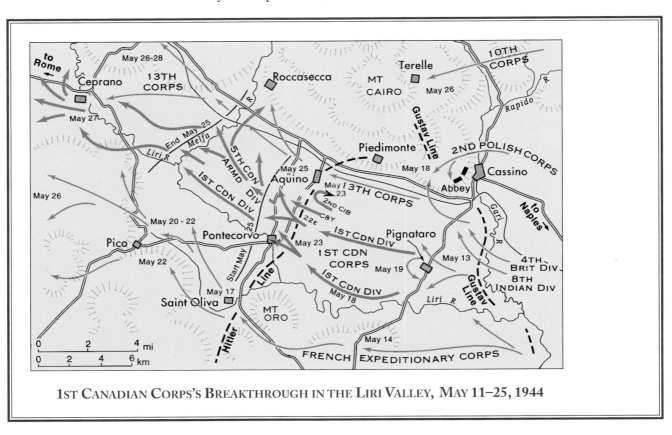

1ST CANADIAN CORPS'S BREAKTHROUGH IN THE LIRI VALLEY, MAY 11–25, 1944

First into action on May 11 was 1st Canadian Armoured Brigade in support of 8th Indian Division's attack on the Gustav Line. The Calgary Tank Regiment established a tenuous bridgehead by crossing the Gari River on a Canadian-designed and -built Bailey Bridge secured to the base of a Sherman tank, then driven into the river to position the bridge firmly on both banks. Despite heavy infantry losses, 8th Indian Division succeeded in breaking the Gustav Line, opening the way for a new attack against the next line of defence, known as the Hitler Line. Like the Gustav Line, the Hitler Line was a formidable defensive system bristling with pillboxes, tank turrets mounted on concrete emplacements, and vast concentrations of barbed wire and minefields that fronted the entire line.

The job of cracking the Hitler Line fell to 1st Canadian Corps. Movement toward the line began on May 18. Knowing a set-piece attack against the fortified line was likely to result in heavy casualties, 1st Division's Major General Chris Vokes made several attempts to pierce the line with impromptu attacks by individual battalions. When these were stopped cold by the German defenders, he implemented Operation Chesterfield.

On May 23, 1st Canadian Infantry Division attacked immediately on the heels of a massive artillery barrage. All three battalions of 2nd Canadian Infantry Brigade attacking on the division's right flank were soon tangled in the German defences and shredded by enemy fire. The supporting British tanks, the North Irish Horse Regiment, proved easy prey for the tank guns. In this single day of fighting, 2nd Canadian Infantry Brigade lost 162 men killed, 306 wounded, and 75 taken prisoner — the highest loss rate suffered by any brigade in a day's fighting in Italy. On the left flank, however, 3rd Canadian Infantry Brigade's Carleton & York Regiment pierced the line. The brigade's remaining two regiments and the Three Rivers Regiment's tanks rushed into the narrow gap. Soon they widened this sufficiently to enable 5th Canadian Armoured Division to advance tank regiments with supporting infantry past the Hitler Line.

With the Hitler Line breached, Eighth Army could fight its way up the Liri Valley to Rome. It was soon joined by elements of the U.S. Fifth Army that broke through the line elsewhere and out of Anzio beachhead. The Germans continued to offer fierce resistance, frustrating hopes that 5th Canadian Armoured Division would be able to achieve a lightning-fast breakthrough in the valley. The advance stalled briefly at the Melfa River in a costly battle by 5th Canadian Armoured Brigade, supported by the Westminster (Motor) Regiment of mounted infantry for a river crossing. Only after Ceprano fell on May 27 did German resistance begin to crumble. On June 4, Rome fell. Three weeks of action for 1st Canadian Corps brought with it a high price in casualties: about 800 dead, 2,500 wounded, 4,000 sick, and 400 evacuated for battle exhaustion. Two days after Rome fell, the Allies invaded Normandy and Italy became a largely forgotten theatre of war except to the soldiers fighting there.

The Allied march northward continued, reaching the Gothic Line in August. First Canadian Corps was given the task of breaking the line at Pesaro on the Adriatic coast. On August 25, 1st Canadian Infantry Division struck, aiming to open a breach which 5th Canadian Armoured Division could exploit. The battle proved costly as the Canadians encountered line after line of heavily defended ground.

At a pivotal moment, on the verge of the Gothic Line proper, the 5th Division commander Major General Bert Hoffmeister discovered that the massive defensive system was only weakly held. Instead of adhering to the original plan for a slow artillery softening of the defences, the Canadians launched a hasty assault on August 30. The gamble paid off and the line broke, allowing the Canadians to fight their way to the heights overlooking the Po River Valley by September 21. In their wake, the Canadians left 4,511 casualties, of whom 1,016 were killed.

The Allies hoped that breaking into the Po Valley would allow a rapid advance north into Austria, assisting in the decisive collapse of Germany. By September, however, autumn rains had set in and mud soon mired the region, hindering armoured movement and enabling

Canadian infantry advance during the Gothic Line battle in September 1944.

the Germans to continue their strategy of turning each river crossing into a bitterly contested battle. This pattern continued until February 1945, when 1st Canadian Corps was withdrawn from Italy and reunited with the rest of Canada's troops in northwest Europe.

Total Canadian casualties in Italy were 408 officers and 4,991 men killed. A further 1,218 officers and 18,268 men were wounded and 62 officers and 942 men were captured. Another 365 died of other causes. Of a total of 92,757 Canadians who served in Italy, fully 26,254 became casualties.

D-Day Invasion

Canada's involvement in the June 6, 1944, D-Day invasion of Normandy was extensive. Of the 7,016 ships involved, 110 were RCN vessels. Throughout the night before the landing, RCAF No. 6 Bomber Group attacked strategic land targets. A further 16 RCAF fighter squadrons, organized as No. 83 Group, provided close support to the British Second Army from the time it landed on the beaches to its eventual march through Germany.

During the invasion night, a 450-man Canadian Parachute Battalion contingent joined the many paratroops landing inland from the Normandy beachheads to destroy bridges, seize vital transportation links, knock out coastal batteries, and disrupt German communication and movement. Strong winds and evasive action taken by the planes badly scattered the parachutists. Many ended up fighting alone or wandering lost in the darkness until linking up with others to form small, mobile bands that continued to undertake assigned missions. 'C' Company succeeded in destroying a bridge across the Divette River. The Canadian paratroops suffered 117 casualties on D-Day, of whom 20 were killed. A further 81 were captured.

By dawn, the first waves of 3rd Canadian Division were boarding landing craft for the assault on the Canadian beach, Juno. Two of its three brigades constituted the first wave, with 7th Canadian Infantry Brigade, supported by 6th Canadian Armoured Regiment, to land on Mike sector to the right and the 8th Canadian Infantry Brigade, supported by 10th Canadian Armoured Regiment, to land at Nan sector on the left. In reserve was 9th Canadian Infantry Brigade and 27th Canadian Armoured Regiment. Behind the Canadian beach stood three small villages which the Canadians were to seize immediately.

Rain and high seas hampered the landing crafts' progress, causing a 30-minute delay. It was 8:12 a.m. when the Queen's Own Rifles led the way ashore at Nan. The regiment was badly mauled by well-emplaced German machine guns and an 88-millimetre gun while trying to cross 200 yards of open beach between the shoreline and a seawall. After a two-hour battle, however, the regiment captured the village of Bernières-sur-Mer, but resistance by several 88-millimetre guns delayed any further advance inland for hours. To the Queen's

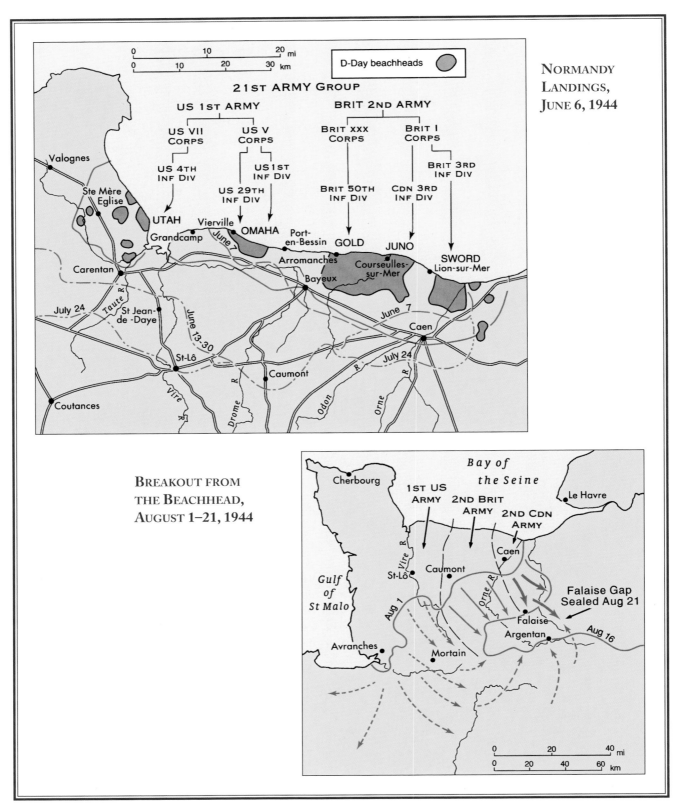

NORMANDY LANDINGS, JUNE 6, 1944

21ST ARMY GROUP

US 1ST ARMY

BRIT 2ND ARMY

US VII CORPS

US V CORPS

BRIT XXX CORPS

BRIT I CORPS

US 4TH INF DIV

US 1ST INF DIV

BRIT 3RD INF DIV

US 29TH INF DIV

BRIT 50TH INF DIV

CDN 3RD INF DIV

D-Day beachheads

Valognes

Ste Mère Eglise

UTAH

Vierville

Grandcamp

OMAHA

Port-en-Bessin

GOLD

JUNO

SWORD

Lion-sur-Mer

Arromanches

Courseulles-sur-Mer

Carentan

Bayeux

Taute R.

June 7

July 24

St Jean-de -Daye

June 13-30

June 7

Caen

July 24

St-Lô

Caumont

Odon R.

Orne R.

Vire R.

Drome R.

Coutances

BREAKOUT FROM THE BEACHHEAD, AUGUST 1–21, 1944

Cherbourg

Bay of the Seine

1ST US ARMY

2ND BRIT ARMY

2ND CDN ARMY

Le Havre

Caen

Gulf of St Malo

Vire R.

St-Lô

Caumont

Orne R.

Falaise Gap Sealed Aug 21

Aug 1

Falaise

Argentan

Aug 16

Avranches

Mortain

Own left flank, the North Shore (New Brunswick) Regiment quickly cleared the beach and captured St. Aubin-sur-Mer.

At Mike sector, the Regina Rifle Regiment landed on the east shore of the River Seulles and the Royal Winnipeg Rifles on the west. Both faced strong opposition from fiercely defended concrete pillboxes, but covering fire from the 1st Hussars tanks enabled the infantry to clear these and push into the village of Courseulles-sur-Mer. By nightfall, all three of the division's brigades were ashore and had advanced further inland than any other Allied troops, although no Canadians had reached and secured their assigned objectives. More ominous was the fact that the British Second Army to which 3rd Canadian Division was linked had failed to occupy Caen, its primary objective for the day. About 14,500 Canadians landed on D-Day; of these 340 were killed, 574 wounded, and 47 captured.

The next morning, 7th Brigade reached its final objective for the previous day astride the road and railway between Caen and Bayeux, the first unit in Second Army to do so. On the Canadian left flank, the North Nova Scotia Highlanders took Buron in house-to-house fighting and then pushed on to Authie. Here they became entangled in the first major German counterattack against the Normandy beachhead, led by the elite 25th SS Panzer-Grenadier Regiment of the 12th SS Panzer Division. The Sherbrooke Fusiliers' tanks were badly battered by the Germans' more heavily gunned and armoured Panthers and the Canadians were thrown back. Until June 12 the Canadians fought off SS counterattacks and managed to cling to most of the ground won during the invasion's first two days.

On June 12 they took the offensive, but achieved only limited success and were badly mauled trying to capture le Mesnil, abandoned

Canadians aboard a Landing Craft, Tank (LCT) during the June 6, 1944, invasion of Normandy

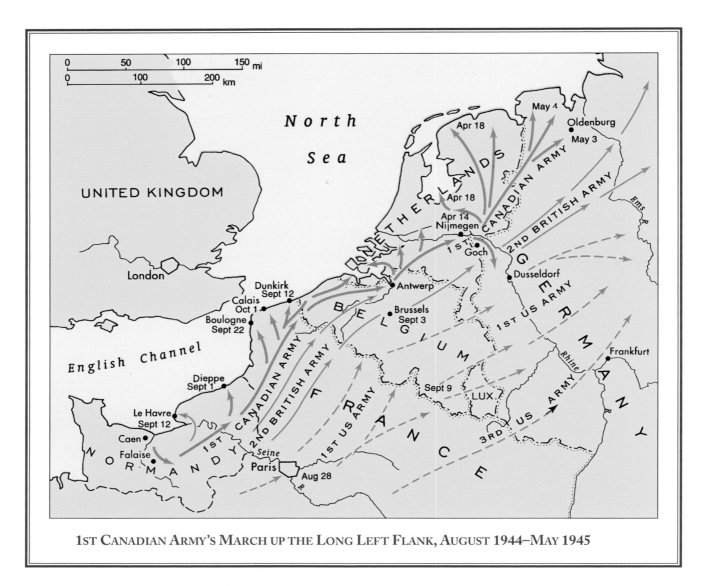

1ST CANADIAN ARMY'S MARCH UP THE LONG LEFT FLANK, AUGUST 1944–MAY 1945

earlier by the Canadian Parachute Battalion. Losses incurred in this fight led to the Canadians being withdrawn from action for two weeks. In six days of fighting, 3rd Canadian Division suffered 1,017 killed and 1,814 wounded.

THE FALAISE GAP

On July 4, 3rd Canadian Division attempted to capture Carpiquet and its airfield as part of the overall Caen offensive. The village fell, but only a toehold was secured on the airport and the entire area remained hotly contested until British divisions cleared Caen on July 9 to the bank of the Orne River. Across the river, the industrial suburb of Faubourg-de-Vancelles remained in German hands. On July 11, 3rd Division reunited with 2nd Division as Major General Guy Simonds brought up the rest of 2nd Canadian Corps to take over control of the Caen sector.

Twenty-one miles south of Caen lay Falaise, the next major objective in the Anglo-Canadian attempt to break out of the Normandy

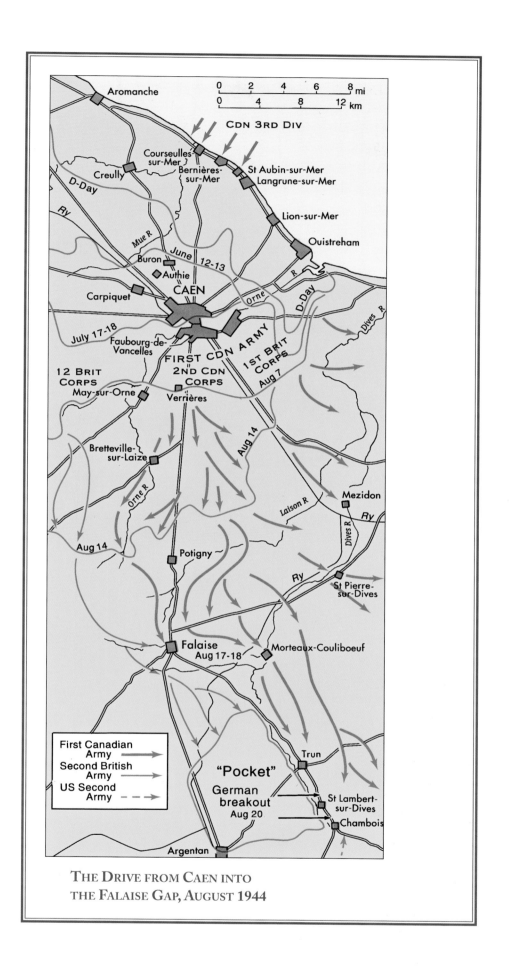

**The Drive from Caen into
the Falaise Gap, August 1944**

beachhead. The attack kicked off on July 18. After two days of fighting, the Canadians reached the kidney-shaped foothill called Verrières Ridge. On July 20, 2nd Division attacked the ridge. On the right and left flanks, the attacks succeeded and heavy counterattacks were repulsed. In the centre, the attack crumbled and was driven back. The involved regiments were nearly destroyed before the situation stabilized the following day with the Canadians left clinging to the lower slopes.

On July 25, Simonds tried again at 3:30 a.m. His men advanced with the aid of "artificial moonlight" created by bouncing searchlights off clouds. The light worked for some but proved hazardous for others, including the North Nova Scotia Highlanders, who were silhouetted and rendered easy targets. All along the ridge the fighting, which failed to secure the ridge crest, was vicious. The resulting 1,500 casualties made this Canada's worst day for casualties suffered during the war. The Black Watch Regiment was decimated — only 15 men were unscathed out of 325. Not until August 8 was the ridge crest won as part of a larger Anglo-Canadian offensive, Totalize.

Totalize was the inaugural battle in which First Canadian Army fought as a single entity. Previously there had been insufficient room in the beachhead for the entire army to deploy. It was an ambitious scheme that envisioned four regimental-sized columns of tanks and infantry in vehicles converted into Armoured Personnel Carriers (APCs) advancing rapidly and bypassing enemy concentrations that would be mopped up later by follow-on forces. The objective was Falaise.

Starting at 11:30 p.m. on August 7, the attack quickly became confused, but despite all four columns becoming lost and suffering heavy casualties, most reached their initial objectives by midday. The second phase quickly ran out of steam, particularly after U.S. bombers blasted Canadian units by mistake. By August 10, the attack was abandoned well short of Falaise.

Dubbed Tractable, the next offensive involved two large concentrated wedges of armour and infantry, with 4th Armoured Division making up one wedge and 3rd Canadian Division and 2nd Armoured Brigade the other. The improvised APCs again provided mobility for the infantry. The attack went forward at noon on August 14 against immediate heavy resistance, because the Germans had captured a map detailing the objectives. Once again, high-altitude bombers dropped much of their payload on the Canadians and supporting Poles, resulting in 400 casualties. Despite these setbacks, the advance continued and, after winning a crossing of the Laison River, the Canadians started taking great numbers of German prisoners.

By August 16, the Canadians had advanced far enough that several hundred thousand Germans were in danger of being cut off inside a pocket. To close the gap, Simonds needed to sever the narrow

18-mile-wide neck and link up with First American Army to the south. The Germans were desperately trying to escape through here but were hampered by poor transport, mud-choked roads, and relentless strafing by fighters and fighter-bombers, some piloted by Canadians of 2nd Tactical Air Force.

On August 17, the Canadians drove through Falaise and on to Trun the following day, with 4th Canadian Armoured Division leading. The next target was St. Lamber-sur-Dives, not far from where 90th U.S. Infantry Division waited on the outskirts of Chambois to effect the linkup. But the 4th Division was desperately short of men and could only send a South Alberta Regiment tank squadron and an Argyll and Sutherland Highlanders company to effect the closure. This small force was too weak for the task assigned. Despite meagre reinforcement that night by two half-companies of infantry, the force was soon left fiercely hanging on to its positions within St. Lamber-sur-Dives as successive German units escaped through the gap. However, on August 21 the gap was decisively closed.

Since June 6, the Germans had lost 200,000 killed or wounded and a further 200,000 taken prisoner. Only about 18,000 managed to escape from the pocket. Allied losses from D-Day to the end of August were 206,000 killed or wounded. Of these, 18,444 were Canadians, with 5,021 killed.

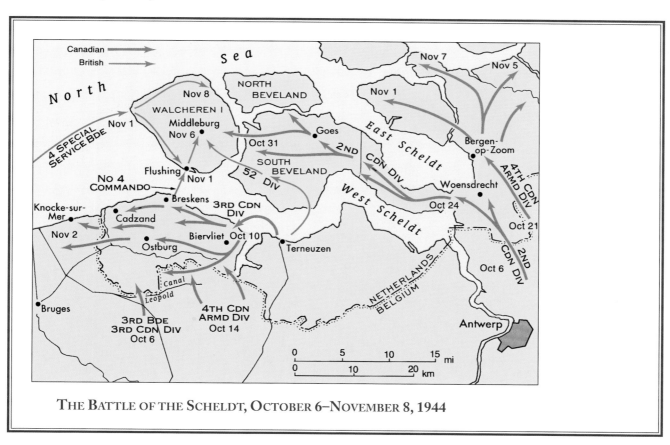

THE BATTLE OF THE SCHELDT, OCTOBER 6–NOVEMBER 8, 1944

THE SCHELDT

After Falaise, First Canadian Army undertook capture of a succession of ports stretching up the coast to Antwerp. On September 1, 2nd Canadian Division entered undefended Dieppe. At Boulogne, however, 3rd Division met stiff resistance that delayed the advance for six days before about 9,500 Germans surrendered on September 23. On October 1, Calais fell in another six-day battle that yielded 7,500 prisoners. As the Canadians crossed into Belgium, the Allies launched Operation Market Garden, a bold dash to reach the Rhine River. Market Garden was a disaster and, because of the supplies and men diverted to its execution, no attempt was made to clear the 65-mile Scheldt River estuary running from Antwerp to the sea. With the Germans holding the estuary, the fact that the British had taken Antwerp on September 5 was meaningless, for the harbour could not be used by Allied shipping. The task of opening the port fell to the Canadians.

As General Henry Crerar had contracted dysentery, Simonds commanded. He developed a simple plan whereby 2nd Canadian Division would cut the Beveland isthmus north of the Scheldt River while 3rd Canadian Division and 4th Canadian Armoured Division cleared the Breskens pocket to the south. The soldiers advanced into a sodden nightmare where mud was thigh-deep, much of the ground was deliberately flooded, and the Germans were well entrenched. The attack started on October 6 with 2nd Canadian Division driving up the narrow isthmus toward Woensdrecht and 3rd Canadian Division attempting to create a bridgehead over the Leopold Canal. Casualties were heavy and gains minimal. Futile attack followed attack.

On October 13, 2nd Canadian Division's Black Watch tried to cross 1,200 yards of open fields in broad daylight and was cut to pieces, suffering 145 casualties, of whom 56 died. Not until October 24 was the isthmus finally cut. By October 31, only Walcheren Island on the estuary's north side remained in German hands. After a series of bloody attempts to cross a causeway from Beveland to Walcheren Island, the Canadians were so shredded British units had to take over. Finally Simonds organized an amphibious operation and the island fell on November 8.

South of the estuary, the fighting proved just as bloody, but by November 3 the south bank had been cleared. In five weeks, the Canadians suffered 6,367 casualties fighting a battle that, had the British cleared off the light German presence earlier instead of forcing the Allied launching of Market Garden, would have been unnecessary.

YEAR OF VICTORY

In January 1945, Allied strategy set First Canadian Army marching southeast from Nijmegen into Germany along the southern shore of

the Rhine, to link up with a U.S. drive northeast from the Maas River to Wesel. The intent was to destroy German forces concentrated south of the Rhine. Operation Veritable started on February 8 with good initial progress, but soon mired the Canadians in heavy fighting within the Reichswald forest. The weather was appalling and the Germans had deliberately flooded much of the countryside. The situation did not improve after the Reichswald was cleared on February 13, because strong pockets of resistance were well entrenched in Moyland Wood and along the Goch-Calcar road. Casualties among 2nd Canadian Corps were heavy clearing these objectives, particularly when the Canadian Scottish Regiment lost 140 men during a counterattack on February 18–19. Beyond these objectives, cleared by February 22, lay Hochwald forest.

Second and Third Canadian divisions kicked off Operation Blockbuster on February 26 at 3:45 a.m. As the Germans used a porous defensive technique to lure Canadian battalions into predesignated

Sherman tanks of the Fort Garry Horse follow the Beveland Canal during the final days of the Battle of the Scheldt.

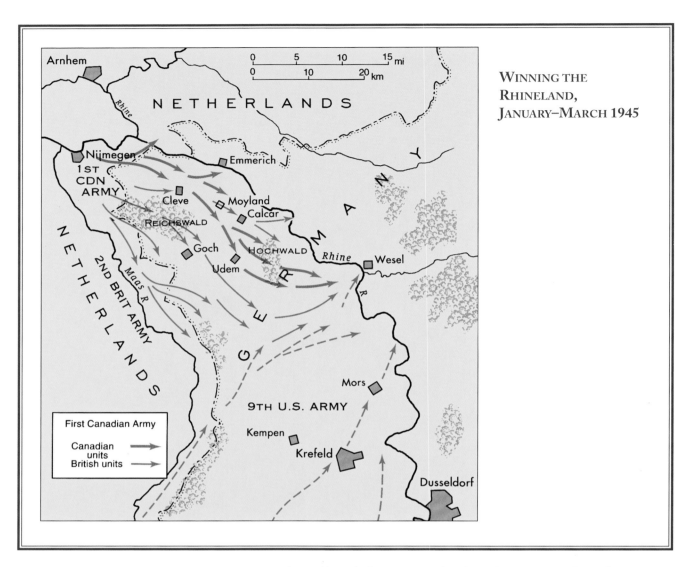

mortar-and-artillery killing grounds, the advance was slow, despite determined attacks. Clearing the forest took until March 4 and not before March 10 did German resistance west of the Rhine cease. By that time, the two operations had cost 5,304 Canadian casualties. Against that, the Germans had lost an unknown but heavy number of casualties, and a further 22,000 men taken prisoner.

In early March, 1st Canadian Corps arrived from Italy, putting all major Canadian army units in Europe under unified command. On March 23, the much expanded First Canadian Army crossed the Rhine against light resistance in Operation Plunder and swung north and northwest into Holland. In early April, the Canadians advanced rapidly against a crumbling German army. For the liberated Dutch, April was the "Sweetest of Springs," while for the Canadians the spring was bittersweet, for each casualty suffered in the sporadic skirmishing that marked this phase of rapidly advancing operations might well be the last. From May 1 to May 5, the last day of fighting, 114 died, including 12 on May 5. On May 7, the Germans surrendered.

Victory in Europe did not end the war. In the Pacific, Japan fought on and Canada organized Canadian Army Pacific Force comprised of 24,000 men. Before this force could be deployed, however, the atomic bombing of Hiroshima and Nagasaki on August 6 and 9 respectively brought Japan's surrender.

Of the 1,086,343 Canadians who saw full-time service in World War II, 42,042 died.

Total army casualties were about 81,000, of whom 23,000 died. The navy counted 1,600 killed from a total of 2,000 casualties and the air-force had approximately 18,000 casualties, of whom 17,000 died. Slightly more than 9.5 percent of all Canadians had seen active service.

Infantry of the South Saskatchewan Regiment caught in a skirmish with German troops during the long advance through Holland into Germany

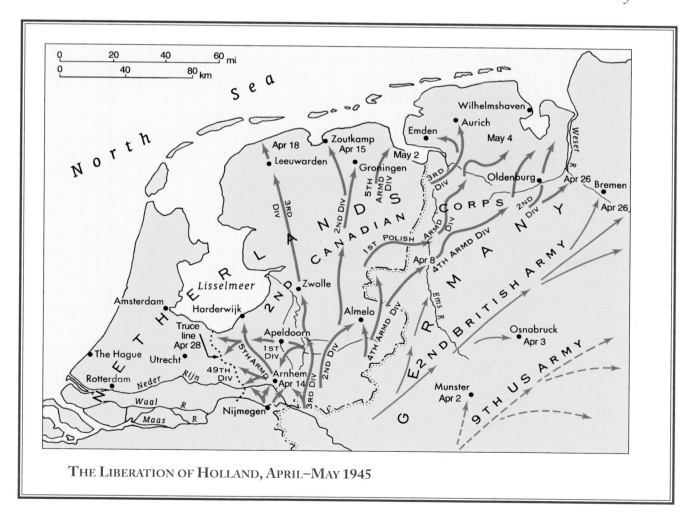

THE LIBERATION OF HOLLAND, APRIL–MAY 1945

Chapter Nine

Korea and the Cold War
1950–1965

TASK GROUP 214.1

On June 25, 1950, two North Korean corps totalling about 90,000 men slashed through the thin 15,000-strong Republic of Korea (ROK) force guarding the 38th parallel boundary and plunged into South Korea. At 7:00 p.m. the following day, the North Koreans were eight miles from the capital, Seoul. Five hours earlier, the United Nations General Assembly had started debate on a three-point U.S.-sponsored resolution calling for the UN to ensure South Korea's survival. The resolution passed and the United States immediately deployed army, navy, and air force units to South Korea. The UN intervention was proclaimed a "police action." Neither the participating countries nor the UN declared war on North Korea. Therefore, technically the intervention was a UN peacekeeping operation and Canadian troops there were not considered to have fought in a war.

Seoul fell on June 28 and the ROK, lacking modern equipment such as tanks and trucks, reeled southward before the North Korean juggernaut. On June 30, Prime Minister Louis St. Laurent told the House of Commons that Canada would contribute three destroyers based at Esquimalt, British Columbia. The 828 officers and men aboard *Athabaskan, Cayuga,* and *Sioux* were to constitute Canada's total contribution. At 3:00 p.m. on July 5, the ships, jointly designated Task Group 214.1, put to sea.

On July 12, the UN Secretary-General accepted Canada's offer to put the task group under UN operational command, but two days later he also requested commitment of ground troops. Lieutenant General Charles Foulkes, chief of the General Staff of Canadian Forces, reported to Cabinet that the army, possessing only three understrength infantry battalions, would be hard pressed to send even a modest regular-force unit to Korea. Despite this lack of readiness, the House of Commons, Canadian media, and the general public clamoured for deployment of ground troops.

Meanwhile, U.S. General Douglas MacArthur, commander-in-chief of United Nations forces in Korea, made it clear in a telegram to Task Group 214.1 commander Captain Jeffry V. Brock that he had little use for warships. However, when the task group arrived at Sasebo, Japan, on July 30 the *Athabaskan* was assigned the next day to escort a convoy from Japan to Korea.

SPECIAL FORCE

By the end of July, ROK and UN troops were clinging desperately to a small bulge of land centred on Pusan. The rest of South Korea was in North Korean hands. As the primarily American UN ground force was poorly trained and equipped, only sheer numbers prevented the North Koreans eliminating the bulge and destroying the army there. With the situation worsening daily, mounting pressure from both the U.S. government and popular opinion led St. Laurent to announce on August 7 that a Canadian Army Special Force of about 4,960 men with a 2,105-man reserve would be formed for Korean service. The next day, recruiting offices across the country started processing volunteers. About 75 percent of those accepted had prior militia, cadet, or regular military service. Half this number had served in World War II, as had most of the force's officers and non-commissioned officers. As training began, the government still hoped the Korean crisis would be resolved before the force was ready to ship overseas.

This outcome appeared certain when U.S. marines seized the Korean port city of Inchon on September 15, establishing a firm beachhead within a day, from which they immediately pressed inland. With the North Korean flank now turned, U.S. and ROK divisions at Pusan counterattacked and quickly routed the enemy. Within two days of the Inchon landings, Seoul was liberated.

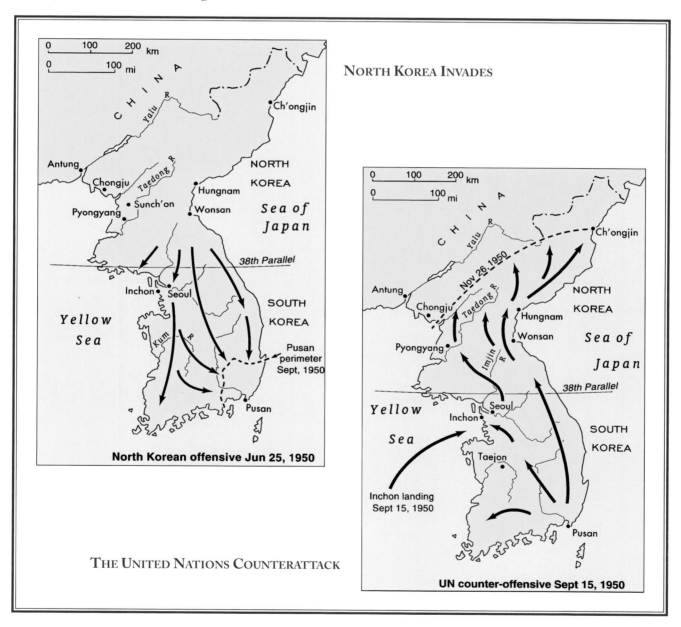

NORTH KOREA INVADES

North Korean offensive Jun 25, 1950

THE UNITED NATIONS COUNTERATTACK

UN counter-offensive Sept 15, 1950

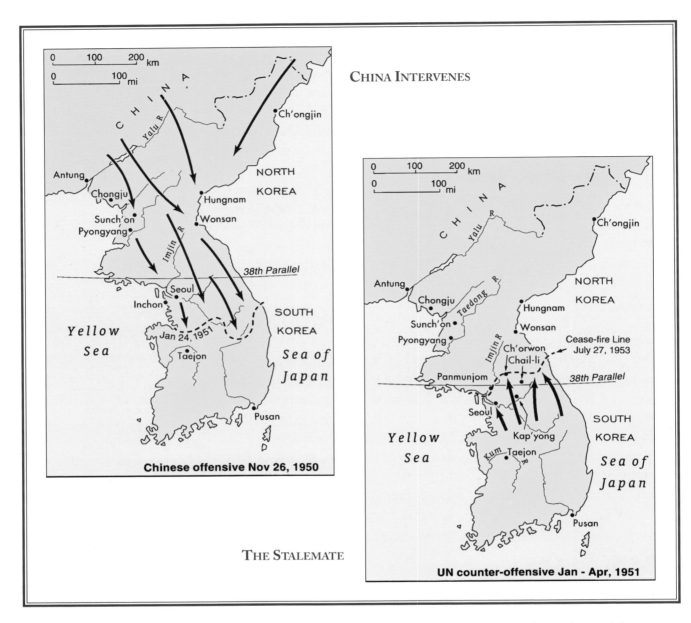

CHINA INTERVENES

Chinese offensive Nov 26, 1950

THE STALEMATE

UN counter-offensive Jan - Apr, 1951

Prior to the Inchon landing, *Athabaskan* undertook naval bombardment operations against North Korean–held islands controlling entrance to the port, in support of ROK Marines seizing Tokchok-To and Yonghung-Do. After Inchon, *Sioux* shelled North Korean installations on the north coast and *Cayuga* and *Athabaskan* conducted several skirmish raids near the Yalu River, including knocking out heavy shore guns at Beijaa Bay.

By the end of the first week of October, all North Korean troops had retreated across the 38th parallel. On October 7, the UN General Assembly authorized invasion of North Korea to unify the peninsula as one nation. Two days later, American divisions entered North Korea and marched northward against light resistance.

The military successes in Korea convinced the Canadian government that deploying the entire force was unnecessary. Instead, it decided to send only 2nd Battalion Princess Patricia's Canadian Light Infantry

(PPCLI). To facilitate training of the force's infantry component, it had been divided into three battalions, each attached to one of the permanent force battalions. The other two battalions were 2nd Battalion Royal Canadian Regiment and 2nd Battalion Royal 22e Regiment.

The 1,383-man PPCLI battalion, commanded by Lieutenant Colonel Jim Stone, sailed from Seattle on November 25. The previous day, MacArthur had launched an offensive across the breadth of Korea to eliminate North Korean opposition and enable UN occupation of the entire peninsula. On November 26, UN and ROK troops advanced into the maw of a massive counterattack by Chinese Communist Forces (CCF) that crossed the Yalu River into North Korea to ensure North Korea's survival and prevent American forces closing on its border. When 2nd Battalion PPCLI landed at Pusan on December 18, the UN and ROK were retreating in disarray to points well south of the 38th parallel. The Canadians would have to fight.

Not until February 17, 1951, was 2nd Battalion PPCLI sufficiently trained and equipped to join the 27th British Commonwealth Infantry Brigade (BCIB), serving as part of 9th U.S. Corps. At this point, the initiative had shifted slightly in favour of the UN–ROK forces and for the next two months the PPCLI battalion engaged in several company-sized attacks as part of a slow return to the 38th parallel. Heavy snow and frequent blizzards hampered movement in the rugged, mountainous countryside. The troops endured perpetually drenched clothing, rampant dysentery, and poor rations. Casualties in the sporadic fighting were low, except for one botched attack against Chinese troops dug in on Hill 532 that resulted in 6 killed and 28 wounded.

'B' Company, 2nd Battalion PPCLI, on the march in February 1951. The hill in the background is typical of those, like Hill 677, whose occupation could determine which side controlled a section of front line.

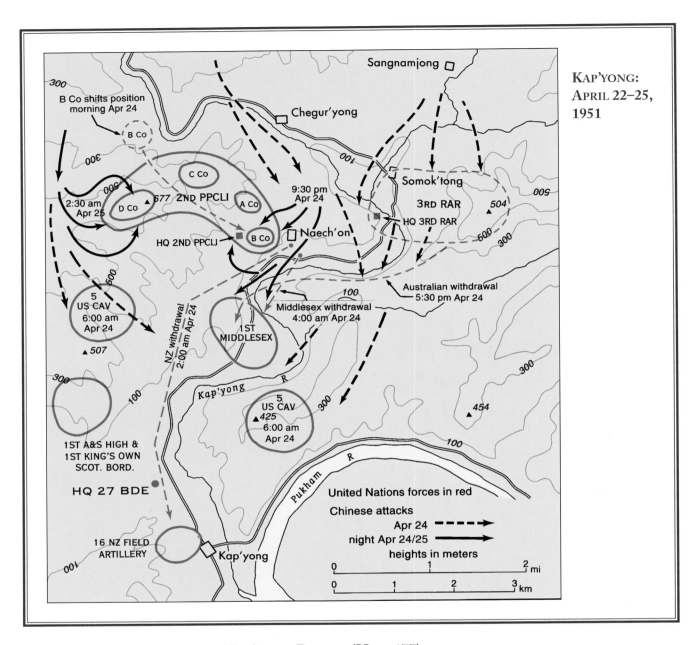

Map labels:

Sangnamjong

KAP'YONG:
APRIL 22–25,
1951

300

B Co shifts position
morning Apr 24

Chegur'yong

B Co

300

C Co

9:30 pm
Apr 24

100

Somok'tong

3RD RAR

504

500

677 2ND PPCLI

A Co

2:30 am
Apr 25

D Co

500

HQ 3RD RAR

HQ 2ND PPCLI

B Co

Naech'on

600

Australian withdrawal
5:30 pm Apr 24

300

600

5
US CAV
6:00 am
Apr 24

NZ withdrawal
2:00 am Apr 24

Middlesex withdrawal
4:00 am Apr 24

100

507

1ST
MIDDLESEX

R

300

300

300

Kap'yong

5
US CAV
425
6:00 am
Apr 24

454

100

100

1ST A&S HIGH &
1ST KING'S OWN
SCOT. BORD.

R

Pukham

HQ 27 BDE

United Nations forces in red

Chinese attacks

Apr 24

16 NZ FIELD
ARTILLERY

Kap'yong

night Apr 24/25

heights in meters

100

0   1   2 mi

0   1   2   3 km

KAP'YONG BATTLE (HILL 677)

On April 22, the CCF launched another massive counterattack across the entire UN front with the major attack against 9th U.S. Corps falling on 6th ROK Division, which quickly broke and retreated south through the Kap'yong River valley. The following day, 27th BCIB was ordered to establish a blocking position about three miles upriver from the town of Kap'yong, which lies northeast of Seoul. The PPCLI battalion was assigned the defence of Hill 677 on the river's west bank. The 3rd Royal Australian Regiment dug in across the river on Hill 504 and the British 1st Middlesex Regiment set up to the south behind the Canadian position. The 16th New Zealand Field Regiment artillery withdrew from its position at Naech'on at 2:00 a.m. on April 24 and fell back to a supporting position west of Kap'yong.

Covered in scrubby woods, cut by gullies, and about one and a half miles wide, Hill 677 could not be defended by deploying companies, so they would mutually support each other. Stone quickly realized his infantry companies would have to deploy as islands with the platoons covering all approaches, while medium-machine gun (MMG) sections, battalion mortars, and artillery field guns provided heavy defensive fire as required to stop major CCF attacks. Accordingly, he deployed 'A' Company on the right flank, 'C' Company along the ridgeline in the centre, 'D' Company on the left, and 'B' Company to the north of 'D' Company. Each company received one two-gun MMG section.

The initial CCF offensive against the brigade's front fell on the Australians at 10:00 p.m. April 23. It was soon evident that Hill 504, which was low lying and easily attacked on wide fronts, would be overrun. To protect his right flank in this eventuality, Stone shifted 'B' Company to the right of 'A' Company so it could overlook the valley of Kap'yong. This move was completed by 11:00 a.m. April 24, shortly before the Australians, having suffered 155 casualties, under-took a successful fighting withdrawal from Hill 504. Five hours earlier, elements of the American 1st Cavalry Division had moved up to assume positions to the rear of the PPCLI, creating a defensive line shaped like a wedge, with the Americans on the back end of each flank and the Canadians holding the point position.

At 9:30 p.m., 'B' Company began taking light mortar and machine-gun fire. A few minutes later, about 400 Chinese were observed concentrating for an attack on the company position. Mortar and artillery fire was immediately directed on the enemy, but it failed to deter an attack at 10:00 p.m. against the company's forward pla-toon. Soon overrun, the platoon was forced to scramble back to the main company position, where the CCF and Canadians locked in a fierce firefight. Meanwhile, a strong CCF attack against Stone's Headquarters unit was shredded by machine-gun fire that killed about 70 Chinese soldiers.

Shortly after midnight, 'D' Company's forward platoon faced enemy probing attacks. At 1:30 a.m., the Chinese launched another mass attack against the platoon and the medium-machine guns were overrun, the two men manning one gun probably killed by friendly fire. Soon all platoons of 'D' Company were engaged and hard-pressed No. 12 platoon retreated to the company headquarters. With the Chinese in among the defenders, company commander Captain Wally Mills called for an air burst artillery salvo on his own position. For 20 minutes, 'D' Company's position was subjected to heavy shelling that decimated the exposed Chinese soldiers while the Canadians hunkered safely in their slit trenches. About 2,300 artillery rounds were fired on the company position and enemy approach paths. At first light, the Chinese melted away, except for some desultory har-rying by small patrols. The battle was over.

OVER:
A 2nd RCHA battery provides supporting fire to two companies of 2nd RCR as the 28th Commonwealth Brigade advances toward Ch'orwon.

Despite its ferocity, 2nd Battalion PPCLI lost only 10 killed and 23 wounded. The number of Chinese killed or wounded is unknown. The battalion was awarded a United States Presidential Citation — the first Canadian unit so honoured — for its stand, which undoubtedly contributed to the Chinese offensive's general collapse.

CANADA'S EXPANDED ROLE

From the summer of 1951 to the end of the war, Canada's naval contribution remained strong, with five more destroyers being rotated through service in Korean waters so that at least three ships were deployed at any given time. The ships added to the rotation were *Nootka*, *Iroquois*, *Haida*, *Huron*, and *Crusader*. One aspect of their operations was shelling trains that attempted to use coastal railways to supply North Korean and Chinese troops. Of 28 trains destroyed by UN naval vessels, 8 fell victim to the guns of Canadian ships.

On May 4, 1951, the rest of Canadian Army Special Force, renamed 25th Canadian Infantry Brigade Group, arrived at Pusan. It included two infantry battalions, 2nd Royal Canadian Regiment (RCR) and 2nd Royal 22e Regiment, 2nd Royal Canadian Horse Artillery (RCHA) regiment, and 'C' Squadron (anti-tank) of the Lord Strathcona's Horse (Royal Canadians) Regiment. The tank squadron quickly swapped its anti-tank weapons for Sherman tanks provided by the U.S. Army. On May 17, the RCHA joined 28th Commonwealth Brigade north of the Han River and began firing support missions the same day. A week later, it rejoined the Canadian brigade in time for the brigade's advance into the front line on May 24 to participate in the plodding UN advance toward Ch'orwon.

The brigade's first major action came on May 30, when 2nd Battalion RCR, supported by Lord Strathcona tanks, attempted to capture Hill 467. Heavy rain and thick fog combined to reduce visibility, and determined, strong Chinese counterattacks disorganized the attack. Thirteen hours after it began, the Canadians broke off the engagement. The RCR lost 5 killed and 31 wounded.

OPERATIONS MINDEN AND COMMANDO

The next three months were spent primarily conducting patrols along a fixed line, as UN forces ceased major offensive operations in anticipation of a successful outcome to armistice negotiations started in June. During this time 2nd Battalion PPCLI rejoined the brigade, and on July 25 the Canadians were integrated into the newly formed 1st Commonwealth Division. The division's operations focused on containing a Chinese salient adjacent to the Imjin River. In late August, the talks collapsed and the UN resumed the offensive with Operation Minden, which involved 1st Commonwealth Division crossing the Imjin in an attempt to straighten the UN line by eliminating the salient.

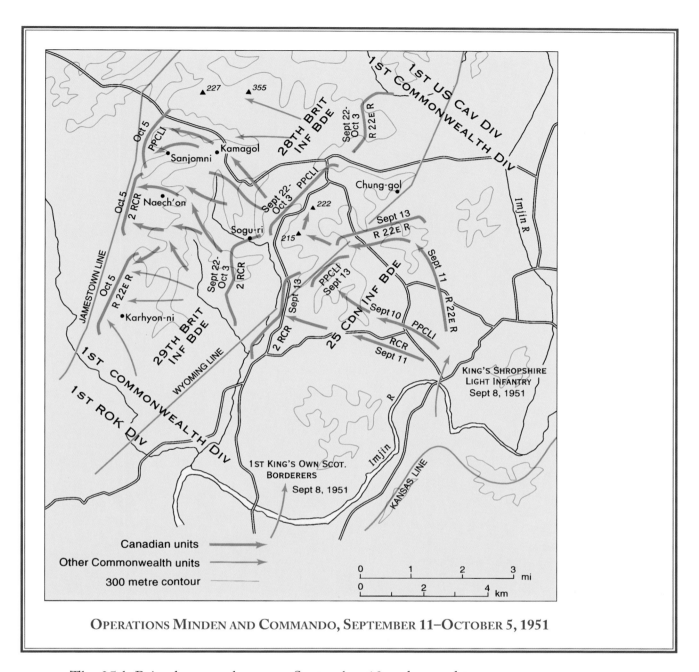

OPERATIONS MINDEN AND COMMANDO, SEPTEMBER 11–OCTOBER 5, 1951

The 25th Brigade crossed over on September 10 and moved to positions facing Chinese positions on Hill 222. Hill 222 was the high point of a facing ridge, with a knoll at the other end identified as Hill 215. On September 13, the Royal 22e Regiment attacked Hill 215 on the heels of a heavy aerial and artillery bombardment. Although the infantry gained the summit, it was unable to hold and withdrew with the loss of two dead and two wounded. The following day, the regiment attacked again and cleared both Hill 222 and 215. The defensive line established after this advance was called Wyoming Line, with Hills 222 and 215 about a mile ahead of the main line.

Wyoming became the base for a further six-mile advance west to control the heights overlooking the Nabu-ri valley, directly beyond

Royal 22e Regiment infantrymen scramble for cover during Operation Commando on October 3, 1951. The Bren gun held by the man furthest back and the bayonet-mounted Lee Enfield carried by the soldier at the front mirror those that Canadians carried in World War II.

which intelligence sources indicated the Chinese hoped to establish a winter defensive line. On September 22, the RCR and PPCLI moved out from Hill 222 and 215 to establish advance positions around Sogu-ri through which the main assault could pass.

Operation Commando kicked off on October 3 with a 27,000-round artillery bombardment accompanied by aerial strafing and bombing. The Canadian attack went forward with 2nd Battalion PPCLI on the right, 2nd Battalion RCR in the centre, and 2nd Battalion Royal 22e on the left. While resistance elsewhere was light, the PPCLI was soon heavily engaged in hand-to-hand fighting amid a trench system protecting Hill 187. They took the hill in two hours of bitter combat at a cost of one killed and six wounded. Total brigade casualties for the day numbered 4 dead and 24 wounded. On October 5, Commando ended when the division reached its objective overlooking the valley and established the Jamestown Line.

HOLDING THE JAMESTOWN LINE

On November 2, 1951, Chinese infantry launched massed attacks against the section of the Canadians' five-and-a-half-mile front held by the RCR. Concentrated artillery support prevented the battalion from being overrun and the attack was repelled. Three days later, the CCF started shelling and mortaring the PPCLI front in the late afternoon. At 6:15 p.m., the Chinese attacked PPCLI's 'D' Company, holding the brigade's extreme flank where its boundary met that of British 28th Brigade. Fighting was at close quarters and continued into the early morning as the Chinese sent about 800 men in against the approximately 100 Canadians. 'D' Company held, losing 3 killed and 15 wounded.

Repeated Chinese offensives against the division eventually resulted in development of an enemy salient inside the line when the British 28th Brigade lost Hill 227 on November 17. To meet the Chinese threat, the Canadian brigade shifted to the right on November 21, with the Royal 22e moving into a saddle running from the west slope of Hill 355 to the foot of Hill 227. Hill 355 was American-held. Almost immediately, Royal 22e was brought under intense artillery and mortar fire. At 4:20 p.m. on November 23, two Chinese infantry companies struck at the regiment's 'D' Company. Although fighting was fierce and at close quarters, 'D' Company held out, but the American companies on Hill 355 were forced off by a battalion-strength attack. This left the Canadian right flank perilously open. The Chinese mounted repeated attacks against the Royal 22e, but it held on while control of Hill 355 seesawed back and forth between U.S. and Chinese units. Finally, at dawn November 26, the battle ended with the United States again in control of Hill 355. The Royal 22e lost 16 killed, 44 wounded, and 3 men missing and presumed dead.

Once again the line stalemated, as both sides resorted to vigorous patrolling and raiding. This state persisted throughout 1952. Such operations proved as costly as the preceding 1951 battles. In four consecutive nights of patrolling in June 1952, for example, 25th Brigade had 8 men killed, 45 wounded, 1 captured, and 1 declared missing. Occasionally the Chinese launched major offensives, as was the case on October 22 when they attacked Hill 355, now held by the RCR. When the fierce battle finally ended in a Chinese withdrawal on October 24, 18 Canadians were dead, 35 were wounded, and 14 had been captured.

Meanwhile, at sea on October 2, 1952, *Iroquois* was hit by shore battery fire while attacking a series of tunnels between Songjin and Sinpo in Korea. Three sailors were killed and eleven badly wounded. In all, 3,621 officers and men served in Korea and, of these, only the three killed on *Iroquois* were lost in combat — although three others were lost at sea and two died in vehicle mishaps.

The war ground into 1953 with the Canadians holding various sections of the Jamestown Line, never far from where they had first arrived during Operation Commando. On May 2, 1953, the Chinese launched a nighttime assault in successive waves against the RCR

Sherman tanks of 'B' Squadron Lord Strathcona's Horse rumble out of the deadlocked Jamestown Line for a break on July 16, 1952.

front protecting the approaches to Hill 187. Although the battalion repelled the attack, it suffered the heaviest Canadian casualty rate in one day of the war — 26 killed, 27 wounded, and 8 taken prisoner. This was also the Canadians' last major engagement in Korea.

Twenty-two Royal Canadian Air Force pilots attached to United States Fifth Air Force also served in Korea, flying Sabre jet fighters on combat missions between November 1950 and July 1953. Canadian Flight Lieutenant E. A. Glover shot down three enemy fighters and damaged another three. He was awarded the Distinguished Flying Cross, the first time the medal was awarded during a peacetime mission.

On June 8, 1953, an armistice was concluded. Following the ceasefire, 25th Canadian Infantry Brigade assumed responsibility for guarding the demarcation line along a section of front previously held by the entire 1st Commonwealth Division. Tensions flared later in the month when South Korea's government attempted to manufacture a confrontation that would force a UN offensive to effect Korean reunification. When this crisis passed, a final ceasefire was agreed on July 27, 1953, and the war ended.

In all, 21,940 Canadians saw service in the Canadian army in Korea. Of these, 309 were killed and about 1,200 were wounded.

THE COLD WAR

The Korean War was not Canada's only military operation abroad during the early 1950s. On April 4, 1949, Canada became a signatory to the North Atlantic Treaty Organization (NATO), but this remained largely a paper entity until the Korean War and the Soviet Union's domination of eastern Europe raised concerns of Communist worldwide expansionism. These fears led the Canadian government in January 1951 to commit itself to a major military buildup.

On February 5, 1951, the government announced an expansion of the Royal Canadian Navy to 100 ships, the creation of 40 Royal

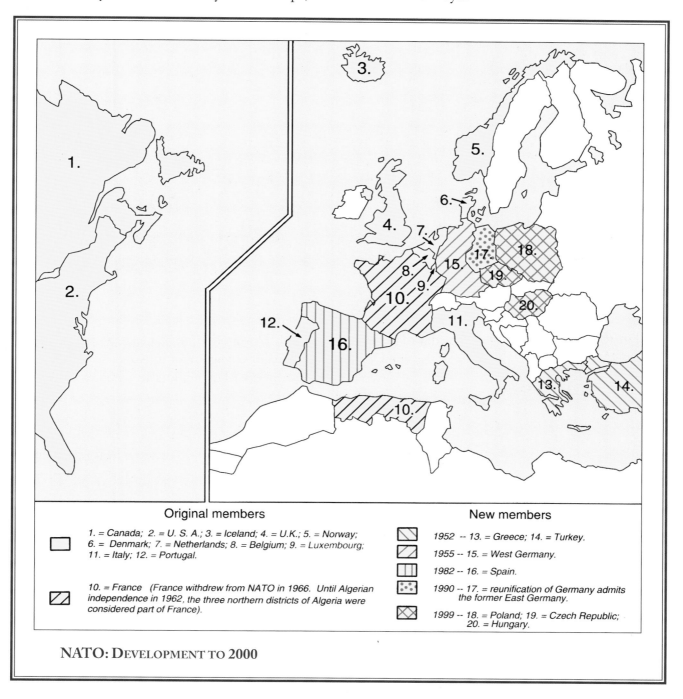

Original members

1. = Canada; 2. = U. S. A.; 3. = Iceland; 4. = U.K.; 5. = Norway; 6. = Denmark; 7. = Netherlands; 8. = Belgium; 9. = Luxembourg; 11. = Italy; 12. = Portugal.

10. = France (France withdrew from NATO in 1966. Until Algerian independence in 1962, the three northern districts of Algeria were considered part of France).

New members

1952 -- 13. = Greece; 14. = Turkey.

1955 -- 15. = West Germany.

1982 -- 16. = Spain.

1990 -- 17. = reunification of Germany admits the former East Germany.

1999 -- 18. = Poland; 19. = Czech Republic; 20. = Hungary.

NATO: DEVELOPMENT TO 2000

Canadian Air Force squadrons, and the building of a full army division. The RCAF also undertook responsibility for training NATO pilots and navigators on Canadian bases. An army brigade group of 10,000 men and 12 RCAF F-86 fighter squadrons were promised for deployment to Europe. By late October 1951, the army brigade was in Europe and in summer of 1953 the last of the RCAF squadrons arrived. Canada's military expanded from about 47,000 men in 1950 to 104,000 in 1953 and its budget increased tenfold to $1.9 billion annually.

When the Soviet Union conducted its first nuclear test on September 14, 1954, the threat of a nuclear missile attack against the United States loomed, with Canada caught in the middle. Air defence and early-warning radar detection lines became a priority. The first constructed was the Pinetree Line, with an initial count of 33 stations, which eventually numbered 44. It followed the 49th parallel with a line extending up the east coast to the southern part of Baffin Island.

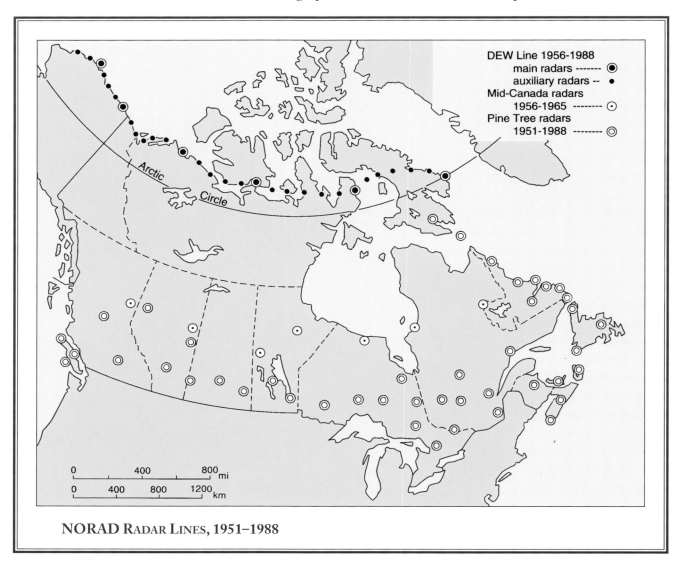

NORAD RADAR LINES, 1951–1988

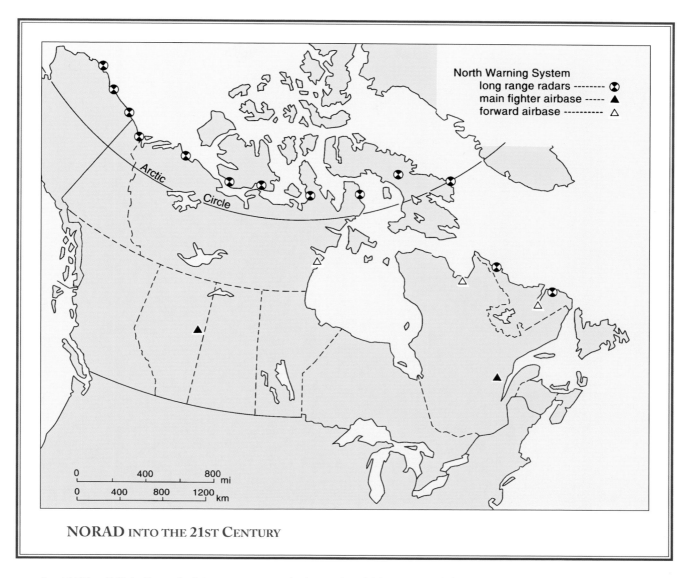

NORAD INTO THE 21ST CENTURY

In 1955, a Mid-Canada Line was started along the 55th parallel. This 98-station system was completed in 1957. Meanwhile, since 1954 the United States and Canada had been jointly developing plans to construct the Distant Early Warning (DEW) Line along the Arctic coast from Alaska to Baffin Island. DEW's 22 stations were funded entirely by the United States and completed in 1957. The American-Canadian cooperation required for construction and operation of these radio lines was expanded on August 1, 1957, by formation of the North American Aerospace Defence Command (later renamed North American Air Defence Agreement or NORAD).

NORAD integrated American and Canadian air defence radar and fighting forces into a single unified defence. Although the operational structure, number of radar sites, and importance of various lines have changed much since its creation in the 1950s (the Mid-Canada Line was phased out in 1965, for example), NORAD continues through the North Warning System to link the physical defence of Canada with that of the United States.

CHAPTER TEN

Peacekeeping Operations
1948–2001

When the United Nations was formed in the summer of 1945, part of its mandate was to maintain international peace and security. From the outset, Canada was well positioned in the international community to play a pivotal UN peacekeeping role. The first such operation was authorized on January 20, 1948, when the newly independent dominions of Pakistan and India clashed over control of Jammu and Kashmir, particularly the latter state. The UN's initial attempts to establish a UN commission to mediate a resolution failed and the war heated up. Previous experience in Palestine indicated a lasting

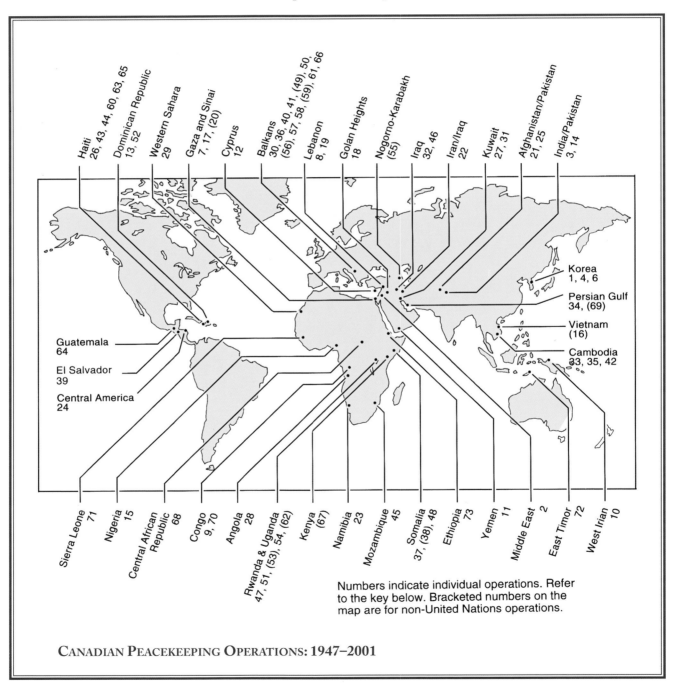

Haiti
26, 43, 44, 60, 63, 65

Dominican Republic
13, 52

Western Sahara
29

Gaza and Sinai
7, 17, (20)

Cyprus
12

Balkans
30, 36, 40, 41, (49), 50, (56), 57, 58, (59), 61, 66

Lebanon
8, 19

Golan Heights
18

Nogorno-Karabakh
(55)

Iraq
32, 46

Iran/Iraq
22

Kuwait
27, 31

Afghanistan/Pakistan
21, 25

India/Pakistan
3, 14

Korea
1, 4, 6

Persian Gulf
34, (69)

Vietnam
(16)

Cambodia
33, 35, 42

Guatemala
64

El Salvador
39

Central America
24

Sierra Leone
71

Nigeria
15

Central African Republic
68

Congo
9, 70

Angola
28

Rwanda & Uganda
47, 51, (53), 54, (62)

Kenya
(67)

Namibia
23

Mozambique
45

Somalia
37, (38), 48

Ethiopia
73

Yemen
11

Middle East
2

East Timor
72

West Irian
10

Numbers indicate individual operations. Refer to the key below. Bracketed numbers on the map are for non-United Nations operations.

CANADIAN PEACEKEEPING OPERATIONS: 1947–2001

1. 1947–48   UNTCOK: United Nations Temporary Commission on Korea
2. 1948–present   UNTSO: United Nations Truce Supervision Organization
3. 1949–96   United Nations Military Observer Group in India and Pakistan
4. 1950–53   United Nations Command Korea
5. 1953–present   UNCMAC: United Nations Command Military Armistice Commission
(6.) 1954–74   ICSC: International Commission for Supervision and Control (not UN)
7. 1956–67   UNEF l: United Nations Emergency Force (Middle East)
8. 1958   UNOGIL: United Nations Observor Group in Lebanon
9. 1960–64   ONUC: *Operations Nations Unies au Congo*
10. 1962–63   UNTEA: United Nations Temporary Executive Authority in West New Guinea
11. 1963–64   UNYOM: United Nations Yemen Observation Mission
12. 1964–present   UNFICYP: United Nations Peacekeeping Force in Cyprus
13. 1965–66   DOMREP: Mission of the Representative of the Secretary-General in the Dominican Republic
14. 1965–66   UNIPOM: United Nations India-Pakistan Observation Mission
(15.) 1968–70   OTN: International Observer Team to Nigeria (not UN)
(16.) 1973   ICCS: International Commission on Control and Supervison (not UN)
17. 1973–79   UNEF ll: United Nations Emergency Force (Middle East)
18. 1974–present   UNDOF: United Nations Disengagement Observer Force (Golan Heights)
19. 1978   UNIFIL: United Nations Interim Force in Lebanon
(20.) 1986–present   MFO: Multinational Force and Observers (Middle East) (not UN)
21. 1988–90   UNGOMAP: United Nations Good Offices Mission in Afghanistan and Pakistan
22. 1988–91   UNIIMOG: United Nations Iran-Iraq Military Observer Group
23. 1989–90   UNTAG: United Nations Transition Assistance Group
24. 1989–92   ONUCA: United Nations Observer Group in Central America
25. 1990–92   OSGAP: Office of the Secretary-General in Afghanistan and Pakistan
26. 1990–91   ONUVEH: United Nations Observer Group for the Verification of Elections in Haiti
27. 1990–91   Operations in Support of UN Resolutions Persian Gulf and Kuwait (Gulf War)
28. 1991–93   UNAVEM ll: United Nations Angola Verification Mission
29. 1991–94   MINURSO: United Nations Mission for the Referendum in western Sahara
(30.) 1991–94   ECMM: European Community Monitoring Mission in Yugoslavia (not UN)
31. 1991–present   UNIKOM: United Nations Iraq-Kuwait Observation Mission
32. 1991–present   UNSCOM: United Nations Special Commission (Iraq)
33. 1991–92   UNAMIC: United Nations Advance Mission in Cambodia
34. 1991–present   MIF: Multinational Interdiction Force Operations (Persian Gulf)
35. 1992–93   UNTAC: United Nations Transitional Authority in Cambodia
36. 1992–94   UNCOE: United Nations Committee of Experts
37. 1992   UNOSOM: United Nations Operations in Somalia
(38.) 1992–93   UNITAF: United Task Force (Somalia) (not UN)
39. 1992–94   ONUSAL: United Nations Mission in El Salvador
40. 1992–95   UNPROFOR: United Nations Protection Force in Yugoslavia
41. 1992–96   Sarajevo airlift
42. 1993–present   CMAC: Cambodia Mine Action Centre. UNDP: United Nations Development Program
43. 1993–94   UN Maritime Sanctions against Haiti
44. 1993–96   UNMIH: United Nations Mission in Haiti
45. 1993–95   UNOMOZ: United Nations Operations in Mozambique
46. 1991–present   AWACS (Airborne Warning and Control Systems): monitoring of no-fly-zone over Northern Iraq and Southern Iraq
47. 1993–94   UNOMUR: United Nations Observer Mission Uganda-Rwanda
48. 1993–95   UNOSOM ll: United Nations Operations in Somalia
(49.) 1993–present   Operation DENY FLIGHT (Bosnia-Hercegovina) (not UN)
50. 1993–96   Enforcement of United Nations Embargo of the former Yugoslavia
51. 1993–96   UNAMIR: United Nations Assistance Mission in Rwanda
52. 1994   Military Observer Group Dominican Republic
(53.) 1994   Provision of humanitarian aid to Rwanda (not UN)
54. 1994   United Nations Assistance Mission to Rwanda
(55.) 1995–96   Peacekeeping mission in Nogorno-Karabakh (not UN)
(56.) 1995–96   IFOR: NATO Implementation Force (not UN)
57. 1995–present   UNMIBH: United Nations Mission in Bosnia-Hercegovina
58. 1995–present   UNPREDEP: United Nations Preventive Deployment Force in the Former Yugoslav Republic of Macedonia
(59.) 1996   SFOR: NATO Stabilization Force (not UN)
60. 1996–present   UNSMIH: United Nations Support Mission in Haiti
61. 1996–present   UNMOP: United Nations Mission of Observers in Prevlaka
(62.) 1996   African Great Lakes Multinational Force (not UN)
63. 1997   UNTMIH: United Nations Transition Mission in Haiti
64. 1997–present   MINUGA: *Mission Nations Unies Guatemala*
65. 1997–present   MIPONUH: *Mission de Police des Nations Unies en Haiti*
66. 1997–present   OSCE (Organization for Security and Cooperation in Europe): Operation Mentor / Bosnia-Hercegovina
(67.) 1998   Care Canada Secondment to Kenya (not UN)
68. 1998–present   MINURCA: United Nations Mission to the Central African Republic
(69.) 1998–present   Operation Determination (Persian Gulf) (not UN)
70. 1999–present   MONUC: United Nations Mission in the Democratic Republic of the Congo
71. 1999–present   UNAMSIL: United Nations Mission in Sierra Leone
72. 1999–present   UNTAET: United Nations Transitional Administration in East Timor
73. 2001–present   UNMEE: United Nations Mission in Ethipia and Eritrea

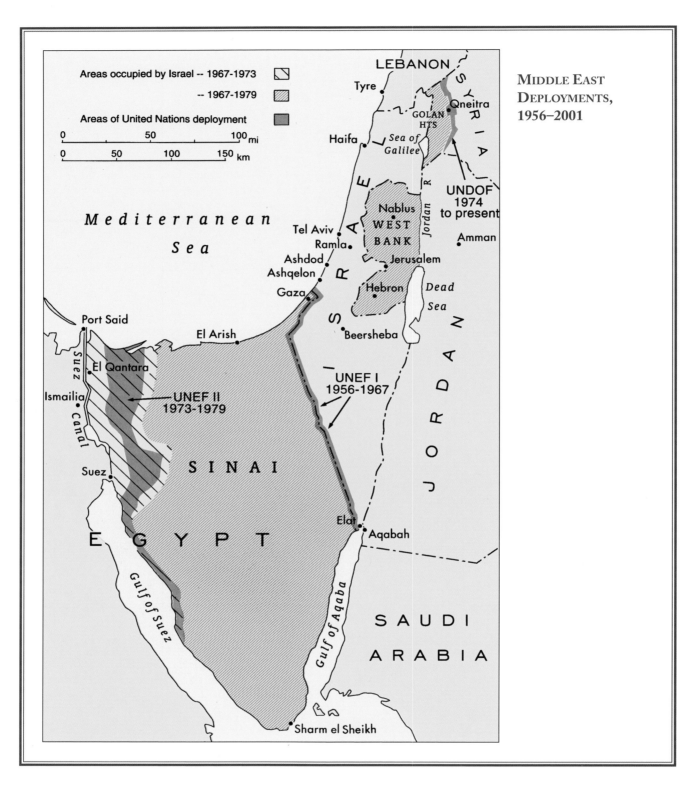

Areas occupied by Israel -- 1967-1973

-- 1967-1979

Areas of United Nations deployment

| 0 | 50 | 100 mi |

| 0 | 50 | 100 | 150 km |

LEBANON

Tyre

Haifa

Sea of Galilee

GOLAN HTS

Qneitra

SYRIA

UNDOF 1974 to present

Mediterranean Sea

Nablus

WEST BANK

Jordan R.

Amman

Tel Aviv

Ramla

Ashdod

Ashqelon

Gaza

Jerusalem

Hebron

Dead Sea

Beersheba

Port Said

El Arish

El Qantara

UNEF II 1973-1979

UNEF I 1956-1967

Ismailia

Suez

S I N A I

JORDAN

Elat

Aqabah

E G Y P T

Gulf of Suez

Gulf of Aqaba

S A U D I

A R A B I A

Sharm el Sheikh

MIDDLE EAST DEPLOYMENTS, 1956–2001

ceasefire was most likely to develop if UN observers were posted with the opposing military forces to report violations. In February 1949, a 35-man observer team, including four Canadians, deployed to the region.

The UN's long involvement in Middle East affairs began on May 14, 1948, when the State of Israel was proclaimed and was attacked the following day by Arab Palestinians and bordering Arab states. The eventual truce resulted in 572 unarmed UN military observers taking up positions on the Armistice Demarcation Line between Israel and Egypt and Syria. Canada's involvement in the UN Truce Supervision Organization (UNTSO), as this operation was called, started in 1954 when Major General E. L. M. Burns and three other officers arrived, with Burns becoming UNTSO Chief of Staff. Canadians have served as peacekeepers on the Israeli border ever since. The observers here have always been unarmed.

SINAI PEACEKEEPING

On July 26, 1956, Egypt nationalized the Suez Canal, co-owned by Britain and France and considered vital to their national interests. On October 29, Israel, acting in accordance with a tripartite strategy developed by Israel, Britain, and France, advanced into the Sinai Peninsula. The next day, Britain and France used this attack as a pretext to order both Israel and Egypt to cease hostilities and for both to move 10 miles in opposite directions away from the canal. French and British troops would then deploy to control the canal. Egypt rejected this ultimatum, and on October 31 air attacks were launched against Egyptian targets and an Anglo-French force seized Port Said.

Canadians of 56th Reconnaissance Squadron monitor the Israeli withdrawal from Sinai during the deployment of UNEF I to bring an end to the Suez Crisis of 1956–57.

The British-French action was condemned in a motion presented to the UN Security Council that demanded a cessation of hostilities and an Israeli withdrawal from the Sinai. The motion was vetoed by France and Britain. For the first time, the General Assembly consequently legally overrode the Security Council by passing with a two-thirds majority a motion calling for withdrawal of troops. Although Canada abstained from this resolution, which passed on November 2, Secretary for External Affairs Lester B. Pearson explained it did so because the motion did not go far enough. He called for a UN army composed of national contingents large enough to stand between opponents and impose a ceasefire. The General Assembly approved Pearson's plan on November 4 and Burns was immediately made its commander.

The first United Nations Emergency Force (UNEF I) was legalized on November 7, one day after Britain and France agreed to a

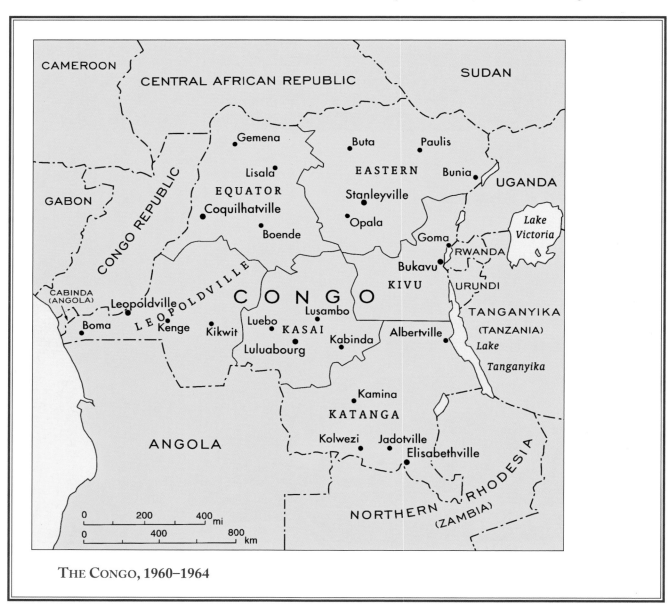

THE CONGO, 1960–1964

ceasefire. Canada initially planned to contribute 1st Battalion, Queen's Own Rifles, but Egypt protested that the Canadian infantrymen and even their battalion identity seemed too British. After much haggling, Egypt agreed to Canada deploying technical, communication, engineering, and transportation units provided by both the army and the Royal Canadian Air Force. Canada added the 56th Canadian Reconnaissance Squadron, which oversaw the Israeli withdrawal from the vast Sinai. UNEF's authorized strength was 6,000 men and of these about 1,000 would be Canadian. All were in place by early January 1957, the last arriving aboard aircraft carrier HMCS *Magnificent*.

Although the Anglo-French force withdrew on December 22, 1956, UNEF remained, shifting its operational boundaries to the Sinai region of Sharm el Sheikh on the western side of the mouth of the Gulf of Aqaba and the Gaza strip as the Israelis withdrew from the rest of the peninsula. It continued to provide an Egyptian-Israeli buffer until May 1967, when the Egyptian government ordered its withdrawal. This had not been entirely completed when Egypt and Israel went to war on June 5 and 15 UN troops (none were Canadian) were killed in the crossfire before final evacuation on June 17.

UNEF would be resurrected as Second United Nations Emergency Force (UNEF II) after Egypt and Syria launched a surprise attack against Israel on October 6, 1973, that soon backlashed into a rout of Egyptian troops back to and beyond the Suez Canal. On October 25, the UN passed a resolution demanding an immediate ceasefire in what has become known as the Yom Kippur War and the return to prewar boundaries. Canada contributed 1,000 logistics personnel to UNEF II, which continued until its withdrawal in July 1979. The UN also established a buffer zone maintained by peacekeepers serving as the United Nations Disengagement Observer Force (UNDOF) on the strategically important Golan Heights between Syria and Israel, to which Canada has provided personnel through to the present day.

The Congo

UNEF and the UN Truce Supervision Organization (UNTSO) represented two distinct approaches to international peacekeeping — UNEF placed a military force directly between combatants while UNTSO required unarmed observers to maintain peace through persuasion and moral censor. Both, however, were designed to deal with nation-versus-nation conflicts. The Congo crisis forced the UN to attempt to restore public order within a sovereign state.

Within a week of Patrice Lumumba's government assuming power over the former Belgian colony on June 30, 1960, elements of the 25,000-strong military police mutinied. On July 11, Belgium intervened militarily without Congolese government consent. This prompted Provincial President Moïshe Shombe to declare Katanga

M-113 Armoured Personnel Carrier patrolling the Green Line in Nicosia in 1984

province independent. Lumumba pleaded for UN military assistance on July 12. A UN Security Council resolution was passed July 14 demanding the withdrawal of Belgian troops and authorizing UN Secretary-General Dag Hammerskjöld to provide military assistance to Lumumba's government.

On the evening of July 15, UN troops landed at Leopoldville and the next day the Belgians agreed to withdraw. Contingents for United Nations Operation in the Congo (UNOC) came initially from European and African nations. By the time the Belgian withdrawal was complete in early August, about 14,000 UN troops drawn from 24 countries were deployed. Eventually 35 countries contributed to build a 20,000-strong force — the largest UN operation until Cambodia in 1992–93. Canada contributed about 500 men, principally logistical experts. Small detachments drawn from 200 Canadian signallers were scattered to UNOC units throughout the Congo during the four-year peacekeeping operation. Although 234 peacekeepers died in the operation, Canadian casualties were relatively light. Two Canadians died of illnesses and 33 were injured, 12 in beatings by Congolese gangs.

The issue of Katangan independence remained largely unresolved when UNOC withdrew in 1964. While order had been mostly restored, UNOC's withdrawal resulted primarily from UN inability to continue financing the $400 million operation, to which Canada contributed $8 million. Financing major UN peacekeeping deployments would prove increasingly difficult. UNOC was the first time UN peacekeepers intervened directly in a sovereign state's internal affairs.

Although soon commonplace, such operations generally proved more difficult to resolve and more hazardous for UN personnel than was the case with international conflicts.

CYPRUS

Three years after the Republic of Cyprus gained independence from Britain in 1960, the delicate constitutional balance between the

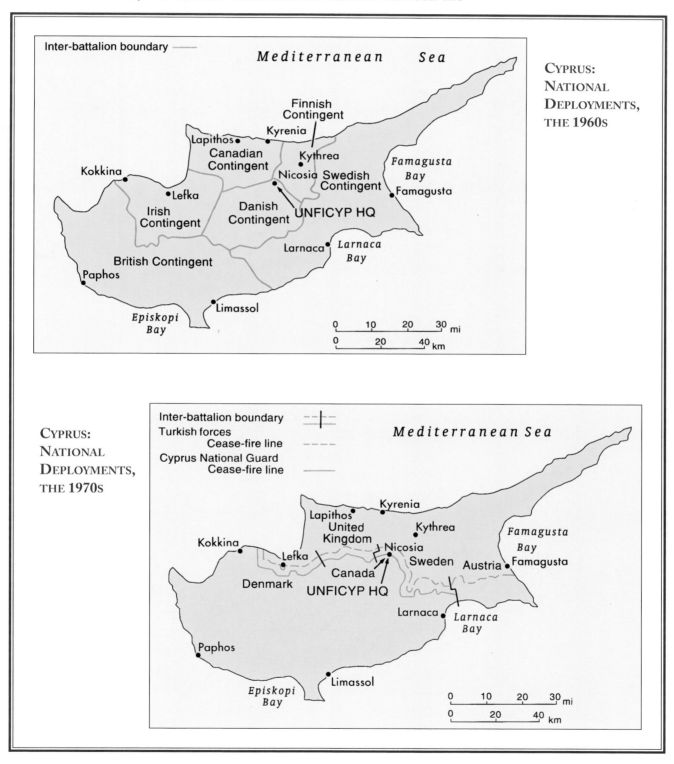

CYPRUS: NATIONAL DEPLOYMENTS, THE 1960S

CYPRUS: NATIONAL DEPLOYMENTS, THE 1970S

dominant Greek majority and the Turkish minority collapsed when the president attempted to amend the constitution to strengthen Greek control. His proposals sparked general rioting and Turkey massed troops on its neighbouring coast preparatory to invasion.

Open warfare was averted only when Cyprus agreed to accept a three-power Turkish, Greek, and British peacekeeping force operating under British command. The UN provided an observer. The tripartite force proved incapable of preventing growing violence in early 1964 that led to heavy civilian casualties and fighting between guerilla forces. Britain and Cyprus jointly called for UN intervention on February 15, 1964, which was approved on March 6.

By this time, the situation was desperate as Turkey threatened on March 12 to invade unless attacks on Turkish Cypriots ceased. UN Secretary-General U Thant pushed an emergency resolution through the following day that authorized the immediate deployment of a mostly Canadian force designated the United Nations Peacekeeping Force in Cyprus (UNFICYP). On March 15, an advance party commanded by Colonel E. A. C. Amy entered Nicosia, followed the next day by an RCAF Air Transport lift that included a component of the 1,100-man contingent of 1st Battalion, Royal 22e Regiment, and a Royal Canadian Dragoons reconnaissance squadron. By month's end, the entire contingent was in Cyprus patrolling Nicosia's Green Line buffer zone, created between Greek and Turkish populations and a 100-square-mile territory in the island's north-central part.

By December 1965, UN troops from Sweden, Finland, Britain, Ireland, Denmark, and Canada numbered 6,500 and had divided the entire island into six sectors of control. Initially mandated to serve in Cyprus for only three months, Canadians have been there ever since.

For the first 10 years, peacekeepers prevented a major war but were unable to prevent outbreaks of Greek and Turkish guerilla operations. The two island populations became increasingly segregated, with Turkish enclaves developing, particularly in the port area of Famagusta on the east coast and between Nicosia and Kyrenia. This partitioning only served to harden ethnic hatred.

On July 15, 1974, a botched military coup staged by Greece's junta was met by a Turkish invasion on July 20. Within a matter of days, 40,000 Turkish troops seized 40 percent of the island and engaged in bitter fighting with Greek Cypriots. With initially only about 2,000 troops present, the UN could do little to intervene. Reinforcements, including 400 more Canadian paratroops and reconnaissance soldiers, brought the force up to only 4,444 by August 14. Overwhelmingly outnumbered, the peacekeepers could only try to negotiate localized ceasefires to enable civilian evacuation from battle zones.

The Canadians were also responsible for operations in most of Nicosia, including preventing either Greeks or Turks from controlling the international airport. With so much of the island under Turkish control, thousands of Greek refugees poured across the Nicosia Green Line into the Greek-controlled sector, putting extreme pressure on the Canadian security operations. Canadians also came under fire several times while trying to protect or escort refugees.

By the end of August, a ceasefire was negotiated, but throughout September violence was frequent. On August 6, a Canadian was killed by sniper fire and another was fatally shot on September 19. Thirteen other Canadians were wounded. The ceasefire did not bring about Turkey's withdrawal. Instead, UN peacekeepers began patrolling a 135-mile-long demarcation line between the island's Turkish-army controlled sector and that controlled by Greek Cypriot fighters. Across this line, about 200,000 Greek Cypriot refugees passed some 37,000 Turkish Cypriot refugees, as people sought refuge in their own ethnic enclave.

Although there are still occasional outbreaks of violence, the 1974 boundaries remain largely unchanged, as does the role of UN peacekeepers. The fragile peace has resulted in slow strength reductions to about 1,500 UN personnel in 2000, of whom only two were Canadians.

PEACEKEEPING AT HOME: OKA

On July 11, 1990, the Sûreté de Québec (provincial police) attempted to remove armed Mohawks from the Kanesatake Reserve who were trying to stop an Oka community golf course expansion into a Mohawk sacred site. Gunfire ensued and one police officer died. Soon after, other Mohawks from the Kahnawake Reserve blocked Mercier Bridge, closing a prime Montreal commuter route. Members of the Mohawk Warriors Society, an unofficial militant tribal faction, manned the barricades at Oka and the bridge. The situation at the bridge quickly turned ugly, with residents of Chateauguay and disgruntled commuters confronting the Mohawks behind the barricades. Rocks and racial epithets were aimed at the Mohawks, while police largely stood by. Meanwhile, support in the Mohawk community was sharply divided between those who sanctioned the Warriors' actions and those who condemned them.

Police and warriors dug in on either side, effecting a stalemate neither could win without bloodshed. To break the stalemate, the Canadian government authorized the army to replace the police on August 8, but before the transfer could be effected a series of riots at Mercier Bridge between August 12 and 14 resulted in about 40 people being injured.

The 5th Mechanized Brigade based at CFB Valcartier moved in about 1,800 troops on August 20. A week later, Quebec Premier Robert Bourassa asked the army to remove the barricade of Mercier

Media scrum with Canadian officer (left) and Oka warrior (right) facing each other.

Bridge because negotiations were deadlocked. Since the Mohawks were heavily armed, it was assumed that the bridge had been booby-trapped with explosives and that the barricade would be violently defended. For this reason, Leopard tanks mounted with dozer blades were deployed so their armoured bodies could protect soldiers advancing and the blades could clear obstacles. However, the undefended barricades were easily removed and the bridge opened on August 27.

When they withdrew, the Mohawks took refuge in a reserve treatment centre which the military quickly surrounded. Elsewhere on the reserve, a group of women, children, and elders attempting to evacuate from the embattled Kahnawake Reserve were attacked by a rock-throwing mob while police did little to prevent the violence.

As the military extended its control over the reserve and replaced the ineffectual police, another standoff set in, with tensions heightened by the army's utilization of a combined strategy of negotiation and vigorous patrolling to demonstrate to the warriors that the army controlled the situation. Occasional shots were fired and several minor clashes resulted. There were, however, no casualties until 300 Mohawks blocked a combined police-army search of Tekakwitha

Island on September 18. About 140 troops attempted to contain the Mohawks with tear gas, rifle butts, and warning shots. Some 75 warriors and 22 soldiers were injured in the subsequent fighting. Seized during the search were 48 weapons and about 5,000 rounds of ammunition.

The siege at Oka ended on September 26 with some warriors taken into custody and others attempting to evade capture. When a crowd of about 350 Mohawks advanced on an army checkpoint manned by only 6 soldiers and attacked them with lead pipes and baseball bats, the troops responded with tear gas, fixed bayonets, and warning shots. Soon 25 reinforcements arrived and the commander ordered the selection of individual Mohawks as targets for immediate rifle fire. Realizing the army's intentions, the Mohawks retreated. No attempt to pursue was made and fortunately there were no casualties on either side. This was the closest the troops came to applying lethal force and marked the end of the crisis.

In the fall of 2000, a tentative settlement was reached by the government and the Mohawks that would transfer most of the disputed lands to the Mohawk people. Oka's successful resolution demonstrated the overlap of international peacekeeping operations with those involving the maintenance of security within Canada. Many soldiers at Oka had peacekeeping experience. Their ability to maintain a visible and determined security net, while conducting protracted negotiations with the warriors, led to the crisis being successfully defused.

THE GULF WAR

While the Oka crisis played out in Canada, an international crisis erupted when Iraq invaded Kuwait on August 2, 1990. The UN Security Council demanded unconditional withdrawal of Iraqi troops. Embargoes, sanctions, and other non-military measures followed without success, resulting in a November 29 UN resolution authorizing UN member states to use "all necessary means" to force an Iraqi withdrawal. Iraq was given until January 15, 1991, to comply.

Within days of the invasion, a multinational detachment was enforcing the trade sanctions. Canada agreed on August 11 to send ships into the Persian Gulf. On August 24, Canadian Task Group, consisting of two destroyers, *Athabaskan* and *Terra Nova*, and the supply ship *Protecteur*, sailed from Halifax with a combined crew of 934. It arrived in Manamah, Bahrain, on September 30. Meanwhile, 419 Squadron's 18 CF-18s moved from Canada's NATO base at Baden, Germany, to Doha, Qatar, to provide air cover.

On October 1, *Athabaskan* challenged seven ships that were suspected of carrying prohibited goods to Iraq. Twelve days later, Canadian fighters flew their first combat air patrols. As the deadline for Iraq's withdrawal neared, Canada's ships continued patrolling, boarding 20 ships, which amounted to about 25 percent of all inspections undertaken by the 100-strong multinational fleet.

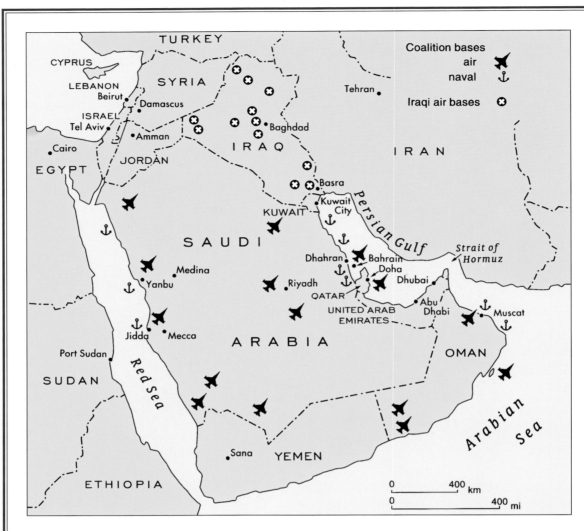

GULF WAR: AREA OF OPERATIONS, 1990–1991

Coalition bases
air
naval

Iraqi air bases

TURKEY

CYPRUS

LEBANON
Beirut
ISRAEL
Tel Aviv
Damascus
SYRIA

Amman
JORDAN

Cairo

EGYPT

IRAQ
Baghdad

Basra
Kuwait
City
KUWAIT

SAUDI

Medina

Yanbu

Riyadh

Dhahran   Bahrain
Doha
QATAR   Dhubai

UNITED ARAB
EMIRATES   Abu
Dhabi   Muscat

ARABIA

Jidda   Mecca

Port Sudan

SUDAN

Red Sea

OMAN

Arabian
Sea

Tehran

IRAN

Persian Gulf

Strait of
Hormuz

Sana   YEMEN

ETHIOPIA

0   400 km
0   400 mi

THE ALLIED LAND OFFENSIVE AGAINST IRAQ, FEBRUARY 1991

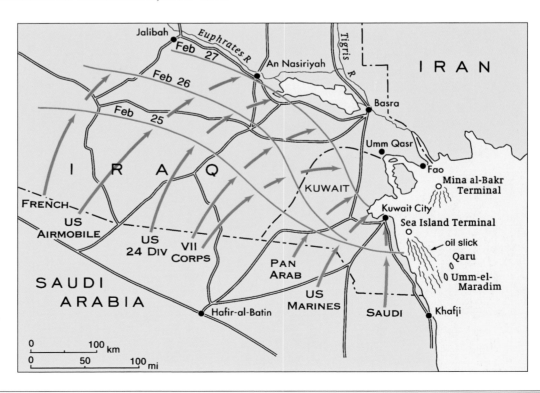

Jalibah
Euphrates R.
Feb 27
Feb 26
An Nasiriyah
Tigris R.

IRAN

Feb 25

Basra

Umm Qasr

I R A Q

Fao

KUWAIT

Mina al-Bakr
Terminal

FRENCH

US
AIRMOBILE

US
24 DIV   VII
CORPS

PAN
ARAB

Kuwait City

Sea Island Terminal

oil slick

Qaru

SAUDI
ARABIA

US
MARINES

SAUDI

Umm-el-
Maradim

Hafir-al-Batin

Khafji

0   100 km
0   50   100 mi

A massive military buildup was taking place, as about 750,000 military personnel from 37 countries gathered preparatory to an attack on Iraqi forces bordering Saudi Arabia. About 500,000 were Americans. Canada contributed 1,700 people.

On January 16, American, British, Kuwaiti, and Saudi aircraft undertook an extended air war against Iraq that continued until the February 24 ground invasion. Iraq responded with sporadic firing of Scud missiles against targets in Saudi Arabia and Israel and by releasing massive, environmentally catastrophic oil slicks into the Gulf from two oil-storage terminals. These actions only hardened the Allied determination to oust Iraq from Kuwait. Initially, Canadian fighters were limited to patrolling, but on February 1 the squadron, now numbering 24 CF-18s drawn from 416 Squadron out of Cold Lake and 439 Squadron from Baden, was authorized to "engage and eliminate enemy aircraft." On February 20, the CF-18s were assigned ground-attack tasks using regular iron bombs and cluster bombs.

No Canadians participated in the 100-hour ground attack, code-named Operation Desert Sabre, that was launched on February 24. While a quick, massive armoured envelopment destroyed the effectiveness of the Republican Guard and Iraq's armoured reserves and

Leading seaman from HMCS Regina *(background) searches a vessel during Persian Gulf blockade operations.*

plunged deep into Iraq, a direct frontal assault smashed the Iraqi forces in Kuwait. The Canadian CF-18s continued performing a ground-attack role until Iraq's February 27 surrender. Iraq suffered at least 30,000 dead, 70,000 wounded, and had 60,000 to 65,000 soldiers taken prisoner against fewer than 1,000 Allied losses. No Canadians were killed during operations against Iraq.

On April 14, Canadians shifted to participating in the United Nations Iraq Kuwait Observation Mission, contributing about 300 engineers to clear mines from the Iraqi-Kuwait border. This was a task Canadian peacekeepers would soon also be performing in Cambodia, many parts of former Yugoslavia, and other nations. In the aftermath of the war, the United Nations deployed a Maritime Interception Force comprised of naval ships from many nations whose orders were to prevent the supplying of contraband arms and supplies to Iraq that could be used for military purposes. Canadian ships, such as the destroyer *Regina* which deployed to the Gulf in 1997, have participated in this operation on a regular basis.

SOMALIA

Since Canada's first peacekeepers deployed in 1948, its armed forces enjoyed a reputation for both professionalism and the ability to work effectively with a variety of ethnic, racial, and political communities. On December 28, 1992, a change to that reputation was set in motion when the 850-strong battle group of the Canadian Airborne Regiment, 'A' Squadron Royal Canadian Dragoons, and an engineer squadron arrived at Belet Huen, Somalia, to take up peacekeeping duties in the civil war–stricken state. The situation in Somalia had collapsed the previous November when the government effectively lost control and a variety of clans and sub-clans fought to dominate parts of the capital, Mogadishu, and other regions. Combined with a devastating drought, the increasing violence brought about 4.5 million people — roughly half the national population — to the brink of starvation. By the end of 1992 about 300,000 people had died.

UN attempts in early 1992 to restore order had failed, and on December 3 a resolution was adopted to deliver humanitarian aid to Somalia even if this required engaging Somalian clans in combat. Unified Task Force (UTF), of which the Canadians were part, deployed 37,000 troops into southern and central Somalia. About 28,000 were American, with the rest drawn from 20 other countries.

The Canadians set up base a few kilometres from Belet Huen and undertook standard UTF tasks of protecting neighbouring villages and towns, escorting aid convoys, helping local police, seizing heavy weapons, and attempting to mediate between the various factions while also trying to prevent looting of their own compound. On February 17, 1993, a Somalian was killed when Canadian soldiers fired on demonstrators from one clan trying to force their way across a bridge into a rival clan's sector. Then paratroopers patrolling outside the camp's perimeter wire shot two Somalian men on March 4. One was killed at close range by a bullet in the back of the head.

On March 16, a patrol was ordered to capture a looter to serve as a warning to others. At 8:45 p.m., 16-year-old Shindane Abukar Arone was arrested and detained in a bunker where two soldiers subsequently beat him to death, while 15 others watched without intervening. This disturbing incident brought about the termination of Canada's involvement in the Somalian peacekeeping mission by month's end, resulted in a series of criminal prosecutions, and led to the disbanding of Canadian Airborne Regiment.

THE BALKANS

Following World War II, Yugoslavia became a federation of six republics — Croatia, Slovenia, Bosnia-Herzegovina, Macedonia, Serbia, and Montenegro — and two provinces — Vojvodina and Kosovo. After President Marshal Tito's death in 1980, serious ethnic division

The thin blue line between warring factions in the Balkans is often little more than a lightly manned checkpoint such as this.

threatened the nation's stability. In June 1991, Croatia and Slovenia declared independence, followed by Macedonia in September 1991, and Bosnia-Herzegovina in March 1992. Serbia and Montenegro united as the Federal Republic of Yugoslavia on April 27, 1992.

Croatia and Bosnia-Herzegovina were immediately torn by ethnic violence. In Croatia in December 1991, the Serbian minority declared independence over 25 percent of the country. Fighting broke out between Croatian government troops and paramilitary Serbs supported by Serbia. About 10,000 people were killed and another 500,000 became refugees before 14,000 UN troops arrived in March 1992, following the establishment on February 15, 1992, of United Nations Protection Force (UNPROFOR). As part of UNPROFOR, Canada deployed a 1,200-strong force to western Slovenia. Canadian Battalion One was drawn from the Royal 22e Regiment and elements of the Royal Canadian Regiment and 4th Canadian Engineer Regiment. Restoring the breakaway Serb area to Croatian control proved impossible for UNPROFOR to effect through negotiation. Finally, Croatia attacked in May 1995, setting off a war that ended only on January 15, 1998, in Croatian victory and the displacement of most Serbs from Croatia or their elimination by genocide.

In 1991, Bosnia-Herzegovina's ethnic mix was 44 percent Bosnian Moslems, 31 percent Serbs, 17 percent Croats, and 8 percent unidentified. When the Moslem faction won the presidential election, the Serbs and Croats formed a coalition and revolted. Serbia supported the rebels and soon 70 percent of the new nation was Serbian-dominated, with the Croats controlling a further 20 percent. The Croats then switched allegiance to the Bosnian Moslems because the Serbs were gaining too much strength in the region. After several battlefield reversals, the Serbs retained only about 50 percent, with the Moslem-Croat coalition controlling the other half.

Endeavouring to contain the combat violence and ethnic "cleansing," UNPROFOR intervened and in October 1992 Canadian Battalion Two (CANBATT Two) prepared to enter central Bosnia. Due to the intense fighting, however, it was not until February 1993 that the battalion could begin operations in its designated sector in the Visoko region northwest of Sarajevo. Once deployed, CANBATT Two was also assigned to monitor a 20-kilometre weapons exclusion zone around Sarajevo and to verify compliance with previously negotiated ceasefire terms. Canada also provided airlift capacity for the movement of humanitarian supplies into Sarajevo between 1992 and 1995, moving 11,600 passengers and 23,150 tons of relief supplies.

On December 14, 1995, the Dayton Peace Accords established a borderline between Bosnia-Herzegovina and the Bosnian Serb Republic. To ensure the agreement's maintenance, a heavily armed 60,000-strong NATO-controlled multinational force (IFOR) was formed. Canada contributed an initial strength of 1,000 personnel to

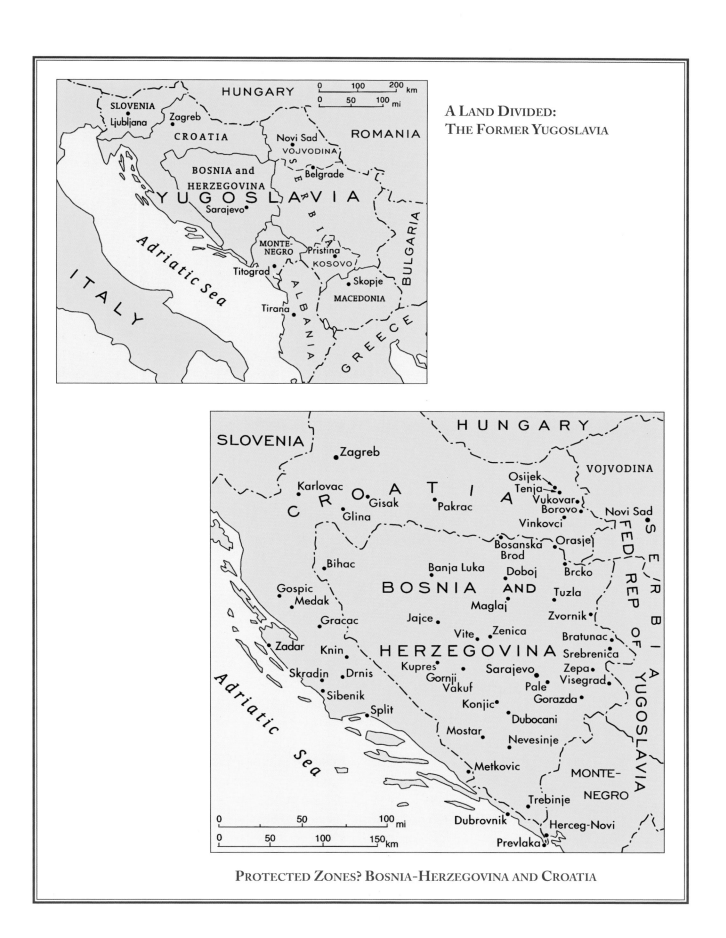

A Land Divided:
The Former Yugoslavia

Protected Zones? Bosnia-Herzegovina and Croatia

Grizzly armoured car on patrol amid ruins in Dubocani, Bosnia-Herzegovina

IFOR. On December 12, 1996, the UN renewed IFOR's operational mandate, redesignating it Stabilization Force (SFOR). The next day, Canada committed 1,200 personnel and Canadians have served with SFOR ever since.

In 2001, SFOR numbered some 21,000 troops, including nearly 1,700 Canadians. Between 1992 and 1996, 12 Canadians died serving with UNPROFOR and IFOR.

Kosovo

On October 16, 1998, Yugoslavian President Slobodon Milosevic agreed to a ceasefire between Serbian forces and the Kosovo Liberation Army (KLA) and to withdraw its estimated 40,000-strong Serbian military and police forces from the province. Although Kosovo's population was 90 percent Albanian, it had been forcibly annexed to Serbia for many years. The ceasefire was to be verified by about 2,000 unarmed civilian personnel operating under the auspices of the Organisation for Security and Cooperation as the Kosovo Verification Mission (KVM). Canada contributed 100 personnel to this mission, which was finally composed of only 1,350 men and women.

It was soon evident to KVM personnel that Serbia was violating the agreement at will, with Serbian police and soldiers conducting mass murders throughout the province. As fighting between the KLA and Serbian forces in early 1999 engulfed the province, the KVM monitors withdrew on March 20, 1999, to Albania. Here they helped local officials attempting to cope with thousands of Kosovar refugees fleeing the violence.

Three days later, against strong opposition from the UN, NATO ordered air attacks against Yugoslavia to force its compliance with the peace agreement. On March 24, NATO aircraft, including four Canadian CF-18s operating out of Aviano, Italy, struck against Yugoslavian targets. For 79 days and nights, a total of 18 Canadian CF-18s were operational, flying 678 combat sorties involving 2,600 flying hours and dropping 532 bombs containing about 500,000 pounds of explosives. There were no Canadian losses.

On June 10, 1999, the air campaign ended when Yugoslav authorities agreed to withdraw from Kosovo. The following day, Canada authorized the deployment of 1,300 troops to Kosovo as part of NATO's Kosovar Force (KFOR). On June 12, 25,000 troops were in Kosovo enforcing the ceasefire. By June 20, Canadian troops had advanced on the heels of withdrawing Serbs to their area of operation southeast of Pristina, which included Pristina Airport, the major air facility in Kosovo. Soon the Canadian presence expanded to include the Drenica Valley.

Over the ensuing months, peacekeeping responsibility shifted from NATO to the UN and Canada's role in Kosovo was slowly scaled back through 2000, until by year's end only about 100 Canadians served in the UN contingent.

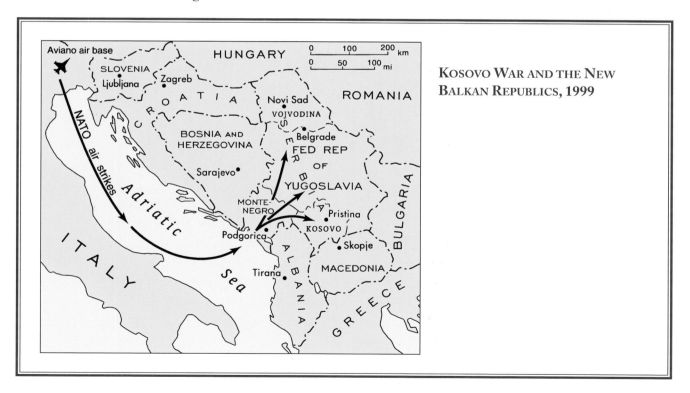

KOSOVO WAR AND THE NEW BALKAN REPUBLICS, 1999

Canadian CF-18s armed with missiles and bombs struck against Serbian targets during the Kosovo air war launched by NATO forces.

THE FUTURE

Since 1948, Canada has participated in about 90 peacekeeping missions varying greatly in size, duration, and strategies adopted to maintain peace. Some, such as Bosnia where major security incidents dropped from 14 in April 1999 to only one the following October, have evolved with painful slowness toward a potentially favourable and lasting outcome. Others, such as the October 1999 intervention to stabilize East Timor and secure its independent status, were accomplished smoothly in mere months. Still others, such as the 1993 to 1995 Rwanda mission, have proven incapable of preventing mass violence and call into question the selective process of authorizing large-scale UN or NATO intervention. Why the Balkans, but not Rwanda?

Somalia aside, Canadian performance in peacekeeping theatres garners generally high international praise. But peacekeeping is a costly venture, both in terms of meeting personnel commitments and in funding their deployment and overseas operations. In the future, it is probable that Canada will remain a committed participant in UN peacekeeping and NATO security operations. However, as of 2001, Canada began transforming its peacekeeping role to one of providing rapid-deployment, quick-stabilization forces, which will normally hand over the task of overseeing the implementation and monitoring of peace to other nations possessing larger military forces. Such an approach will probably result in the overall numbers of Canadian personnel involved in peacekeeping duties at any given time being reduced from the beginning of the century, when about 3,100 men and women were involved in 19 overseas peacekeeping missions.

Royal 22e Regiment troopers splash ashore in East Timor in October 1999.

Bibliography

OVERVIEW WORKS

Brebner, John Bartlet. *North Atlantic Triangle: The Interplay of Canada, the United States, and Great Britain.* Toronto: Ryerson Press, 1945.

Burpee, Lawrence. *An Historical Atlas of Canada.* Toronto: Thomas Nelson and Sons Ltd., 1927.

Canada in the Great World War, Vol. 1, *Military History of Canada, 1608–1914.* Toronto: United Publishers of Canada, 1917.

Israel, Fred L., ed. *Major Peace Treaties of Modern History, 1648–1967.* New York: Chelsea House, 1967.

Kingsford, William. *History of Canada.* 10 vols. 1887–98.

Langer, William L., ed. *An Encyclopaedia of World History.* Boston: Houghton Mifflin, 1948.

Marteinson, John, et. al. *We Stand on Guard: An Illustrated History of the Canadian Army.* Montreal: Ovale Publications, 1992.

Morris, Richard B., ed. *Encyclopaedia of American History.* New York: Harper and Brothers, 1953.

Morton, Desmond. *A Military History of Canada.* Toronto: McClelland & Stewart, 1992.

Stanley, George F. G. *Canada's Soldiers, 1604–1954: The Military History of an Unmilitary People.* Toronto: The Macmillan Company of Canada, 1954.

CHAPTER ONE

Champlain, Samuel de. H. P. Biggar, ed.; John Squair, trans. *The Works of Samuel de Champlain.* Toronto: The Champlain Society, 1925.

Eccles, W. J. *Canada Under Louis XIV: 1663–1701.* Toronto: McClelland & Stewart, 1964.

———. *The Canadian Frontier: 1534–1760.* Albuquerque: University of New Mexico Press, 1974.

Miquelon, Dale. *New France 1701–1744: "A Supplement to Europe."* Toronto: McClelland & Stewart, 1987.

Trigger, Bruce. *The Children of Aataentsic: A History of the Huron People to 1660.* Montreal: McGill–Queen's University Press, 1976.

———. *Natives and Newcomers: Canada's Heroic Age Reconsidered.* Montreal: McGill–Queen's University Press, 1985.

Trudel, Marcel. Patricia Claxton, trans. *The Beginnings of New France, 1524–1663.* Toronto: McClelland & Stewart, 1973.

Verney, Jack. *The Good Regiment: The Carignan-Salières Regiment in Canada, 1665–1668.* Montreal: McGill-Queen's University Press, 1991.

CHAPTER TWO

Bird, Harrison. *Battle for a Continent.* New York: Oxford University Press, 1965.

Donaldson, Gordon. *Battle for a Continent, Quebec 1759.* Toronto: William Collins Sons & Co., 1972.

Frégault, Guy. Margaret M. Cameron, trans. *Canada: The War of the Conquest.* Toronto: Oxford University Press, 1969.

Knox, John. *An Historical Journal of the Campaigns in North America for the Years 1757, 1758, 1759, and 1760.* Champlain Society Publications, nos. 8–10. Toronto, 1914–1916. Facsimile ed., Greenwood Press, 1968.

Stanley, George F. G. *New France: The Last Phase, 1744–1760.* Toronto: McClelland & Stewart, 1968.

Warner, Oliver. *With Wolfe to Quebec: The Path to Glory.* Toronto: William Collins Sons & Co., 1972.

Wood, William. *The Logs of the Conquest of Canada.* Champlain Society Publications, no. 4. Toronto, 1909. Facsimile ed., Greenwood Press, 1968.

CHAPTER THREE

Clark, Ernest. *The Siege of Fort Cumberland, 1776.* Montreal: McGill–Queen's University Press, 1995.

Hatch, Robert McConnell. *Thrust for Canada: The American Attempt on Quebec in 1775–1776.* Boston: Houghton Mifflin Co., 1979.

Lanctot, Gustave. Margaret M. Cameron, trans. *Canada & the American Revolution, 1774–1783.* Toronto: Clarke, Irwin & Co., 1967.

Smith, Justin H. *Arnold's March from Cambridge to Quebec.* New York: Putnam, 1903.

———. *Our Struggle for the Fourteenth Colony: Canada and the American Revolution.* New York: Putnam, 1907.

Stanley, George F. G. *Canada Invaded: 1775–1776.* Toronto: A. M. Hakkert, 1973.

CHAPTER FOUR

Berton, Pierre. *Flames Across the Border: 1813–1814.* Toronto: McClelland & Stewart, 1982.

———. *The Invasion of Canada: 1812–1813.* Toronto: McClelland & Stewart, 1981.

Hannay, James. *History of the War of 1812*. Toronto: Morang & Co., 1905.

Hitsman, J. M. *The Incredible War of 1812: A Military History*. Toronto: Robin Brass Studio, 1999.

Southern, Victor. *The War of 1812*. Toronto: McClelland & Stewart, 1999.

Stanley, George F. G. *The War of 1812: Land Operations*. Canadian War Museum Historical Publication No. 18, Macmillan of Canada, 1983.

Turner, Wesley B. *The War of 1812: The War That Both Sides Won*. 2nd ed. Toronto: Dundurn Group, 2000.

Wood, William, ed. *Select British Documents of the Canadian War of 1812*. 4 vols. Champlain Society Publications, nos. 13–15, 17. Toronto, 1920–1928. Facsimile ed., Greenwood Press, 1968.

CHAPTER FIVE

Beal, Bob, and Rod Macleod. *Prairie Fire: The 1885 North-West Rebellion*. Edmonton: Hurtig Publishing, 1984.

Bumstead, J. M. *The Red River Rebellion*. Winnipeg: Watson & Dwyer, 1996.

"Correspondence Respecting the Recent Fenian Aggression upon Canada." *British Parliamentary Papers*, vol. 26, *Correspondence and other papers relating to the unification of the provinces and other affairs in Canada 1867*. Shannon, Ireland: Irish University Press, 1985.

Fryer, Mary Beacock. *Volunteers, Redcoats, Rebels & Raiders: A Military History of the Rebellions in Upper Canada*. Toronto: Dundurn Press, 1987.

Greer, Allan. *The Patriots and the People: The Rebellion of 1837 in Rural Lower Canada*. Toronto: University of Toronto Press, 1993.

Hildebrandt, Walter. *The Battle of Batoche: British Small Warfare and the Entrenched Métis*. Ottawa: Environment Canada, 1989.

Morton, Desmond. *The Last War Drum: The Northwest Campaign of 1885*. Toronto: Hakkert, 1972.

Read, Colin Frederick. *The Rising in Upper Canada, 1837–8: The Duncombe Revolt and After*. Toronto: University of Toronto Press, 1982.

———— and Ronald J. Stagg eds. *The Rebellion of 1837 in Upper Canada*. The Champlain Society in cooperation with the Ontario Heritage Foundation and Carleton University Press, 1985.

Schull, Joseph. *Rebellion: The Rising in French Canada, 1837*. Toronto: Macmillan Canada, 1996.

Senior, Hereward. *The Last Invasion of Canada: The Fenian Raids, 1866–1870*. Toronto: Dundurn Press, 1991.

Sessional Paper No. 6, 1886: *Report Upon the Suppression of the Rebellion in the North-west Territories, and Matters in Connection Therewith, in 1885*. Ottawa: 1886.

Stanley, George F. *The Birth of Western Canada: A History of the Riel Rebellions*. Toronto: University of Toronto Press, 1960.

CHAPTER SIX

Amery, L. S., ed. *The Times History of the War in South Africa 1899–1902*, 7 vols. London: Sampson, Low, Marston, and Co., 1909.

Carver, Michael. *The National Army Museum Book of the Boer War*. London: Sidgwick & Jackson, 1999.

Miller, Carman. *Painting the Map Red: Canada and the South African War, 1899–1902*. Montreal: McGill–Queen's University Press, 1993.

Pakenham, Thomas. *The Boer War*. New York: Random House, 1979.

Reid, Brian A. *Our Little Army in the Field: The Canadians in South Africa*. St. Catharines, Ontario: Vanwell Publishing, 1996.

Sessional Paper No. 35a, 1901: *Supplementary Report; Organization, Equipment Despatch and Service of Canadian Contingents during the War in South Africa, 1899–1900*, Ottawa, 1901.

Sessional Paper no. 35a, 1902: *Further Supplementary Report; Organization, Equipment Despatch and Service of Canadian Contingents during the War in South Africa, 1899–1902*, Ottawa, 1903.

CHAPTER SEVEN

Berton, Pierre. *Vimy*. Toronto: McClelland & Stewart, 1986.

Dancocks, Daniel. *Welcome to Flanders Fields: The First Canadian Battle of the Great War, Ypres 1615*. Toronto: McClelland & Stewart, 1988.

Duguid, Arthur Fortescue. *Official History of the Canadian Forces in the Great War, 1914–1918*, 2 vols. Ottawa: J.O. Patenaude, 1938.

Edmonds, J. E. *Military Operations in France and Belgium*, 1915, 4 vols. London: Macmillan and Co., 1927–28.

Freeman, Bill, and Richard Nielsen. *Far From Home: Canadians in the First World War*. Toronto: McGraw-Hill Ryerson, 1999.

Livesay, J. F. B. *Canada's Hundred Days: With the Canadian Corps from Amiens to Mons, Aug 8–Nov 11, 1918*. Toronto: Thomas Allen, 1919.

Morton, Desmond, and J. L. Granatstein. *Marching to Armageddon: Canadians and the Great War, 1914–1919.* Toronto: Lester & Orpen Dennys, 1989.

Nicholson, Col. G. W. L. *Canadian Expeditionary Force, 1914–1919.* Ottawa: Queen's Printer, 1962.

Overseas Military Forces of Canada: Report of the Ministry 1918. London.

CHAPTER EIGHT

Copp, Terry, and Richard Nielsen. *No Price Too High: Canadians and the Second World War.* Toronto: McGraw-Hill Ryerson, 1996.

Douglas, W. A. B. *The Creation of a National Air Force.* Toronto: University of Toronto Press, 1986.

Granatstein, J. L., and Desmond Morton. *A Nation Forged in Fire: Canadians and the Second World War, 1939–1945.* Toronto: Lester & Orpen Dennys, 1989.

Greenhous, B., et al. *The Crucible of War, 1939–1945.* Toronto: University of Toronto Press, 1994.

McAndrew, Bill. *Canadians and the Italian Campaign, 1943–1945.* Montreal: Éditions Art Global, 1996.

McAndrew, Bill, Bill Rawling, and Michael Whitby. *Liberation: The Canadians in Europe.* Montreal: Éditions Art Global, 1995.

Milner, Marc. *The North Atlantic Run: The Royal Canadian Navy and the Battle for the Convoys.* Toronto: University of Toronto Press, 1985.

———. *The U-Boat Hunters.* Toronto: University of Toronto Press, 1994.

Nicholson, Lt.-Col. G. W. L. *The Canadians in Italy, 1943–1945.* Ottawa: Queen's Printer, 1956.

Stacey, Col. C. P. *The Canadian Army, 1919–1945: An Official Historical Summary.* Ottawa: Queen's Printer, 1948.

———. *The Victory Campaign.* Ottawa: Queen's Printer, 1960.

CHAPTER NINE

Barris, Ted. *Deadlock in Korea: Canadians at War, 1950–1953.* Toronto: Macmillan Canada, 1999.

Bercuson, David Jay. *Blood on the Hills: The Canadian Army in the Korean War.* Toronto: University of Toronto, 1999.

Melady, John. *Korea: Canada's Forgotten War.* Toronto: Macmillan Canada, 1983.

Meyers, Edward C. *Thunder in the Morning Calm: The Royal Canadian Navy in Korea, 1950–1955.* St. Catharines, Ontario: Vanwell Publishing, 1992.

Thorgrimson, Thor, and E. C. Russell. *Canadian Naval Operations in Korean Waters, 1950–1955.* Ottawa: Queen's Printer, 1965.

Wood, Herbert Fairlie. *Strange Battleground: The Operations in Korea and Their Effects on the Defence Policy of Canada.* Ottawa: Queen's Printer, 1966.

CHAPTER TEN

Coulon, Jocelyn. Phyllis Aronoff and Howard Scott, trans. *Soldiers of Diplomacy: The United Nations, Peacekeeping, and the New World Order.* Toronto: University of Toronto Press, 1998.

Farrar-Hockley, Anthony. *A Distant Obligation. Official History the British Part in the Korean War*, vol. 1. London: HMSO, n.d.

———. *An Honourable Discharge. Official History the British Part in the Korean War*, vol. 2. London: HMSO.

Gaffen, Fred. *In the Eye of the Storm: A History of Canadian Peacekeeping.* Toronto: Deneau & Wayne Publishers, 1987.

Granatstein, J. L., and David Bercuson. *War and Peacekeeping: From South Africa to the Gulf — Canada's Limited Wars.* Toronto: Key Porter Books, 1991.

United Nations. *The Blue Helmets: A Review of United Nations Peace-keeping.* 3rd ed. New York: United Nations Reproduction Section, 1996.

Photo Credits

We gratefully acknowledge the National Archives of Canada for the use of the following photographs: pages 5, 13, NAC C-29485; p. 7, NAC C-5749; p. 10, NAC C-74102; p. 21, NAC C-1090; p. 24, NAC C-2644; pp. 27, 42, NAC C-7222; p. 37, (top) NAC C-4664, (bottom) NAC C-2645; pp. 45, 52–53, NAC C-5415; p. 51, NAC C-6046; pp. 59, 64–65, NAC C-7762; p. 64, NAC C-273; p. 68, NAC PA-21304; p. 72, NAC C-3297; p. 78, NAC C-12094; pp. 81, 90–91, NAC C-18737 ; p. 84, NAC C-396; p. 85, NAC C-11322; p. 97, NAC C-3455; p. 99, NAC C-3463; p. 100, by James Peters, NAC C-4522; pp. 103, 108–9, by James Cooper Mason, NAC PA-173037; p. 110, NAC PA-181414; p. 113, from the Borden Clarke Collection, NAC C-24623; pp. 116–17, by William F. Athawes, NAC PA-113027; pp. 119, 132–33, by Henry Edward Knobel, NAC PA-1020; p. 124, by William Ivor Castle, NAC PA-648; p. 128, NAC PA-1012; p. 129, NAC C-15366; p. 134, from the Strathy Smith Collection, NAC PA-1182; p. 135, NAC PA-1326; p. 137, by William Rider-Rider, NAC PA-2162; p. 141, NAC PA-3133; pp. 145, 171, by Ken Bell, NAC PA-138429; p. 150, NAC PA-202794; p. 153, NAC C-14160; p. 155, by Herb Nott, NAC PA-107903; p. 159, by T. Rowe, NAC PA-141671; p. 162, NAC PA-173437; p. 165, by Dennis Sullivan, NAC PA-129053; p. 173, by Daniel Guravich, NAC PA-138284; pp. 175, 182–83, by Paul E. Tomelin, NAC PA-128280; p. 179, by Bill Olson, NAC PA-115034; p. 186, Paul E. Tomelin, NAC PA-128848; p. 188, by Paul E. Tomelin, NAC PA-115496; p. 197, NAC PA-122737.

We also acknowledge the Department of National Defence for the use of the following photos: pp. 193, 209, CFPU ISC93-5316-15; p. 200, CFPU ISC84-351; p. 204, CFPU ISC90-660; p. 207, CFPU ISC97-071; p. 212, CFPU ISD97-022; p. 214, CFPU BNC98-300-329; p. 215, CFPU ISD99-433.

Index